FLYING INTO DANGER

The story of Paul Brickhill RAAF

Published by Brolga Publishing Pty Ltd
ABN 46 063 962 443
PO Box 12544
A'Beckett St
Melbourne, VIC, 8006
Australia

email: markzocchi@brolgapublishing.com.au

National Library of Australia
Cataloguing-in-Publication data
Ramsland, John (author)
Flying into Danger: The story of Paul Brickhill
ISBN: 9781925367683 (paperback)
Subjects: Brickhill, Paul, 1916-1991.
Fighter pilots--Australia--Biography
Authors--20th century--Biography.
Soldiers--Australia--Biography.

Printed in Australia
Cover design by Working Type Studio
Artwork by Mark Postlethwaite, c/- Sidewinder Publishing, Enderby, Leicester, UK
Typeset by Tara Wyllie & Elly Cridland

FLYING INTO DANGER

The story of Paul Brickhill RAAF

The Australian who wrote *The Great Escape,*
The Dam Busters and *Reach for the Sky*

JOHN RAMSLAND

To Marie
With love

TABLE OF CONTENTS

INTRODUCTION

Yes, the decent people of this world would have to remember war. Movies and radio records should remind this and the future generations of what happened… It should be possible to keep this danger in everyone's mind so that we can never be caught on the wrong foot again. So that our children will have a chance to live. After all, that is why we are born. We aren't born to die.

– Guy Gibson, *Enemy Coast Ahead – Uncensored*, 273

Innumerable authors have written fictitious stories in which their characters make breathtaking escapes in a variety of circumstances, some realistic, some fanciful. Yet no matter how fertile a writer's imagination or how convincing they can be, for many readers a fictional escape does not surpass those that happen in real life, especially after World War II. Paul Brickhill (1916-1991) was the supremo of such writers and the most favoured by such readers in the 1950s.

As schoolchildren of the post Second World War era, we graduated from escape stories in Baroness Orczy's *The Scarlet Pimpernel* and her other novels of historical romance concerning the same mysterious protagonist[1] to Charles Dickens' *A Tale of Two Cities*, Alexander Dumas' *The Count of Monte Cristo* and Anthony Hope's *The Prisoner of Zenda*; through fast-paced thrillers like John Buchan's *The Thirty-Nine Steps* to Ian Fleming's James Bond secret service series. Such adventures were reinforced visually in the cinema – all became popular feature films that we enjoyed watching regularly on a weekly basis in the 1950s and beyond.

Ultimately, however, fictitious escapes did not completely satisfy and, with the turn into later adolescence and a growing maturity of outlook, authenticity was demanded and looked for and we turned to what was called "faction", especially wartime faction which was much published in the late forties and the 1950s. We were close to the lived imagined experience of World War II. We were compulsively drawn as the youth of the immediate post-war period to the genre of real life writing about the experiences of heroic figures in the desperate situation of modern industrial war. And given the number of

1 *Triumph of the Scarlet Pimpernel, The Way of the Scarlet Pimpernel, Eldorado, I will Repay, Lord Tony's Wife, Sir Percy Hits Back, Sir Percy Leads the Band, Mam'zelle Guillotine.*

bestselling true life books of the war, so were plenty of adults and among them some returned servicemen and women who had undergone similar wartime experiences themselves and could relate emotionally and make comparisons with their own lives in a therapy of sorts.

Life narratives that breathed authenticity, like those of Paul Brickhill's escape stories of World War II, drew us to them like a magnet. Calling such life narrative 'non-fiction' confuses rather than resolves the issue. Both real life narrative and fiction share the features we ascribe to fictional writing: unfolding action, dialogue, setting, characterisation and so on. Authors themselves were interested in blurring the edges of the boundaries between real life narrative and fictional narration in the first-person novel.[2] The writing of Paul Brickhill, the once celebrated famous best-selling author, is particularly situated to this type of definition as he uses such devices throughout his work.

We were taken up in adolescence with the frightening excitement of escape in *The Count of Monte Cristo* when the hero replacing the dead man is sewn up in a canvas bag and thrown in the outer harbour of Marseilles from the Château d'If. He then managed to cut his way out of the body bag and swim to shore to freedom and revenge. It seemed dramatic and authentic. But when we are more mature the once monstrous Château looked improbably small, almost a toy castle floating in the water compared with the vast dark foreboding fortress we once imagined. Eventually this fictitious escape from dreaded prison became an improbable fantasy and its authenticity was lost.

The extreme popularity of so-called wartime non-fiction about daring escapes got off to a splendid beginning in readers' imagination with Eric Williams' *The Wooden Horse*, first

---

2 G Thomas Couser, 'Genre matters: form, force and filiation', *Life Writing*, vol. 2, no 2, 2005, 130.

published in 1949. It was quickly reprinted for several years to rave reviews. Even before the war was over, Williams published in 1943 *Goon in the Block*, the story of Peter Howard, an airman who was shot down over Germany, taken prisoner and later managed to escape to Sweden. But the war was still being fought and he could not reveal the vivid details of the escape plan and information that would have aided the enemy. With *The Wooden Horse*, however, it could be claimed that Williams was one of the creators of a new sub-genre of wartime non-fiction. The story in *Goon in the Block* became fact thinly disguised as fiction and any reference to the escape was intentionally misleading. With *The Wooden Horse* (*The Tunnel Escape*) immediately after the war, Williams was freed as a writer and able to open up and provide authentic compelling detail. In doing so he used a little of the material from *Goon in the Block*.[3]

When *The Wooden Horse* was released, it sold so well internationally in the English-speaking world that, only a year later, it was made into an extremely popular motion film of ninety-eight minutes directed by Jack Lee and starring Leo Genn, David Tomlinson and Anthony Steel. Williams began his book evocatively with:

> It was January when they had first come to Stalag-Luft III, and for the whole of that month the ground was under snow. Snow lay thickly on the roofs of the barrack blocks and gave an air of gaiety to the barbed wire which sparkled and glittered in the sun.[4]

The film is now considered a gripping British War Classic

---

3 Eric Williams, Preface, *The Wooden Horse*, The Reprint Society, London, 1950.
4 Williams, *The Wooden Horse*, 9.

based on a true story, Eric Williams' novel *The Tunnel Escape* also called *The Wooden Horse*. It was nominated for Best Film for the 1951 BAFTA Awards and also featured Peter Finch, Paul Brickhill's schoolboy friend, in a supporting cameo role. Both Leo Genn and Anthony Steel were particularly well chosen for the main roles in the film as they both had wartime experiences, thus heightening the authentic feel.

Born in Chelsea, London in 1920, Anthony Steel was the son of an officer in the Indian army. He served throughout the Second World War in the Grenadier Guards. *The Wooden Horse* established his name as a screen actor in the 1950s and he played in several other war films including *Albert RN* (1953), *The Malta Story* (1954), *The Sea Shall Not Have Them* (1955) and *Storm Over the Nile* (1955).

Leo Genn was born in London in 1905. With the advent of World War II he joined the Royal Artillery rising to the rank of Lieutenant Colonel. After the war as a barrister, he served as a prosecutor in real life on the Nuremberg Trials, securing confessions from the Belsen concentration camp commanders. As an actor, he appeared in Laurence Olivier's *Henry V* and other important films of the 1950s.[5] In *The Wooden Horse*, Genn, as the more experienced and nuanced actor, had the top billing above the title. Williams was permitted to write the screenplay based on his own novel. This reinforced the social realism of the film with documentary flair. The production was mainly filmed in Germany and Denmark where the actual events took place.

The story of *The Wooden Horse*, both as book and film, tells about three desperate British prisoners-of-war (POWs) who hatched a daring, highly original plan loosely based on

---

5 Ann Lloyd & Graham Fuller (eds), *The Illustrated Who's Who of the Cinema*, Child-Henry, Hornsby, 1983, 168, 415.

the Trojan horse legend of Greek mythology. They plotted to escape using a gymnastic vaulting horse with covered-in sides to conceal their tunnelling activities. They constructed the large strong wooden vaulting horse with sliding-in handles to allow several men to carry it with the person inside. It was placed over the concealed tunnel entry, but in full view of the enemy guards in the parade ground. It was placed in exactly the same place each day and a team of athletes jumped over it for a prescribed time of several hours. The film's publicity claimed prominently that it was based on a true story – the book by Williams, *The Tunnel Escape* (a less romantic title). The film was to become a gripping British war classic expressing British values and traditions.

Starting the tunnel in this manner was a great advantage over tunnelling from under one of the barracks buildings as the men were much closer to the exterior barbed wire fence: 'After week after week of dogged and courageous work', Paul Brickhill later wrote, 'they broke through outside the wire one night and all three of them got back to England by way of Sweden'.[6] Soon that effort was acknowledged as one of the classic escapes of history. The vaulting horse was strong enough to contain inside the three diggers who eventually became acclaimed escapees. The 1950 classic film glorified their work in a dramatic way, but followed the narrative of the book closely. Both the book and the film created and reinforced each other as the sub-genre of true life escape stories.

Paul Brickhill – the subject of this book – soon entered the fray by himself in the immediate post-war period with spectacular success in 1950 with the release of *The Great Escape*. Before this was published, *Escape to Danger* (1946), co-written

6 Paul Brickhill, *The Great Escape*, Reprint Readers Union, Faber & Faber, London, 1952, 83.

with a fellow prisoner-of-war Conrad Norton, appeared based on some of their wartime experiences and those of others and the manuscript Brickhill prepared while in Stalag Luft III. It was a fine collection of wide-ranging wartime escape stories including the embryo of the mass escape which became *The Great Escape* in a more detailed form soon after. *Escape to Danger* appeared three years before Eric Williams' *The Wooden Horse* (1949). Brickhill, therefore, with Conrad Norton was an original pioneering spirit in creating or reviving the sub-genre of wartime escape literature of a factual nature.

Brickhill's *The Dam Busters* appeared in 1951; *Escape – or Die* came out in 1952 and *Reach for the Sky* in 1954. All this achievement was coupled with being a foreign correspondent with the Sydney *Sun* and writing detailed feature articles on the impact of the war in Europe. These were crowded years for Brickhill in which he established himself boldly as a prolific international writer.

Brickhill's books made him one of the most successful non-fiction writers of his time and were translated into several foreign languages. As well, he was sought after for film rights. *The Dam Busters*, starring Richard Todd and Michael Redgrave, and *Reach for the Sky* with Kenneth More became hit movies in the 1950s, as did *The Great Escape* in 1963. All were acknowledged in the film titles as being based on Brickhill's books. In particular, *The Dam Busters* became a world bestseller, a radio feature (also written and narrated by Brickhill), a newspaper serial and a most popular film. It told the breathtaking story in the three media forms of the 617 Squadron and its attacks on the German network of dams in the Ruhr Valley. *The Great Escape* as a book and film told the graphic story of "X" organisation in Stalag Luft III and the tragedy of the mass escape. *Reach for the Sky* was a fine biographical study of Douglas Bader, the limbless fighter pilot, prisoner-of-war and escapologist. The actor Kenneth More magnificently captured the character of the protagonist and the optimistic mood of the book. In this highly competitive genre of wartime faction as a whole, Paul Brickhill had instant success and quickly became a larger-than-life celebrated, even legendary personality, especially amongst London's social sets. He was a highly skilled promoter of his own books and worked hard in a particularly public arena of the publishing world.

This present book is a historical biography of the man behind the public mask and explores the mysteries of his Sydney childhood in Greenwich, his experiences as a young outstanding journalist for the Sydney *Sun* in the late 1930s, his adventures in the RAAF and the RAF as a courageous elite fighter pilot, his time as a prisoner-of-war in Stalag Luft III and his post-war celebrity as an extremely popular and well-regarded author in the 1950s.

In the early 1960s with the publication of his first novel (and final book) *The Deadline* (1962, called *War of Nerves* in the United States when it was published in 1963), Paul Brickhill suddenly stopped writing – or at least publishing – and he seemed to become a virtual recluse until his death in 1991 at the age of 74. Had wartime trauma, especially the prolonged period he spent as an inmate, a prisoner-of-war in the terrors of Nazi Germany, finally taken its toll after a period of frenetic celebrity researching and writing in London and Sydney of the 1950s? What further evidence is there of nervous breakdowns and psychiatric treatment in the 1950s and 1960s that show post-war traumatic stress or what was labelled at the time as 'war neurosis'? How did the experience of prolonged incarceration (six hundred days) affect the rest of his life and his memory? What part did his divorce in 1964 play in all of this? How did he play out the rest of his life in a well-appointed art deco flat in Sydney's Balmoral Beach, Mosman? All of these questions and more are played out in this book. An attempt is made to evaluate his real, but largely forgotten contribution to Australian literature as an Australian author.

Few writers other than Brickhill have celebrated so strongly the war experiences and adventures of RAAF and RAF pilots of the Second World War and captured the essence and importance of their existence in a fading British Empire. He had a commanding knowledge of how the air force culture and traditions operated with all their nuances.

While Paul Brickhill almost instantly became the doyen of the sub-genre of true life escape stories using the fictitious techniques as were also used by Eric Williams and others at about the same time – such as recreating conversation in the form of direct speech and unfolding the narrative and the plot dramatically, as in John Buchan's thrillers like *The Thirty-Nine Steps* (also about escape, but into the Scottish Highlands by an innocent fugitive from justice just prior to World War I). Brickhill was generous enough to recognise the influence on his literary work and style of Eric Williams whose writing he described as 'brilliant'.[7]

In the popular literary culture of the 1950s, it seems true that almost every schoolboy in the English-speaking world, especially of the British Commonwealth, as well as many adults took great pleasure in World War II escape stories of a factual kind like those of Paul Brickhill. Copies of *The Great Escape*, *The Dam Busters*, *Escape – or Die* and *Reach for the Sky* were found on many family bookshelves and in most local public libraries. For progressive Australian parents, Brickhill's works were considered wholesome reading for older children and teenagers. They taught decency, courage and reliability. All were adapted as children's literature and set as standard texts in

---

7 Brickhill, *The Great Escape*, 83.

English and History lessons in the classroom.

After being a prisoner-of-war in dangerous Nazi Germany for six hundred days, Brickhill soon after demobilisation suddenly found himself at the pinnacle of fêted success in what was a huge popular non-fiction movement. Some people believed, with a degree of justification at its perhaps unconscious level or essence, a new form of war propaganda was being developed and directed to a great extent at the rising generation – the youth of English-speaking peoples of the British Commonwealth of nations. Or, at least in Brickhill's work of constantly using stories of exciting or dangerous real life experiences, was it to evoke once again in the post-war era the tradition of British fictitious heroes? Characters who were akin to those in Rudyard Kipling's short fiction, like *The Man who would be King*, or Richard Hannay, the intrepid escapologist of John Buchan's *The Thirty-Nine Steps*, or EW Horning's gentleman thief and cricketer AJ Raffles or even WE Johns' hero Biggles, the heroic aviator detective. Such an idea will need to be teased out at various times in the following chapters.

In all of Paul Brickhill's books, as in all non-fiction, there is a degree of autobiography, of telling what it was like from personal experiences. He draws on vivid unforgettable memories of what happened to him and how he felt. This made his writing so compelling. Readers frequently believe that only those who have experienced war can write about it in the way Brickhill did.

Fictitious tales will no longer do, such readers often claim. The author tells the tale of one who survived out of ten in World War II as well as those who did not quite make it – that completely dwarfed the wildest flights of adventure fiction. He provides a sheer, sustained drama of war by capturing incidents or cameos of courage mixed with blood, misery and pain. He chronicles the great untold personal adventures of war for those pilots who were exiled for weary years in POW camps behind the barbed wire and in the midst of the enemy. He brings to life again, in dramatic unfolding terms, some of the ten thousand lives who fell with their aircraft over hostile soil. They paid for their survival by 'dreary imprisonment' and years spent 'in those barren cramped compounds' of 'numbed misery'; life marked time, but 'despair and emotion didn't', as Brickhill explained concisely and frequently.

Many extraordinary true-life stories were there to be concisely and plainly told with vivid use of telling detail. One was the cameo account of "Chuck" Charles Lark, the short wiry observer from Sydney who trained in Ottawa and went on to a Wimpy squadron. Mid-1942 found Lark coming back from what was called 'Happy Valley' – over Germany. The Dutch coast was almost in sight when an enemy night-fighter attacked them. Chuck was on lookout in the astro-dome.[8] He received a bullet in the right shoulder, another in the right hip and then a third which went through the right temple and came out of the eye socket leaving the right eyeball dangling down his cheek, suspended by 'stringy, bloody strips of muscle, or tendon'. A great hole was blown in the side of the fuselage, one engine was put out and the Wimpy – the nickname for the Vickers Wellington bomber[9] – was burning fiercely and dangerously. Half-blinded and 'pretty faint', Chuck baled out of the hole in the fuselage after being stuck halfway and forced to squirm free, energetically and urgently.

8 Or 'astrodome', usually made of Perspex (trademark), a transparent dome on the top of the fuselage of the aeroplane for astronomical observations.
9 The Vickers Wellington was a British twin engine long range medium sized bomber designed in the mid-1930s at Brookland in Weybridge, Surrey, by Vickers-Armstrong's designer Rex Pearson. It was widely used for night bombing over Europe in World War II. The nickname "Wimpy" by RAF personnel was from the character J Wellington Wimpy in the then popular Popeye the sailor man cartoons. They claimed the Wellington was as portly as Wimpy in shape.

Good fortune was 'still against him': he landed in the middle of a large deep saltwater lake north of the famous Zuyder Zee, forcing him to swim about a quarter of a mile to shore. It wasn't until he was in the water that he felt the 'sharp stinging in the right eye socket' and 'caught a glimpse of something flopping on his cheek'. With his good eye, he saw the mangled eyeball 'floating bloodily' in the water by his nose. Later, Lark could not remember much more of the heart-stopping swim. Eventually, he staggered ashore covered in blood and somehow made it to a nearby house, barely able to drag himself there. He knocked on the door. A woman opened and saw a horrific sight before her. She promptly slammed the door in his face.

He dragged himself to the next house where a Dutch family 'tenderly' assisted him in and hastily brought in a doctor. The Germans took over and he received treatment in a church hospital for five weeks before he was sent to Stalag Luft III in Sagan where Brickhill met him and obtained his story along with a host of others.[10] His story was used in *Escape to Danger*, but it was only a cameo of two paragraphs.

Through his writing career, Brickhill replaced fictitious escape-artist characters, like the Count of Monte Christo, the Scarlet Pimpernel, Richard Hannay, Biggles and Raffles, with real life characters. But they were just as dashing and determined. They became almost the super-heroes of the Second World War as major protagonists of his books. There were the more documented daring exploits of Wing Commander Douglas Bader, the legless ace whose story Brickhill followed through from a chapter in *Escape to Danger* into a full-scale biography in *Reach for the Sky*; the famed leader of the "X" Organisation at Stalag Luft III Wing Commander Roger Bushell, the great

10 F/Lt Paul Brickhill and Conrad Norton, *Escape to Danger*, Faber and Faber, London, 1946.

South African barrister and intrepid escapologist (*Escape to Danger* and *The Great Escape*); Wing Commander Guy Gibson VC, the famed leader of the Dambusters (*The Dam Busters*) as well as Leonard Cheshire VC and the Australian Micky Martin (also in *The Dam Busters*), Wing Commander HA "The Dodger" Day OSO, OBE, MC (*Escape to Danger, The Dam Busters* and *The Great Escape*).

Through their real life characterisations, Brickhill created a veritable galaxy of revered World War II heroes for eager post-war readers to admire and to relate to. Some were mere cameos; others were fully detailed. In their time, they became as big as Ian Fleming's James Bond, but without the sexual fantasy, the fantastically unbelievable adventure episodes and daring escapes.

Similar heroes to Gibson, Bushell, Martin, Cheshire and Bader – but lesser known – took the same shape and had a place of honour in Brickhill's *Escape – or Die* sponsored by the Royal Air Force Escaping Society, led by Air Marshal Sir Basil Embry. It came out immediately after *Escape to Danger, The Great Escape* and *The Dam Busters* and had immediate acclaim and huge books sales.

HE Bates, the popular English novelist, saw Brickhill's RAF and RAAF fighting men and heroes as sophisticated new Elizabethans with a special attitude of their own. They excelled in 'pure cussedness' and were rich in invention and 'defeatless humour'.[11]

The fall of France to Germany in 1940 created special circumstances for them as they were not infrequently shot down and captured, placed in concentration camps (like Brickhill) and sought fearlessly to escape against all odds. Brickhill was able deftly to capture the nuances of their culture as, like Eric Williams, he was one of them.

11 HE Bates, 'Escape', Paul Brickhill, *Escape – or Die. Authentic Stories of the RAF Escaping Society*, Evans Brothers Limited, London, 1952, 11-12.

While the characters in his books were reconstructions of the real thing, thus to a degree fictionalised with direct 'made up speech placed on their lips' they still portrayed the general type of the fighter or bomber pilot of the RAF or the RAAF living in what HE Bates described as an abnormal world that they were forced to master to a degree quite separate from the civilian environment most of them had come from, like Richard Hannay, Buchan's fictional hero, and Raffles and some others. They were all, mostly, supreme amateurs in a dangerous world. They were volunteers who had been car salesmen, office workers, school teachers and so on. And now they became unbelievably courageous heroes due to the circumstances of war.

They all brought to their new fighting world a particularly refined attitude, as Bates put it, to understatement, a desire to be casual and low key as expressed in their language. Such men no longer crashed an aircraft, he 'pranged or wrapped it up'. He no longer described a gallant action; it was 'a good show'. He did not simply die; he 'bought it'. Everything easy or straight forward was a 'piece of cake'. All such expressions became united as 'a legendary synonym for acute Britishness': 'The more closely and harshly war impinged on life the more smoothly, casually and cryptically were the fears of it wrapped up in the veil of language and the cloak of behaviour. War was an embarrassment that simply ought not to be mentioned'.[12]

Brickhill's books adhere to these principles and recreate perfectly the 'veil of language' that existed amongst wartime air force people. Even long into his virtual retirement from writing, or at least publishing, Brickhill spoke the RAF 'chokes away' clipped speak. Some things were a 'piece of cake' and everything talked about was so carefully understated, especially when he spoke to curious journalists, so that he seems to others, especially

12 Bates, 'Escape', 12.

in his speech and dress, the impeccable English RAF gentleman type. His personality seems set in aspic like his books until his death at seventy-four in 1991 in his upstairs flat at Balmoral Beach on harbourside Sydney. There was always the age-old British reluctance to make a fuss about things and to always be a straight-shooter and not exaggerate. The man seemed to step out of his own precisely-written books as a larger-than-life character.

The protagonists of his books were most reluctant prisoners-of-war, particularly Douglas Bader: 'it was suddenly', as Bates put it, 'very annoying not to be able to ride home for tea' in the English countryside. They found it infuriating 'to keep a date with a Nazi rifle' instead of one with a brunette in a country café or a wayside English pub. RAF men were singularly unprepared for capture and subjection – it was a situation constitutionally difficult or impossible for them.

When Bates once asked Brickhill why flying men did not go over Germany or occupied France in their bombers or fighters wearing fully-packed civilian disguises under their flying suits so they could immediately begin organising escape on hitting German or French soil in their parachutes, instead of afterwards toiling in tunnels behind barbed wire, he remarked that he supposed no RAF man, with a few exceptions, had a final and absolute belief that he would ever be shot down and that, if by some unfortunate accident he was, he would never be captured anyway – such was his culture of idealistic optimism.

Even the one exception to the rule, Group Captain John Whitley, whose story is found in *Escape – or Die* and who always wore a complete civilian outfit underneath his flying suit, 'healthily refused' to accept the idea of death. Brickhill wrote: 'He violently rejected… the idea of being captured'.[13]

---

13 Bates, 'Escape', 13; Brickhill, 'The Man Who Went Prepared', *Escape – or Die*, 161-82.

And so Brickhill's real life heroes were frequently captured, found themselves behind the barbed wire of compounds from which they looked out intensely towards the open spaces and planned with such meticulous care and risk to get back to the very point from which they had started, a British airfield. All readers of Brickhill's *The Great Escape*, with its meticulous account of the masterly system of pass forging, the corruption and blackmailing of German guards by sheer daylight cheek still today remain fascinated helped by the author's precise and objectively understated writing, or as depicted visually in the Hollywood film classic under the same title – *The Great Escape*.

HE Bates drew it all together in a nutshell as far as British POWs of the Second World War were concerned:

> All that is certain is that as long as there are prisons men will try to escape from them; and that as long as there is an R.A.F. it will bring to the problems of escape the qualities of high resource, pure cussedness and that indefinable, damnably annoying refusal to lie down when dead, of which all the stories in this book [*Escape – or Die*] are such excellent – and, I think, such exciting – examples.[14]

And Paul Brickhill, as a master story-teller, was fully equipped to tell them and many others in the 1950s.

> We whistled over the anti-tank ditches and beach obstacles. We saw the yellow sand dunes slide below us silently, yellow in the pale morning.
> Then we were over the sea with the rollers breaking on

14 Bates, 'Escape', 15.

the beaches and the moon casting its long reflection straight in front of us – and there was England.

We were free.

– Guy Gibson, *Enemy Coast Ahead – Uncensored*, 274

FROM CHILDHOOD TO WAR

Left: The Brickhill boys - Paul, Adrian (Geoff) and Russell
Right: Baby Lloyd with mother, Izitella (Dot), on the same day

The Brickhill boys: LLoyd, Paul, Clive, Russell, and Adrian (Geoff)
(Courtesy of Margaret Brickhill)

CHAPTER 1

EARLY YEARS AT GREENWICH POINT

Boat shed, Greenwich Point

Two boys and a boat

Near a boatshed on Sydney's Greenwich Point, two eleven-year-old scallywag boys discovered an abandoned canoe beside the bush that fell almost to the water's edge from the steep hill above. It was the high summer of 1927-28 and school holidays. Their imaginations were fired enough to take the canoe out into the deep water beyond the Point of the junction of the Parramatta and Lane Cove Rivers. Little did they know the canoe was defective.

As the colourful story went by one of them much later in life, they headed towards the half-built Sydney Harbour Bridge passing by the Greenwich Sailing Club, Manns Point, Balls Head, McMahons Point, Lavender Bay and then Milsons Point under the works of the yet-to-be finished bridge. On they continued their wild adventure, past Kirribilli and Cremorne Point.

But, as they rounded Bradleys Head, the boat started to leak badly.

It suddenly sank underneath them, disappearing into the Davey Dark. Perhaps they had intended to get to Manly, or maybe they didn't have a destination thought out.

Both boys could swim well enough, but they were caught in a life-threatening situation in the waves near the headland rocks. The desperate boys nearly drowned together in the deep, pounding waves open to the harbour's swell opposite the heads.

As luck would have it, a passing workboat rescued them and eventually they got back safely to Greenwich Point – rather bedraggled.[1] Their schoolboy relationship became bonded by such exploits and pranks, by the mysterious twists and turns that make up true friendships in childhood. They became boon companions in many outdoor episodes. Both were born in 1916 at the height of the Great War. They met at Greenwich Point as newly-arrived children.

But who were they?

The more solidly-built boy was Paul Chester Jerome Brickhill, the son of a prominent newspaper editor, George Brickhill and the thinner boy was Peter George Ingle Finch of uncertain parentage. Both boys were to achieve lasting fame in the late 1940s and early 1950s: Paul as the highly celebrated author of *Escape to Danger* (with Conrad Norton), *The Great*

---

1 Elaine Dundy, *Finch, Bloody Finch A Life of Peter Finch*, Holt, Reinhart and Winston, New York, 1980, 53.

Escape, The Dam Busters, Escape – or Die and *Reach for the Sky. The Story of Douglas Bader D.S.O., D.F.C.*. All his books were published to great acclaim between 1949 and 1954 – in the space of five years! *The Dam Busters, Reach for the Sky* and *The Great Escape* were made into highly respected and popular classical war films.

Peter Finch, on the other hand, became a 'dazzling chameleon' of an acclaimed actor in the late 1940s in London.[2]

* * *

Life begins at the beginning. Paul Chester Jerome Brickhill was born on Wednesday, 20 December 1916 at the height of the Great War. At the time, his parents, Tasmanian-born George Brickhill and Izitella Victoria (née Bradshaw) were living at "Elsmere" 133 Burke Road, Camberwell in Melbourne, Victoria. George was a prominent newspaper editor well-known on the national level in the world of the Australian press. Paul was the third son born to the proud parents. His older brothers were Russell[3] and Adrian. The younger brothers were Lloyd and Clive. There were no girls. Russell was six years older than Paul; Adrian three; Lloyd was two years younger and Clive six. It was a band of five brothers close in age. As well as Paul, Lloyd and Clive were to serve as volunteers in the Second World War – all three were to survive. All five brothers were high achievers as adults taking after their father George.[4]

---

2 Trader Faulkner, *Peter Finch. A Biography*, Angus & Robertson, Sydney, 1979, 14.
3 Russell John Brickhill (born in Hawthorne) was Mayor of Lane Cove Council between 1962 and 1963 and alderman from 1954 to 1968. The Brickhill Children's Playground (Reserve) in Rankin Street was established in 1962.
4 Russell George b. 18.4.1911, Melbourne; Adrian Geoffrey b. 11.4.1914, Melbourne; Lloyd Wesley b. 13.10.1918, Melbourne; Clive Desmond b. 10.4.1923, Adelaide. Information supplied by Margaret Brickhill, 11 May 2016.

Greenwich Days

When Paul was a young schoolboy, his family moved to Sydney and he grew up mainly at 41 George Street, Greenwich Point close to the harbour front. Greenwich was in the Municipality of Lane Cove seven kilometres north-west of Sydney on the Lane Cove River where it joins the Parramatta River, but psychologically its location seems part of Sydney Harbour in the broader sense.

Greenwich House, built in 1836, was still standing on the corner of George Street and St Lawrence Street when the family moved there. Greenwich was named after Greenwich on the Thames in London, but derived more directly from the title of Greenwich House, partly because of its geographic location from Sydney and the metropolis, like the original Greenwich on the Thames – almost the same distance by water south from central London.

In the early days in Sydney, Greenwich was a prominent boat-building village because of its close proximity to reliable deep calm water. It had retained much of that ambience when the Brickhills settled there in the late 1920s. It was an idyllic place for Paul to grow up in from about the age of ten. Many of the picturesque houses were still standing and the quiet streets suited childhood play.

By ferry, his father had easy access to metropolitan and the newspaper world in which he was a key figure. Greenwich is still conveniently close to Sydney and is characterised by gracious large homes with an old world charm.[5] Across the Lane Cover River from the Greenwich township was the Gore Bay Installation (The Shell Transport and Trading Company, Burns Phillip Pty Ltd) where the first bulk shipment of kerosene

5 Frances Pollon (compiler & ed.), *The Book of Sydney Suburbs* (original manuscript Gerald Healy), Cornstalk Publishing, Pymble, 1996, 116.

arrived in Australia in 1901.[6] By the time Paul Brickhill was participating in childhood play in the outdoors near his home in George Street, the Shell Company's installation at Gore Cove had become a major storage and distribution centre for petrol for the developing car industry and dominated part of the landscape.[7]

George Brickhill – newspaper man

George Brickhill was born in 1879 in Launceston, Tasmania, and died in Greenwich on 4 September 1965 having witnessed in the 1950s Paul's great international successes as an author and a famous post-war foreign correspondent and feature writer for the Sydney *Sun*. Without a doubt, being a journalist himself from his youth, George Brickhill was enormously proud of his son's success and achievements. George had entered journalism on a friend's newspaper in Launceston. His father James was also in the newspaper game as a private secretary. George married Izitella Victoria Bradshaw in Kensington, New South Wales. He was thirty years of age at the time.

(Johnstone, O'Shannessy & Co, State Library of Victoria)

George went on from Launceston to work as a journalist in a wide variety of places in Victoria and South Australia before arriving in Greenwich, Sydney. He was primarily a prominent newspaper editor for several metropolitan and regional

6 Brian Kennedy & Barbara Kennedy, *Sydney and Suburbs. A History and Description*, Reed, Frenchs Forest, 1982, 74-75.
7 Pollon, *The Book of*, 116.

country newspapers. He moved around a lot with his growing family. He had a stint for a period as an advance agent and business manager for a major Australian travelling circus, Wirth's Circus. In this capacity, George used his journalistic skills to secure grounds, accommodation and other provisions before the circus appeared on the scene in the town in question. He wrote and arranged advertising and announcements in the local press and provided press releases and even wrote extensive feature articles for eager local newspapers.[8] Many of the articles had nutshell biographical studies of star circus performers.

In George Brickhill's time as a circus advance agent, he wrote many what could be now called short "silhouette biographies" of various circus performers to stimulate and inculcate the public's interest with a sense of romance, to draw crowds to the travelling circus while set up in a country town. Such pieces appeared on occasions in local newspapers, usually without naming the author. They were full of hyperbole and excitement. When Wirth Brothers Enormous New United Circus was touring Western Australian towns, a typical "silhouette biography"[9] of May Wirth – who later became the world's greatest lady bareback rider in the United States – appeared in the *Kalgoorlie Miner* on 4 July 1904:

> Clad in spangled silver grey, a young performer rejoicing in the name of Mayazel went through a remarkable contortion act in thoroughly graceful fashion on an elevated staging and concluded a heartily applauded turn by seizing the top of a

---

8 Mark St Leon, 'Circus & Nation', Part II, PhD thesis, University of Sydney, 2006, 266.

9 Leonard Cassuto, 'The Silhouette ad the Secret Self. Theorising Biography in Our Times', *American Quarterly*, vol.58, no 4, December 2006, 1249-61.

> revolving pillar with her teeth raising her body up and doubling it backwards and spinning around while supported only by the hold of teeth on a pillar.[10]

The author deftly combined accuracy of exciting descriptive detail with a suggestion of hyperbole – May was billed on posters by the advance agent as 'The Greatest Contortionist on Earth'. In this fragmented biography, the reader is told that she was born May Zinga, became 'Miss M Masinga' and then May Martin and finally May Wirth after her adoptive parents, the famous circus proprietors.

George Brickhill worked with the travelling circus for a couple of years using his journalistic skills to tell such stories to the general public of circus-goers.[11] With Wirth's he travelled even to India and Burma and had the experience in both places of wild-game hunting.

Paul inherited his father's ability to write an exciting dramatic story and to paint in words character sketches of singular impact in a short space. Throughout his life, he produced many "silhouette biographies", but generally without the hyperbole that was required in the circus world. Rather, he adopted the use of understatement, or 'straight-shooting', common among wartime pilot officers in the RAAF and the RAF along with a carefully clipped moustache. One of Brickhill's straight-shooting "silhouette biographies" later took shape in his book *The Great Escape:*

> The Kommandant had been wounded seven times in the 1914 war and now he was just over sixty, still as

---

10 Mark St Leon, *Circus in Australia Printed Ephemera 1833-2008*, Mark St Leon & Associates, Penshurst, 2008, 57.

11 St Leon, *Circus in Australia*, 57.

> straight as a young lad. He was an Oberst (colonel) and his name was Von Lindeiner. He was a lean, good-looking man with composure in his face, always immaculate in the Prussian tradition, the Iron Cross on his left pocket, tailored tunic, extravagantly cut riding breeches and black riding boots.[12]

In a short space, Brickhill gives a precise and memorable picture of the man from his own monumental imagination as an eye-witness, but this was written after he had matured as a journalist and had endured the conditions in a German prison camp as a young RAAF officer. In it he effectively captures the moment and the immediate emotional context while glancing briefly at the man's past. He carefully selects the interesting or dominant, outstanding physical traits of the man that succinctly capture his personality and character. And yet we are told only a little of his past. Nevertheless, we see the man clearly in terms of how he publically presented himself as a commandant of Stalag Luft III.

There is significant detail of both the moment and the background as imbedded inside a lump of amber, while the secret self remains more elusive than the cultural world around. It is an almost perfect "silhouette biography" placed in a single paragraph. Brickhill has made the effort of reconstructing a life from which 'little information' has survived the passing of time. As a brief eye-witness narrative it is an interplay between cultural currents and the individual psyche.[13] The biography uses the subject's life to explore the history of the present circa 1952 and the lack of detail anchors its biographical subject firmly and fully within his time. Thus Brickhill created a subject

12 Brickhill, *The Great Escape* (1952), 42.
13 Cassuto, 'The Silhouette', 1255-6.

based on a limited fragment of concrete evidence of what he had seen in the concentration camp at Sagan.

George Brickhill worked in Melbourne, Bendigo in Victoria and Port Pirie in South Australia in the newspaper world. Between 1922 and 1927 he was editor of the Adelaide *Mail* before moving to Sydney. He was a vastly experienced newspaper man with a wide range of friendly contact across Australia. He was well-known as a founding member of the powerful Australian Journalist Association (AJA) who awarded him life membership and the Association's gold badge for his many contributions to the newspaper world.[14]

In his prime, George Brickhill was a handsome, well-set-up man and was always immaculately dressed. Paul took after him in both regards. George wrote innumerable leading articles for a variety of regional and city newspapers, including *The McIvor Times and Rodney Advertiser* (Heathcote, Victoria), *The Advertiser* (Adelaide), *The Register* (Adelaide), *Barrier Miner* (Broken Hill, New South Wales), *Zeehan and Dundas Herald* (Tasmania) and *The Mail* (South Australia). As a journalist, he was an intrepid sojourner moving from place to place during the times his five sons were being born. They lived in several households in different places.

When George finally brought his family to the metropolis of Sydney, he at first moved briefly into 8 Mitchell Street, Greenwich, before moving temporarily to Greendale Street. He became a prominent public figure there and was President of the Greenwich Progress Association. For a time, he edited the local *Community Centre News*.

---

14 *Argus* (Melbourne), 23 December 1916; Brickhill, George Russell, A *Biographical Register 1788-1939. Notes from the names index of the Australian Dictionary of Biography*, vol.1 A-K, compiled & edited by HJ Gibney & Ann G Smith, Australian National University, Canberra, 81.

While the Brickhill family settled permanently at 41 George Street, Greenwich Point, they had moved in the same suburb mirroring George's sojourning career as an itinerant journalist and editor. No 41 George Street was, however, a truly palatial residence known as "Blythswood". It faced Upper Serpentine Road – which was in part almost a laneway rather than a road. The property had a dual address as 1 Upper Serpentine Road. As a residence it was more than big enough to hold a large family of growing boys.

So his son Paul came from a long and strongly persuasive newspaper tradition that was to influence profoundly his adult professional life after leaving school to begin work in the early 1930s at the height of the Great Depression and then after his wartime military service in the RAAF when he returned to journalism in 1945 until the mid-1950s. This was the beginning of a splendid, if fairly short, career as a journalist (unlike his father). But like his father, Paul was to place high value in all his writings on real life and real personal stories as what is now termed an investigative journalist frequently using interviews, but also using the fiction writer's techniques in characterisation, plotting, reconstruction of dialogue from imagination and unfolding suspense building in story construction. In much of his journalistic writing he revealed the soul of an imaginative and assured biographer. But, using his own words late in life when he was interviewed by curious journalists, he was at all times a 'straight shooter' like many of his RAAF pals.

Boon Companions

At idyllic, leafy Greenwich Point on a watery headland and small bay with a tidal pool near the junction of the Parramatta and the Lane Cove Rivers, Paul Brickhill's closest boyhood friend and constant comrade of outdoor escapades was Peter Finch who later became a brilliant stage and screen actor and an eminent stage director in England. As a film actor Finch was one of the internationally greatest actors that Australia has ever produced. For many years he dominated the film scene in England as a leading actor with brilliant and diverse performances that garnered many acting awards.

Peter William Mitchell (or George Ingle) Finch was born in 1916, the same year as Paul Brickhill, but in London. Like Paul, Peter was an extraordinary and talented child full of potential and creative imagination. The Greenwich Point streets, coastal bush tracks, tidal swimming pool and boat sheds became their frequent playgrounds.

Ten-year-old Peter Finch

They both belonged to the 2nd Greenwich Boy Scout Troop whose activities they enjoyed. Peter had no friends at school in Greenwich. But one boy of his own age – who went to a different school – lived about seventy-five yards away, Paul Brickhill. Peter lived at 16 Wallace Street on the corner of Wallace and Mitchell Streets opposite a park. Their childhood games and rambles together in the streets surged their creative imaginations about adventure and daring. Peter's restricted miserable home life at Greenwich Point was quite different to the happy steady home life in a nuclear, but large family that Paul enjoyed. Peter lived as a seemingly orphan child with his great Uncle Edward Henry Finch – a retired bank manager aged seventy-three, when the ten-year-old Peter suddenly arrived on his doorstep – and Edward's spinster daughter Bertha in her forties, known to Peter as Betty, as well as her brother Jack, who was blind in one eye. Jack was a reserved shy auditor in the Bank of New South Wales. These three adults struggling in genteel poverty lived in a bungalow a short distance from Paul's street. The Brickhills lived in a magnificent and prominent many-roomed mansion looking out on the busy river scene of ferries and sailing craft, Cockatoo Island and Hunters Hill. It was one of the best residences in Greenwich Point on a comparatively large and manicured block of gardens – a prominent corner block on the crest of the hill.

Peter Finch later referred to his seven years living with his elderly relatives in Greenwich Point, from the age of ten to seventeen, as 'the dark ages'. While a kindly soft man who like Peter hated rows, his elderly great uncle stood apart from the severe supervision of Peter's upbringing which was dominated by the rather bitter Betty who resented Peter's arrival in the household. He had considerably disturbed her staid social life as a housekeeper. Jack supported them all on a small part-time salary.

As a sensitive boy with a healthy imagination, Peter was quick to sense her silent resentment. She was emotionally cold towards him while, as a lonely boy, he was craving for affection. He was heavily disciplined, but not neglected in any material sense by the adults, always led by the fiery Betty.

Before arriving there, Peter had led an undisciplined carefree life, especially in India from 1925 with his romantic grandmother Laura, who was pursuing spiritual enlightenment in the Theosophical Movement in Madras and did not take much notice of him. He was free to wander around the institution and its temples in Buddhist robes. Before that he had lived his infancy in London and then, at the age of two, in an artistic bohemian commune in France near Paris with his Australian natural mother.

Thus Betty found him a strange little boy of ten living within his imagination and she did not have sufficient empathy to understand him. He tended to tell her wild stories that had no basis in fact. She forced him to do – what he regarded – as menial tasks in the household and garden. The Finch and the Brickhill home life were very different.

As Paul became Peter's boon companion he soon noticed this situation and sympathised with his friend's situation. It was unlike his own family. Both were new arrivals from elsewhere and had a natural affinity with one another. As a boy, Paul had a bad stammer. Peter, as a free-flowing articulate speaker, attempted to help his friend overcome his stammer, but it took several years.

Betty viewed Peter as a great embarrassment to her sedate middle-class friends. He wet the bed frequently. Betty's seemingly draconian discipline maddened him. Amongst other pranks in revenge, he urinated on her garden beds just as her guests who had been invited for tea were arriving through the front gate. Peter was exasperated by Betty and she him. As well, he was always playing practical jokes on the hapless Uncle Jack – sometimes in league with Paul Brickhill. At fifteen, Peter used to take his uncle's prized collection of telescopes into the street over in nearby Hunter's Hill and offer to sell them in the main street. His uncle soon found out and was distressed about it. He was forced to buy back those which had been sold.

It was Betty, however, who used to give Peter a good hiding which Peter exaggerated to gain sympathy, calling it a cruel flogging. According to the adult Peter, Betty was 'tyrannical' and the frustration of her sex drive in spinsterhood found its outlet in trying to handle and discipline what proved to be the maverick-spirited Peter.[15] As a colourful unreliable story teller, he implied that she molested him by beating him for no reason at all.

Nevertheless, Betty was kind to Peter in her rigid way and gave him occasional rewards for any unsolicited deeds. She used to require him to mow the lawns and trim the edges every Saturday afternoon as well as look after the backyard (but this would have been a common chore for many schoolboys in Sydney suburbs in more humble homes). All the other privileged boys in the street went to the local cinema including his friend Paul, or they were playing cricket and swimming in the summer or playing rugby in the winter which must have been the source of schoolboy Finch's resentment about Saturdays. Still, he did do most of his aunt's gardening in the large backyard and smaller front garden as well as the household cleaning. He attended Greenwich Public School within walking distance.

The Greenwich Point Baths, a tidal pool in the cove of the headland, was a favourite spot for Paul and Peter when they could get there. They belonged to the amateur swimming club founded there in 1929. Paul, in particular, became a competent competitive swimmer and won several swimming medals and awards from the local club. Paul trained harder and was more regular in his activities than Peter. Consequently, he was the much better swimmer. He also swam there with his brothers. The Brickhill household was a lively, happy one. Swimming champions and local icons Jack McMahon and Ted Lever used the baths for training. Thus with these sporting heroes available, Paul and Peter swam there through the long summers. The

15 Faulkner, *Peter Finch*, 38-39.

swimming club at that time was one of the largest in Sydney and even held an annual carnival.

In the 1920s the internationally famous Dick Cavill, a pioneer of Australian competitive swimming, held the lease of the baths and coached many local children including Peter and Paul.

Swimming pool, Greenwich Point

One of the six famous Cavill competitive swimming brothers, Dick innovated with an alternative version of the Australian crawl swimming long stretches with his head underwater and breathing only when absolutely necessary. Under Cavill's coaching, Paul in particular developed an excellent swimming style – Peter less so as he was unable to attend coaching lessons regularly.

In 1902, Cavill had become the world's foremost swimmer, being the first to swim 100 yards in under a minute (58.6 seconds). He won many Australian and International championships. Between 1900 and 1904, he had won eighteen Australian and twenty-two New South Wales championships.[16] At the time, he was swimming against some of the world's best as Sydney was the mecca of the sport.

In the locality on the same beach were small commercial boat sheds that the two boys spent time hanging around in.

---

16 Judy Washington, 'Tidal Swimming Pools of Lane Cove, 2 Greenwich Baths Pt 2', *Lane Cove Historical Society Newsletter,* no 167, July 2001, 2.

Peter always fooled around wildly with Paul on the infrequent occasions he was let out by his stern aunt. He needed to let off steam, hence their dangerous attempt to row the abandoned boat which led to near disaster for them both. After this occasion, Peter was sent by his aunt to Paul's place to tell him he was banned from playing with him, but this was soon forgotten. They frequently continued to get into trouble and strife on many occasions, but Paul later recounted to Peter's biographer that his friend 'always had a lucky star over him'. Paul reflected with horror Peter's domestic existence with his aunt in stark contrast to his own happy family life. After the war, he claimed: 'He had a tough time. No one ever knew how bad it was. He was a skivvy, a servant – washing, cleaning, sweeping, scrubbing, making beds, working in the garden; he was rarely allowed out'.[17] Paul became determined to rescue his friend – to get him out playing with other boys. In the process they became the closest of boon companions.

North Sydney Boys High

Peter and Paul both left primary school at Greenwich in 1929 and began attending North Sydney Intermediate High School in Falcon and Miller Streets, North Sydney. They travelled there and back by ferry and then walked up Miller Street to the school. At Greenwich they had learned to dodge the local roughs in gangs by running away, dodging and keeping out of trouble as much as possible.

At school in North Sydney the two boys became deft during recess and lunch time at flicking folded cigarette packs or coins against the wall of the school building in various playground petty gambling games with other boys. They were frequently

17 Dundy, *Finch, Bloody Finch*, 53.

successful in such contests. The school recreation yard became their kingdom. They always stuck together at recess and lunchtime when sometimes they would disappear from the school grounds altogether.

At home Peter and Paul loved to go down to the local boatshed. Finch's Uncle Jack made them a little boat. Still Peter felt emotionally homeless. In his imagination he placed himself in a Dickensian situation as a foundling. He was rebellious and often truanted from High School with Paul. They found the classroom a dreary and boring place and the outdoors much more exciting in general. They got on ferries or went down on the foreshore to watch the big cranes moving the two cantilever arcs closer and closer as the Sydney Harbour Bridge took shape in the late 1920s. To them, it was an exciting setting as it was to others. John JC Bradfield's engineering work on the bridge had become a modern marvel for Sydneysiders young and old. To watch the construction was an exciting magnetic sight for schoolboys and worth wagging school for. Peter and Paul, on frequent occasions, preferred to wander the streets than be at home doing jobs for Betty in the house in Greenwich Point.[18]

For the two boys, adventure of all sorts was in the air all around them in the wider sense from 1930 onwards. At the Sydney Cricket Ground Donald Bradman made the world's highest score (452 not out) in first class cricket at the close of New South Wales' second innings on Monday, 6 January 1930. Bradman's score eclipsed the previous record of 437 held by the Victorian and Australian batsman William "Bill" Ponsford. In the previous season Bradman had set a record for the most runs in an Australian cricket season, making seven centuries amongst other good scores. Such sporting achievements were particularly spellbinding for innocent Australian boys of Peter and Paul's age.

---

18 Faulkner, *Peter Finch*, 40.

Equally interesting, particularly for Paul, was that Australian National Airways (ANA) on 1 January 1930 commenced a regular air service between Sydney and Brisbane, the first in Australia. By 1 June that year, ANA also began a regular Sydney to Melbourne air service. On 24 May, Amy Johnson became the first woman to fly solo from Britain to Australia. The flight took nineteen days. Along with Kingsford Smith's 1930 world flight, Paul found it all a fascinating prospect for the future. In the 1930s adolescent Australian boys were commonly addicted to fantasies about flight.

Of particular interest to Peter, however, the Independent Theatre was established on 30 May by Doris Fitton. It was here that he was later to study drama in the mid-1930s.

At 10pm on 19 August 1930, Peter and Paul, watching fascinated, witnessed the two half arches of the Sydney Harbour Bridge, held by steel cables, being joined together. The Bridge was officially opened on Saturday, 19 March 1932 by the New South Wales Labor Premier Jack Lang. The ceremony was earlier dramatically disrupted by the self-styled Captain De Groot, a member of the extreme right-wing New Guard, who had slashed the ceremonial opening ribbon with his sword on horseback in a political demonstration.

For the first time, it was now possible to cross from the south to the north shore of Sydney Harbour and vice versa on foot or by vehicle rather than by ferry. It was still quicker, however, for Paul and Peter to get to the city from Greenwich Point by boat – as it is still today.

In 1932 too, the first talkie feature film by the new Sydney studio Cinesound was released: *On Our Selection* starring Bert Bailey as Dad Rudd and directed by Ken Hall. While it was a huge hit around Australia, little did Peter and Paul realise that Peter would make his film debut in a cameo role in the third film comedy of the series of Dad and Dave stories: *Dad and Dave Come to Town* in 1938 also starring the popular Bert Bailey and directed by Ken Hall.

Peter Finch got his real start in the world of theatre in 1934 in small juvenile parts in the famous Independent Theatre directed by Doris Fitton who realised his great potential. He made more, but still meagre money spruiking in the side shows at the Royal Easter Agricultural Show in Sydney's Moore Park. This activity happened to improve voice projection for acting. Peter soon gained more parts with the Sydney BSA (Broadcasting Service Association) Players and then was discovered by the eminent radio director Lawrence H Cecil. He broke into radio strongly with the ABC. He played a wide range of European and Australian characters in radio plays where his voice was an asset. He was a notable Rene Latour in the popular *The Laughing Women* in 1940, reprising the role seven years later when he won the first Macquarie Award for Best Actor of the Year.

In 1938 as recounted came his film debut in *Dad and Dave Come to Town* as the gormless comic bushie Bill Ryan. He soon was appearing in small parts, particularly for local directors Ken Hall and Charles Chauvel, but they did not yet bring him to fame – that was to come much later and in England after the Second World War.

By the end of the 1930s, Peter Finch had already made a name for himself in Sydney's small theatre world and was prominent in radio drama on the ABC and the Lux Radio Theatre aired on a commercial channel that began in 1939.[19] From the first, he was a fine versatile actor with more than a touch of genius. His debut in feature films came in cameo parts in two Ken G Hall feature comedies the second of which was *Mr Chedworth Steps Out*

---

19 Jacqueline Kent, *The Heyday of Australian Radio. Out of the Bakelite Box*, Angus & Robertson, Sydney, 1983.

(1939). He followed these with diverse parts in Australian films: *The Power and the Glory* (1940), *Rats of Tobruk* (1944), *Red Sky at Morning* (1945), *A Son is Born* (1946) and *Eureka Stockade* (1949).

In 1941 he went to the Middle East with the AIF as a gunner and after many adventures he wound up acting in and producing plays that toured military hospitals and base camps. In Israel he met a Russian group interested in the Stanislavsky acting method. He married Tamara Tchinarova in April 1943. She saw his true potential as an actor.[20]

By 1940 Paul Brickhill was to be influenced by the RAAF recruiting poster 'Coming? – then Hurry! Air crew wanted NOW in the RAAF', illustrated in full colour with a dashingly good-looking pilot-hero climbing aboard a fighter plane. The poster was hung all over Sydney and elsewhere. The RAAF was to report a huge response to their recruiting campaign which drew young Paul in completely and the die was cast – especially with the introduction of compulsory military service.

The next in the feature film Dad and Dave series *Dad Rudd MP* starring Bert Bailey appeared in the same year released in June. Peter Finch was not involved as he was to join up in the 2nd AIF in the artillery. Norman Lindsay's dramatically powerful and understated recruitment poster 'Fall-in' may have influenced him or CB Simmins' poster 'Back Up Your Cobbers!' that showed a keen young recruit in uniform and with pack about to join his towering ship at the wharf for overseas. On 2 June 1941 aged twenty-four, Peter Finch enlisted in the army and soon became Gunner Finch in the Light Australian Artillery Anti-Aircraft Division. Gunner Finch stepped on to the *Queen Mary,* now a troopship bound for the Middle East.

Paul Brickhill, also aged twenty-four, had volunteered for

---

20 Albert Moran and Chris Keating, *Dictionary of Australian Radio and Television,* The Scare Crow Press, Lanham, Maryland, 2007, 161-2.

the Royal Australian Air Force about five months earlier on 6 January. After preliminary training at Narrandera, on 22 May, he embarked by transport ship to Canada for advance pilot training in Ottawa.

In effect, their childhood and adolescence together at Greenwich Point as boon companions was over and then split asunder by war.

Beloved English Teacher

At North Sydney Intermediate High, however, from the age of thirteen to fifteen years, Peter Finch tended to be a mystery to his teachers and his fellow students: 'moody, aloof and remote', apart from his close relationship with Paul Brickhill. Mrs Conybeare, Peter's English teacher, however, had a great affection for him and a strong influence over him. She appreciated his perceptive intelligence and creative imagination. In her class she had Peter, Paul and the rest of the class act in Shakespearean roles. These sessions were much more interesting to Peter and Paul than the normal dull lessons. Conybeare found Peter, in particular, outstanding in acting these parts. His performance of Shylock was especially vivid in her memory. Peter could recite by heart passage after passage of Shakespeare, Latin and French. Nevertheless, he resented the oppressive discipline in the school generally and was frequently and defiantly late for classes, frequently with Paul who went along with the practice. Peter also ran away from home twice when he was at North Sydney Intermediate High – once to Queensland.

At thirteen in First Year High School, Peter and Paul, while travelling from Greenwich Point to Blues Point Wharf and then walking up Blues Point Road and then Miller Street to the school, read a great deal, sharing books (especially the historical romances of Victor Hugo, like *The Hunchback of Notre Dame*, *Les Miserables* and *Toilers of the Sea*, and *The Three Musketeers* and *The Count of Monte Cristo* by Alexandre Dumas, and Charles Dickens' novels such as: *Great Expectations, Oliver Twist, David Copperfield, A Tale of Two Cities* and so on). Finch could play Sydney Carton facing the guillotine to a tee and Quasimodo as the bellringer and other favourites for an instant street or playground performance.

To the two boys, North Sydney Intermediate was a grim, square two-storey brick building that served out a series of unexciting subject-centred lessons. The austere-looking building consisted of eight classrooms, each meant to accommodate thirty-six boys. By the time Paul and Peter started there each class was heavily overcrowded with fifty or more students. The school drew students from the North Shore on the railway to Hornsby, especially from Greenwich, Artarmon, Chatswood and Gordon where there were the larger primary schools of the North Shore.[21] At North Sydney Boys High the Intermediate program the two boys studied was separate from the five-year Leaving Certificate program.

Peter Finch, however, claimed he hated every minute at school, apart from Mrs Conybeare's sessions on Shakespearean drama. Years later when Peter was in Australia shooting *The Shiralee*, Mrs Conybeare received an unexpected phone call from him. They had a most friendly conversation. At the end Peter said: 'I've always loved you. You know I've always loved you, don't you?' For Peter at school she was a major, perhaps the only attraction and influence. This attractive young teacher was, in fact, adored by all the boys in Peter and Paul's class. Her help and encouragement of Peter in drama was indeed a strong

21 Kim Eberhardt, *A Falcon Century. North Sydney Boys High School 1912-2012*, North Sydney Boys High, Crows Nest, 2012, 90.

influence on his future development as a professional stage and screen actor and as a stage director. She no doubt provided a keen support for Paul Brickhill's development as a writer. He excelled in classroom composition under her tuition. The subjects for the Intermediate that both Peter and Paul studied were: English, History, Geography, Maths I and II, Latin and French.[22] No other teachers at the school seem to have had much influence over either of the tearaway boys apart from the vivacious Mrs Conybeare.

Peter Finch was discovered by Laurence Olivier and Vivien Leigh on the Sydney leg of the 1948 Old Vic Tour of Shakespearean plays and, thus encouraged, went to England to seek his fortune. British film parts soon followed with *Train of Events* (1949), *The Wooden Horse* (1950), *The Miniver Story* (1950), *The Story of Robin Hood and His Merry Men* (1952) in which he played his famous screen villain part of the Sheriff of Nottingham and stole the show, *The Story of Gilbert and Sullivan* (1953), *The Heart of the Matter* (1953), *Elephant Walk* (1953/54), *Father Brown* (1954) as the French thief Flambeau, again stealing the show from Alec Guiness as Father Brown, and five other films until one of his greatest roles as the Australian prisoner-of-war in a Japanese prison camp for which he won the British Film Academy Award for Best Actor for 1956 in *A Town Like Alice*.

In the mid-1950s, he met up in London with his old schoolboy pal, the now famous writer Paul Brickhill.

Boy Scouts

Both Peter and Paul found much greater satisfaction and interest in the Boy Scout Movement than in school in their

22 *The Falcon. The Journal of North Sydney Boys High*, no 29, April 1934, 15.

early adolescence. They were both allowed to join the 2nd Greenwich Boy Scout Troop. Peter, with Paul as a slightly quieter accomplice, set about organising the scout troop to form his first acting company from what he had learned in Mrs Conybeare's English class and from his own personal enthusiasm, even obsession, with the art. He knew even then that he wanted to become an actor. Peter and Paul also relished tying knots, stalking, telling yarns around the camp fire by acting them out, learning bushcraft and first aid. They became absorbed in the Scout Movement's progressive and informal educational program with its emphasis on learning-by-doing and its exciting project activities. High School was a very dull place in comparison, a place where you learned not to excel and were totally bored.

Peter and Paul's needs in early adolescence meshed with that of the Boy Scouts activities. As a money-raising project to get a hall for the troop, they put on a show for which the audience were charged admission. They were able to draw an audience of hundreds on a number of occasions. Peter wrote and produced his own play, 'The Tragedy of the Romanoffs'. The production was professionally organised by the two enthusiastic and remarkably creative boys. Peter played the central part wearing Paul's treasured swimming medals around his neck as Russian ceremonial decorations. His fellow creator Paul played an old family retainer who shuffled back and forth in the background of the scenes. Later Paul Brickhill admitted that the play was 'a bit over the heads of the audience', but they applauded enthusiastically at the end. There is no question, however, that Peter Finch was the star attraction of the show.[23] And yet it does not necessarily follow that Paul Brickhill was merely Finch's shadow. The play was presented in 1930 at the

23 Dundy, *Finch, Bloody Finch*, 47-53.

Chatswood Community Hall to adoring parents and friends of the boys' Boy Scout Troop.

* * *

Both boys left North Sydney Boys Intermediate High without any academic distinction to speak of. They never rated a mention in the annual school magazines between 1929 and 1936, although a portrait of Paul Brickhill appeared mysteriously in the school's first history in 1960 after he had achieved fame as an international author, but without comment.[24] Peter Finch was not acknowledged by the same history as being a student at the school. There seems to be no direct evidence that he ever sat for the Intermediate Certificate examination which, in those days, was a passport to a job, but it seems Paul Brickhill completed it. Peter just failed to turn up. Both boys did much better after leaving school with its dull routines.

North Sydney Boys High School

24 A perusal was made of the *Falcon*, the school's journal, from 1926 to 1933; HM Storey, *History of North Sydney High School 1912-1960*, North Sydney Boys High School, Crows Nest, 1962, unpaginated.

Much later, Clive Brickhill recalled his elder brother's boyhood:

> ... I remember Paul as someone with a zest for life, some what of an extravert compared to his brothers. I think he may have had a touch of the Walter Mitty about him, imagining himself in some exciting scene such as being a World War I fighter pilot – this was realised in another context in World War 2. We all have our dreams. Paul wanted to get on with life – not for him the dullness of hard study at North Sydney Boys High School for University matriculation. He left when things were still tough after the depression.[25]

Initially, for a short while after leaving school, Paul worked for his father as a cub reporter on a starting wage of twelve shillings and sixpence per week.

When the family arrived in Sydney George Brickhill founded the United Australia Press. By the 1930s he had set up a chain of Sydney suburban newspapers. Paul, however, soon left his father's employ in favour of situations in the city of Sydney that had appeared.[26]

---

25 Clive Brickhill to Tempe and Tim Brickhill, 11 May 1991 (typescript supplied by Beatrice Brickhill).

26 Typescript Eulogy by Lloyd Brickhill delivered at Paul's funeral service, St Clement's Church of England, Raglan Street, Mosman, 24 April 1991 (supplied by Beatrice Brickhill).

CHAPTER 2

PRE-WAR JOURNALISM

Through the influence of a friend of the middle-class Finch family on Greenwich Point in the North Shore, Peter obtained a junior cadetship with the Sydney *Sun*, a popular mass circulation afternoon newspaper on the rise that included feature articles of a sometimes left-leaning, but sensational nature. Finch ended his schooling when he left North Sydney Boys Intermediate High at the age of sixteen.

Meanwhile, Paul did not succeed in a couple of jobs because his persistent stammer in stressful situations had re-emerged. In early 1932 he obtained a junior clerical position with the Adelaide Steamship Company in its prestigious Sydney office. At the office enquiry counter in dealing with the general public his repeated stammering became an embarrassment and intense irritation to his superior. He considered him a total failure with office work and threatened him with instant dismissal, but other staff members, who found Paul likeable and eager, took his part as he was a mere boy, willing and conscientious. From an office junior, he was a lift driver in the Adelaide Steamship Company's building, but he became discouraged and embarrassed and soon left. He had, however, been treated very sympathetically by the firm's hierarchy.

He was now at a loose end with not much hope of obtaining

other work in Sydney. It was the height of the Great Depression and there were few jobs to be had for the rising generation and those that were available were hotly contested. The open-hearted Peter Finch came to his aid.

Showing his still close friendship with Brickhill, the personable and charming Finch persuaded Norman Johnson, his well-known editor, to hire his friend also as a junior cadet. Finch then persuaded Brickhill about the rich possibilities of becoming a reporter as he knew how to write. Brickhill later claimed: 'If it hadn't been for Peter making Johnson hire me on the newspaper, I would never have become a newspaper man or a writer. I owe Peter a lot'.[1] It is likely that both Peter and Paul got their jobs via the back door through a Finch family connection and, as well, through the influence of Paul's father George who was very well known and highly respected in the Australian newspaper world. To the vast unemployed youth of Sydney at the time cadetships were considered plum jobs and highly sought after. They had a sense of glamour about them together with the hope of a future career as a well-known journalist.

The Sydney *Sun*

The opulently designed *Sun* newspaper building near Martin Place at 60-70 Elizabeth Street (now demolished), where the two young cadets clocked in each working day, was a magnificent art deco affair newly opened in October 1929 to fanfare. The building's impressive entrance which Peter Finch and Paul Brickhill walked through every morning had the newspaper's beautiful logo laid in the tiled floor as well as in the glass lead-

1 Dundy, *Finch, Bloody Finch*, 54.

lighting above the door. It had been designed by the newspaper's Head of the Art Department and layout artist Donald Sackville Bain, who had served in the Great War in the 1st AIF between 1914 and 1919. Bain had returned to Australia with an English war bride, Dorothy (née Bingham), from Surrey who was born in Birmingham.

Donald Bain's logo, etched into the marble floor, depicted a Roman charioteer riding out of the sun astride a chariot with long reins in his hands. In front was a stream of wild horses of different colours in full flight. They were racing from a big brilliant ball representing the sun. While the logo would have fascinated the imagination of the young cadets of the *Sun*, Peter and Paul – still boon companions – the *Sun* building was also a major tourist attraction in Sydney. Many sightseers came to look at it during the 1930s. Work there gave employees a sense of distinction compared to other more unpleasant work situations found in Sydney. The young men were required to dress formally while working for the firm, to consider themselves as gentlemen, but under the rigorous authority of the editor and manager of personnel.

The same design of the *Sun* logo by Donald Bain was featured throughout the elaborate tile walkways of the building, as if to remind the employees that their newspaper articles and features had to hold the same sense of excitement, adventure and direction. On the top of the building was a huge golden ball representing the sun.[2] It stood out as a dominant feature of the skylight of the city for many years.

As an impressionable imaginative young cadet, Paul Brickhill absorbed the symbolism, the sense of direct action and adventure and he captured it effectively in his mature newspaper and book writing that always rolled on with colourful excitement and detail to its journey's end, like the *Sun*'s heroic charioteer of classical mythology. He always wrote symbolically about an intensive heroic chariot of fire.

Bain's design for a logo featured on top of the front page of every issue of the afternoon *Sun* and later on the Sunday *Sun-Herald*. Even after the Second World War, the logo featured on the letterhead of Brickhill's official correspondence paper when he was the *Sun*'s European correspondent immediately after the war.[3] It was one of the most recognised symbols of the city of Sydney.

Donald Bain, the elder statesman as the Head of the Art Department, acted as a mentor to all the young cadets, including Paul and Peter who were frequently sent to his office on errands as part of their daily work. In particular, he would have known George Brickhill, the prominent Sydney newspaper editor and Paul's father. Bain told the boys stories of his life's adventures that they eagerly absorbed. He would have told the two boon companions about his early life before World War I and during it.

Donald and his brother Ian were born in Yorkshire of Scottish heritage. He was twenty-eight years of age when the Great War began and had been previously trained in England

---

2 Correspondence from Janet Ramsland Bain, the daughter of Donald Sackville Bain, the Head of the *Sun*'s Art Department in the 1920s and 1930s, 17.7.2015.

3 Service Record, WWII, Brickhill, F/Lt PCJ, 403313, National Archives of Australia (NAA), Canberra.

for four years as a commercial artist.[4] As young men Donald and his brother Ian had gone to the United States to work and live. For a period, they joined a circus performing as trapeze artists. They also prepared the colourful picturesque backdrops and the illustration of the circus transport. They continued to pursue a commercial art career together as a team in the States. They designed some neon signs in Los Angeles, for example. They then worked on painting backdrops in theatres. They designed the scenery and accessories for performances of various kinds. Once, they prepared the scenic backdrops for the great Caruso, the operatic tenor.

Before the Great War, the two young men migrated to Australia to seek their fortunes. Together they operated a commercial art studio in Sydney.[5] Both men enlisted. Ian Bain was to be killed in action in France; Donald just survived the war fighting in the 13th Company of Engineers. He was a casualty on a number of occasions, including suffering from shellshock, along with many other men in the Australian forces. In later life, he suffered badly from his war injuries, but managed to work prolifically as a prominent commercial artist in Sydney.

His AIF number was 4134. By religion he was a Baptist and single when he enlisted as a volunteer on 29 August 1915. His next-of-kin declared on enlistment was still in Scotland: Miss M Bain, whose address was 54 George Square, Edinburgh. His rank was Private and the unit he was placed in at Holsworthy Training Camp south-west of Sydney was the 13th Battalion, 13th Reinforcement, 11th Field Company of Engineers (Artillery). He was five foot three inches in height and weighed 112lbs, just eight stone. He embarked from Sydney on HMAT A60 *Aeneas*

4 Donald Bain, Service Record, 4134, 1st AIF, NAA.

5 Correspondence, Janet Ramsland Bain.

on 20 December 1915. According to the enlistment papers, he was fair with grey eyes. His training continued in Egypt after Holsworthy before fighting in a variety of situations on the Western Front where he was ill on several occasions and was hospitalised a number of times due to the terrible frontline conditions. Finally, he was taken to a hospital in Boulogne suffering badly from shellshock.

Bain's war experiences maimed him for the rest of his life, but after the Great War he joined the staff of the *Sun* newspaper as Head of the Art Department where Peter Finch and Paul Brickhill met him as young cadets in the early 1930s. They were fascinated with his many stories of overseas, both in the Western Front during the Great War for which he was awarded the 1914/1915 Star, the British War Medal and the Victory Medal, and of his colourful earlier life in America with his brother.[6]

6 Donald Sackville Bain had a distinguished commercial art career. He designed many humorous newspaper cartoons; the logos for Morton Fly Spray, Stamina Trousers for men; Heinz canned food, Madura and Billy Teas (before the war, he and his brother designed logos for Sydney Flour and Arnott's Biscuits). Donald Bain was commissioned to create an advertisement and logo for the Canadian-Pacific Railways that took him six months to complete. The impressive result was displayed in full colour in Sydney in government buses and trams depicting a powerful Indian Chief in magnificent feathered headdress astride a majestic Appaloosa on the cliff of a high mountain top looking down on a steam train depicting a very modern form of luxury transport going through an impressive viaduct. The effort of the large work resulted in Bain, under immense strain from stress and war memories going into Concord Repatriation Hospital for treatment. He eventually returned to work for the *Sun*. Before he joined the *Sun*, he carried out designs and illustrations for the *Bulletin*, designing the front cover. His death occurred in Concord Hospital on 21 November 1954. Information provided by his daughter Janet, Correspondence.

Donald Bain & one of his cartoons from the Sun
(Courtesy of Janet Ramsland Bain)

Working for the *Sun*

In 1932 many boys and girls leaving school would have been envious of Paul Brickhill's plum appointment to the *Sun* newspaper in Sydney. Such appointments were difficult to obtain at the height of the Great Depression. To the youthful cadet, the newly completed building at Elizabeth Street created an exciting new world he was entering – a world in stark contrast with the dull sombre walls of North Sydney Boys High School with its packed classrooms of frequently reluctant schoolboys, stressed, sometimes unpleasant schoolteachers and dull routine lessons.

The new *Sun* building which completely dominated the cityscape with its golden orb on top of its purpose-designed skyscraper was a feverish panopticon of intense and stimulating activity to produce the most famous afternoon newspaper of

Sydney and the *Sunday Illustrated.* When Paul entered the paper's workforce at a junior level, many drastic changes had been recently made in the make-up of the daily and Sunday newspapers by the energetic new management. The name had been changed to its shortened form. The page size of its issue had been altered to the tabloid form to be more in keeping with what was in vogue in America and England for similar popular productions. Improvements were made in the quality of paper and ink. The paper was brighter and more attractive to the newer generation of readers – Paul's generation. And most importantly, the management provided an energetic program of thorough on-the-job training for its cadets, like Peter and Paul. They constantly rubbed shoulders with Sydney's most experienced and successful journalists.

Similar changes were made in the Sunday paper; the name was shortened whilst in both daily and Sunday issues fuller and better display was given to the craft of artist and photographer as led by Donald Bain, chief artist of the newspaper. He was based on the floor below that of Brickhill and the other cadets.

The production of the newspaper was highly and efficiently organised. The building was appropriately designed to suit the wide-ranging culture of the world of popular newspapers. For example, the staff photographer and reporter, along with his cadet, such as Paul, attended say a major rugby union match at the Sydney Cricket Ground and started the ball rolling. The cadet rushed the negative back to the *Sun* building where a print was made on brand new state-of-the-art equipment. The caption writer came onto the scene and, after writing the line that was to accompany the picture, he passed it on to the artist's room where the photograph was prepared for the process department. It was then taken there by the cadet.

The next step was to re-take the photograph through a screen so that it could be printed on metal when the first stage of making the process block was reached. The metal was passed on to the etcher and was etched and cut into the stipulated shape. A proof was then taken from the finished block that then went on to the stereo-department where a "winker" machine came into requisition to make a matrix from which a stereo-plate was carefully moulded. The linotype machine set up the letterpress. One of the giant presses was capable of turning out 72,000 pages per hour for the newspaper. The newspaper was then sold in the streets of the city. Cadets, like Paul Brickhill, had to become familiar in on-the-job training with the complete process from its beginning to its end. Knowledge and understanding were the essence of cadet training in journalism.

The new *Sun* building had a commanding Elizabeth Street frontage which Paul eagerly entered early in the morning of every working day to receive the assignments of an extremely busy day. The magnificent art nouveau entranceway led to a commanding marble-walled vestibule which opened through large doors to the marbled advertising counter beyond with its open access to the general public. As a whole, the building was the perfect work panopticon in design. As well as the huge gilded orb representing the sun, the top featured an observation tower where one could admire the cityscape and the harbour from the elevated position. There was also a large water tank on the roof.

The fourteenth floor was the staff cafeteria that could accommodate the entire staff who worked in the building. Each floor could be reached by electric elevators. The thirteenth below was the Mechanical Department and the Ventilating plant. The twelfth floor was the *Sun Pictorial* General Office housing its experienced reporters. The next floor, the eleventh, was the General Office which Brickhill and the other cadets inhabited when they were not out on assignments. Below was the tenth floor, the Artists Process, Photographic department led in Brickhill's time by Donald Bain, the respected commercial artist.

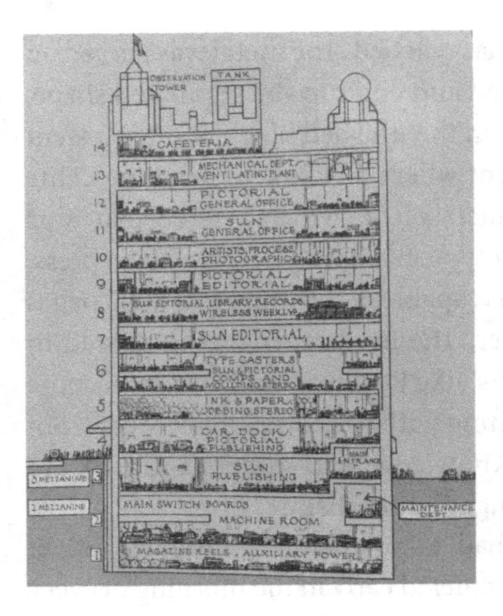

Sun *building c. 1929*

The ninth floor was the *Pictorial* Editorial; the eight floor was the library, Records and *Wireless Weekly*; the seventh floor was the *Sun* Editorial; the sixth, Typecasters *Sun* & *Pictorial* Composers and Moulding Section; the fifth, the Ink and Paper Jobbing, Section and the fourth – the ground floor with the Elizabeth Street entrance, the Car Dock and the *Pictorial* Publishing Office. Below street level were three mezzanine floors: *Sun* Publishing, Main Switch Board and Machine Rooms plus the Maintenance Department and magazine reels, auxiliary power. At the time there was no other building so well equipped in Sydney, particularly for vertical communication. From the basement to the top, it was, in 1932, the tallest building in Sydney. Its golden globe or orb was a landmark for miles around the city.[7]

Paul Brickhill was proud and excited to be part of such a newspaper enterprise and worked hard to climb the ladder of success in journalism during his youth. The symbol of Donald Bain's logo of the chariot of fire in the *Sun* was there to inspire him. He had found his milieu which almost entirely absorbed his working life.

---

7 *Sun Newspaper Ltd 1910-1929*, *Sun* Newspapers Ltd, Sydney, 1929, 1-60.

Fun at the *Sun*

Now working together and earlier schooled together, the two friends Paul Brickhill and Peter Finch remained constant, close companions. For a while they both travelled the short distance to Sydney aboard the Greenwich Point ferry as noisy sixteen-year-olds in their first new or hand-down suits and ties. The *Sun* newspaper demanded high dress standards! (Peter was only a few months older than Paul.) One can imagine that the two spirited and imaginative boys fantasised their way across the water to Circular Quay in intense conversation about their future prospects while they walked up to Martin Place and the Elizabeth Street splendid *Sun* building. One was always going to be an outstanding actor of international stature and the other a pilot, eminent journalist and best selling post-war author. While Finch was ill-suited to the discipline of journalism – a square peg in a round hole – and favoured acting and the theatre above all else, Brickhill came from a solid and influential background of the newspaper world – from both his eminent father and even his grandfather. Brickhill slid easily into the life of journalism which Finch was always uncomfortable with. They were both to have their wishes and dreams of success granted. But it was early days yet and the future with its golden triumphs and darker difficulties lay well before them.

Despite many ups and downs in wartime, by the 1950s both boys had achieved their dreams. At a party in his flat in Dolphin Square in London, the now-celebrated actor Peter Finch arrived late when the crowded party was already in full swing:

> As he came through the door someone handed him a drink and, looking around, he was suddenly startled to see at the other end of the room his earliest

> boyhood mate from Greenwich Point; his fellow copy boy on the Sun with whom he had shared so many youthful fantasies of achievement: Paul Brickhill [now a famous international author]. Peter caught Paul's eye and they looked at each other for a long time, their thoughts going back into the past and then returning to the present. Paul Brickhill was now a successful writer and Peter a successful West End actor.
>
> Slowly Peter raised his glass to Paul in an ironic salute and over the noise he called out with infinite mockery 'Success! Success!' Paul raised his glass in the same spirit and returned the toast, 'Success! Success!'[8]

At the *Sun* newspaper office in 1932 things were different as both were youths just starting out in adult life. Both were fortunate, however, to obtain any sort of job at the time when the number of jobless had risen to 33,700 in Australia. Admittedly they were protégés of their benevolent neighbour, the famous newspaper editor Norman Johnson. Through his influence, Peter and Paul were not just relegated to the copy boy bench at the *Sun*, but were attached and assigned as apprentices to particular outstanding and experienced journalists to learn the trade. They were part of the newspaper's new scheme of on-the-job training in Sydney journalism. Over the next year or so, it became evident to Johnson that Paul was on his way to becoming a top newspaperman while Peter was clearly on way to being sacked – his drive to become an actor was far too strong and suppressed any other ambition. In jobs other than acting, he constantly played the fool.

8 Dundy, *Finch, Bloody Finch*, 170.

The Sydney *Sun* had originally commenced publication on 1 July 1910 when Sir Hugh Denison had acquired the *Star* and the *Sunday Sun* (which began in 1903) as both were in liquidation. This was the same year that the Australian Journalists' Association was formed as a federal body with Paul Brickhill's father George as one of the founders. The Sydney *Sun* soon built up a brisk following with a daily afternoon circulation of note. With no television to watch men and women bought the *Sun* from newsstands on their way home from work in the city.

Sir Hugh Denison, Sun *proprietor*

The same year that Paul Brickhill and Peter Finch began their apprenticeship at the *Sun*, the Labor Premier's opening of the Sydney Harbour Bridge, as already recounted, was marred when mounted New Guardsman Captain Francis de Groot slashed the ceremonial ribbon prematurely. Colonel Eric Campbell's New Guard was a quasi-Fascist, militaristic movement strong amongst certain middle-class Sydney ex-servicemen from the Great War keen to counteract, violently if necessary, the more radical New South Wales Premier, Jack Lang's so-called socialism and his attempts to deal with the Depression by legislation.

Thus Sydney journalists like the budding Brickhill and not so enthusiastic Finch had plenty to report on in such a volatile time culminating in Lang being dismissed by Sir Philip Game, the New South Wales State Governor as part of a plot to overthrow him.

Every lunch hour at the *Sun*, Peter Finch provided other

informal entertainment by performing in the street for a cluster of fellow copy boys. Another copy boy friend of Paul Brickhill David Dixon remembered how all the copy boys at the lunch break would assemble on the pavement and stand out in the street outside the *Sun* building under the awning while the sixteen-year-old Finch entertained them: 'Peter from across the street would yell out "Hitler!", run around the block and reappear impersonating Hitler. Then he would call out "Napoleon!" run around the block again and so forth. Little cameos for lunch'.

As well Finch gave a performance as Quasimodo the Hunchback of Notre Dame encouraged by Brickhill for the benefit of the editorial room inside the building at lunchtime. But it was not much appreciated there by some of the upper office management like Norman Johnson.

One late Friday afternoon, the ebullient Finch seized the hat of the newspaper owner and Director Sir Hugh Denison from its usual stand outside his office and rushed down stairs to the machine room and with it as a distinctive prop stood on the table and gave – to the workers' intense amusement – an amazingly perfect imitation of the great man: his voice, his bearing and his manner of spitting sideways into a corner of a room. In Denison's voice, he raised all their wages, gave out vacations and made bawdy suggestions as to how they should spend them. In the middle of this noisy and most humorous performance, Denison walked in. Finch almost lost his job on the spot, but for Norman Johnson, his mentor, saving his bacon by intervening.

Sir Hugh Denison, who was born near Forbes in New South Wales in 1865, had formed the *Sun* Newspaper Ltd to take over publication of the *Sunday Sun* and the *Australian Star* and renamed it the *Sun*. This became an afternoon daily with a distinctive logo drawn by the newspaper's artist Donald Bain, a war veteran. Denison was a strong believer in the British Empire. In World War I he helped found the Citizens' War Chest and subscribed generously to government war loans and the Australian Red Cross Society. A distinguished-looking man with a neat moustache, Denison was approachable and courteous. He was a gifted public speaker with a resonant baritone voice that the young Peter Finch was able to imitate perfectly along with his distinctive mannerisms. He died in November 1940.[9]

Peter Finch was always mysteriously absent from the newspaper on Wednesday afternoons attending an acting school in Mosman. He got away with this for a while, but was found out eventually. Peter and Paul, who were both earning the princely sum of one pound a week at the *Sun*, had a long argument on the Greenwich Point ferry on their way to work about the dismal future of an acting career. Paul thought it better that Peter stuck to journalism as a viable career. Nevertheless, Finch began acting for some small remuneration in various amateur theatre groups around Sydney to gain experience.

Finally, he was sacked from the *Sun* for inattention to his work. The final situation arose when he poured a jug of water over Norman Johnson's head forcing his boss to take action on the spot.

Without any income, Finch left an unhappy home at Greenwich Point and headed for King's Cross where he lived rough and wild as a homeless person for a while. Paul Brickhill, still a cadet at the *Sun*, was able to give him five shillings a week for a rundown room in the Cross, showing his great friendship and generosity of spirit.[10]

---

9 RB Walker, 'Denison, Sir Hugh Robert (1865-1940)', *Australian Dictionary of Biography (ADB)*, vol.8, Bede Nairn & Geoffrey Serle, (gen. eds), Melbourne University Press, Carlton, 1981, 283-5.

10 Dundy, *Finch, Bloody Finch,* 58-61.

The Budding Journalist

Paul Brickhill, as a budding journalist, absorbed some of the British Empire ambience of the *Sun*'s ideology when he volunteered for the RAAF.

Paul was, however, one of the first to recognise the great acting talent of his schoolboy friend. He shared half his weekly earnings with him recognising that Finch would not be able to receive support from his family who saw him as a troublesome orphan and a worker – a domestic servant – around the home at Greenwich Point. In contrast, Paul's family were supportive, happy and close-knit and Paul was deeply aware of this.

After Peter was sacked from the *Sun* and left for Sydney's turbulent theatre world, Paul Brickhill rose steadily from the ranks of his cadetship to better and bigger things, beginning with court reporting and other fairly routine assignments. His work was so accurate and well-written that he was eventually writing important feature articles for the *Sun*. He was a fully fledged journalist by 1936. By the middle and late 1930s, he had developed an enviable reputation in Sydney as a leading pressman who could never be faulted in his work. He had developed a capacity for story telling beyond the usual. Editors always found his journalism to be of a commendable nature – if a little too detailed at times. He always met the required deadlines. Sub-editors could do the rest.

In the 1930s Peter Finch's acting career had its ups and downs as expected in such a volatile industry, but his raw talent to impress and entertain was always evident. Paul kept in touch with him when he could, but he was sometimes away from Sydney. Peter's acting career began in vaudeville in George Sorlie's famous touring tent show mainly in the outer reaches of country New South Wales and Queensland. With Sorlie's Peter learned the importance of voice projection in the Sorlie tent and audience participation. He soon progressed to radio drama in Sydney where his melodious voice and clear articulation were major assets as well as his ability to play a wide range of character parts from foreign villains to Australian heroes and anti-heroes. He made an impact on the Sydney stage at the same time, but radio provided a more reliable flow of income. Radio had a huge domestic audience in metropolitan and rural Australia. Nevertheless, at times Peter was flat broke like so many would-be actors of the period in Australia. There were tough times when his devoted friend Paul Brickhill needed to help him out. Paul was always there to provide his friend with financial help.

Peter Finch, young radio star

Peter was almost painfully thin with high prominent cheekbones and pimples. His looks gave no real promise of the handsome world-class screen actor he matured into overseas after the Second World War. But from his very beginnings, he was always considered a first-class and compelling actor. He got his first film break in Australia in small cameo parts in two comedies by Ken Hall: *Dad and Dave Come to Town* (1938) and *Mr Chedworth Steps Out* (1939). His debut was actually in an unreleased children's film *The Magic Shoes* (1935). In it he played Prince Charming in a tutu outfit with tights.

It was the 1938 Dad and Dave film, however, that helped him progress in his acting career. When the youthful actor auditioned for the part of the hapless country yokel, he was so impressive he got the part on the spot. At that time, as a close friend of Paul Brickhill, he was mainly an unknown and inexperienced actor of about twenty-one years of age. At the same age and time, Paul was already well established as a Sydney pressman of some repute and high status in the profession.

When Peter played the cameo role in *Dad and Dave...* he was flat broke and got about two days out of filming the scene he was in, but he was launched since the film proved most popular in cinemas across Australia, as was *Mr Chedworth Steps Out* the following year. In this film Finch played the juvenile lead of the eldest son of the main character, played by the experienced actor Cecil Kellaway who later went to Hollywood to score many character roles with RKO. During the filming of *Mr Chedworth...* Finch learnt much from Kellaway.

The Power and the Glory (1941) was Finch's strongest film role thus far as a villainous fifth columnist in early wartime Australia – a role he played with disturbing subtlety as he mingled freely with heroic but naïve men in an RAAF mess room. In Charles Chauvel's *The Rats of Tobruk* (1944) Finch consolidated his acting style on the screen in a powerful support performance as a scholarly AIF soldier, an English migrant who knows his Shakespeare and could entertain his mates reciting it. In the same year he played his first lead as an Irish rebel working as an ostler in an inn in *Red Sky at Morning* (1944) based on a 1938 play by the Australian Dymphna Cusack, set in the early Australian colony. It was his first non-contemporary role.

The film had a troubled release and was not seen by many in Australia. Nevertheless, it was re-released in England as *Escape at Dawn* and ran for 55 minutes as a second feature in country cinemas after Peter Finch had made his name on stage at the West End and in British films.[11]

---

11 Arthur Pike & Ronald Cooper, *Australian Film 1900-1977,* Oxford University Press, Melbourne, 1980, 240-2, 257, 258-9; Ken Hall, *Australian Film. The Inside Story,* Summit Books, Dee Why, 1980, 120.

* * *

As a schoolboy, Finch claimed to Paul: 'I can do anything, be anyone'. Between leaving North Sydney Boys High in the early 1930s to shortly after the Second World War, he was able to achieve his vision and dream. By 1949, he became Australia's leading actor on stage, in film and on radio. In August 1948 when touring Australia with the Old Vic Theatre, Laurence Olivier and Vivien Leigh discovered Peter Finch on an improvised stage at lunchtime in a factory in Sydney. Finch was directing and playing the leading role in Molière's *The Imaginary Invalid*. An extant photograph of the audience shows Olivier and Leigh in a crowded audience eagerly and intensely watching Finch's performance. The Olivier and Leigh acting duo witnessed a performance in the factory which was so brilliant Olivier invited Finch to try his luck in England and offered to sponsor his acting career. It was an offer almost too good to be true, but it was – Finch accepted.

His first major award in England was the British Oscar for his performance in *A Town Like Alice* (1956) as a gritty outback worker and prisoner-of-war of the Japanese who suffers torture, but survives. Finch played Australians in two other British film adaptations of Australian novels: *The Shiralee* (1957) and the gentleman bushranger Captain Starlight in *Robbery Under Arms* (also 1957). Shot on location these two films brought Finch temporarily back to Australia, by then a renowned actor, but he never made another visit. From then on he avoided being typecast as a gritty Australian hero or anti-hero.

Earlier, he had played in other Australian films: *Another Threshold* (1942), *A Son is Born* (1946) and *Eureka Stockade* (1949).

While his friend Paul Brickhill was languishing in Stalag Luft III in World War II, Peter was making significant contributions to Australian culture after a short stint in the Middle East in the 2nd AIF. He contributed to several documentaries made by the Department of Information during the war – several times as narrator. One important contribution was a documentary film about Australia troops on active service, *Jungle Patrol* (1944). After the war he served as Assistant Director of a documentary on Arnhem Land Aborigines, *Primitive Peoples* (1947). He carried out most of the on-location research as well as supervising and narrating the script. Other documentaries he contributed to as narrator were *While there is still time* (1942) and *South West Pacific* (1943).[12]

A high point in Peter's acting career on radio was his performance in the first LUX Radio Theatre Broadcast from station 2GB, Sydney on March 1939. The whole cast were in evening dress, both men and women, although they could only be heard not seen. In an extant photograph Finch at twenty-three years of age was addressing the microphone resplendent in evening suit and a white tie. Such was life then on radio before the introduction of television.

From March 1939 until June 1941 when he enlisted, Peter came under contract with the Australian Broadcasting Commission. He was cast in everything in plays from William Shakespeare to George Bernard Shaw. Through this busy weekly process, he was expanding vocally and receiving a thorough grounding in radio acting working with distinguished directors and casts. He was even able to tackle some of the Greek tragedies as part of an enormous variety of roles he played twice a week.[13] This was Peter Finch's theatre apprenticeship in Australia. But the war and the post-war visit of Sir Laurence Olivier and Vivien

---

12 IM Britain, 'Finch, Frederick George Peter Ingle (1916-77)', *ADB*, vol.14, John Ritchie (gen. ed.), Melbourne University Press, Carlton, 163-4; Brian McFarlane, Geoff Mayer, Ina Bertrand (eds), *The Oxford Companion to Australian Film*, Oxford University Press, Melbourne, 1999, 159.
13 Faulkner, *Peter Finch*, 77.

Leigh changed everything. Later in London, these old school friends Paul and Peter were to meet up again with a toast to 'Success! Success!'

CHAPTER 3

ACTION IN WORLD WAR II

Even while working in a busy, exciting journalistic career with the Sydney *Sun* Paul Brickhill, like several thousands, joined a local army militia as a reservist well before war began. In the 7th Field Artillery he carried out his training locally in the evenings and on weekends. He served in it for three years or so starting at the age of seventeen. Like many others he fell for the dangerous illusion and deception of the widespread pre-World War II belief that Britain 'represented a powerhouse of military protection against any foreign intimidation' for Australia and the rest of the Commonwealth.[1]

The reality was they impersonated a defence system without substance. And yet the drums of war were beating loudly again with the rise of Hitler in Germany and the Fascist movement in Spain and Italy. The young men wore their military uniforms of the various reserves audaciously down the main streets of their suburbs, like that of Greenwich, or in their suburban

1 James Rossison, 'The political decisions and policy leading to the Royal Australian Air Force having no fighters for the coming war against Japan', PhD thesis, Faculty of Creative Industries, Queensland University of Technology, 2015, ii.

shopping centre on the weekend. Instead of sport on weekends, reservists like Paul were driven in trucks to training spots and bases at military establishments dotted in and around the city of Sydney, such as Middle Head. Paul Brickhill's older brother Russell, who had also attended North Sydney Intermediate High, soon became an officer in the reserve military engineers, but Paul was not commissioned – instead he was trained as a gunner.

Joining up

On Sunday, 3 September 1939 the Prime Minister Robert Gordon Menzies explained the situation on national radio:

> Fellow Australians. It is my melancholy duty to inform you officially that, in consequence of the persistence by Germany in her invasion of Poland, Great Britain has declared war upon her, and that, as a result, Australia is also at war.
>
> ...
>
> There can be no doubt that where Great Britain stands, there stands the people of the entire British world.
>
> ...
>
> What may be before us, we do not know; nor how long the journey. But this we do know – Truth is with us in the battle, and Truth must win. In the bitter months to come, calmness, resolution, confidence, and hard work will be required as never before.[2]

2 FK Crowley, *Modern Australia in Documents. Volume 2 1939-1970*, Wren Publishing, Melbourne, 1973, 1.

Robert Gordon Menzies, Australian Prime Minister (Nla.pic-an23217367-v)

Paul Chester Jerome Brickhill, at the age of twenty-four, volunteered on 6 January 1941 for the Australian air force instead of the army. He was single and a roving journalist for the *Sun* in Sydney specialising in aviation and air defence issues. He was a compact five foot six inches tall of medium complexion with startling blue eyes. He maintained a high level of fitness through his favoured sports of squash, swimming and golf. He had a handsome, dapper and stylish appearance and wore a pencil-thin moustache.

He was one of 189,000 men and 27,000 women who enlisted in the Royal Australian Air Force (RAAF). He had decided he wanted to do his part, believing still in the ideology of the British Empire inspired Boy Scout Movement. He may well have been strongly influenced by an attractive recruitment drive poster seen around Sydney for the Volunteer Air Force: 'Make them Mightier Yet'.[3] It is probable that Paul constantly

3 Christopher Mooney, *A Powerhouse of a Man. Tom Farrell,* Brolga Publishing, Melbourne, 2015, 15.

saw the many glamorous patriotic enlistment posters found everywhere in public places: on the ferries, the railway stations, at bus and tram depots and even in city public toilets.

They persuaded him to turn away from the idea of enlistment in the army as a foot soldier to the more glamorous form of enlistment: 'Coming? – then hurry! Air Crews wanted NOW for the R.A.A.F.', shouted one poster, ambiguously depicting a smiling fighter pilot climbing into a solely crewed fighter plane that did not even exist in the RAAF at the time.

Backdrop: the fighterless air force

Even by 1939 Australia was badly equipped and unprepared for the war in the air with what one recent scholar depicted as having a 'fighterless' air force, because key political figures on both sides of politics throughout the 1930s and into the early 1940s had no realisation of the need for air supremacy.

Geoffrey Pentland and Peter Malone in *Aircraft of the RAAF 1921-78* claimed that at the outbreak of the Second World War, Australia's air force was 'almost pitifully weak by world standards' with less than two hundred military aircraft. The RAAF had been built up to a mere strength of between three thousand and four thousand men, but it had reasonably well-established bases in all states except South Australia and Tasmania. Should the security of the country be threatened, however, the twelve existing fighter, bomber and reconnaissance squadrons would find themselves committed to the defence of some 120,000 miles of coastline on the island continent – a major impossible task within the limited resources.[4]

Another popular RAAF recruitment poster implied the romance of travel as well as highly skilled occupations available. It carried the image of a Spitfire and a handsome young pilot standing heroically on the wing and waving his left hand to an apparently admiring audience. The poster shouted the challenge: 'GOING PLACES! How about YOU?' and then below the image: 'R.A.A.F. AIR CREW WANTED AT ONCE! PILOTS • NAVIGATORS • WIRELESS OPERATORS – AIR GUNNERS' and then 'APPLY R.A.A.F. RECRUITING CENTRE OR LOCAL R.A.A.F. COMMITTEE'.

A third poster providing minimal information emphasised the European theatre of war and provided an aerial map of Germany, an exploding fiery bomb in its centre and a squadron of bomber planes overhead. The caption simply and impressionistically read: 'BATTLE OF GERMANY. JOIN AN AIR CREW'.

Yet another recruitment poster provided the portrait of a handsome dashing young pilot (head and shoulders) looking heroically skywards with three Spitfires in the sky. The caption read: 'This is a Man's job! Join the R.A.A.F.'. All the posters misled, especially with the emphasis on the glamour of war and

---

4 Geoffrey Pentland & Peter Malone, *Aircraft of the RAAF 1921-78*, Kookaburra Press Technical Publications, Melbourne, 1971, 45.

of the service. No mention was made of the necessary ground staff or the possibility of being shot down over enemy territory.[5]

The general lack of policy and insight as well as incompetence were found in all the successive federal governments of the period: Lyons, Menzies, Fadden and even the Curtin ministries. Such incompetence culminated dramatically and tragically on 18 January 1942 with the Wirraway disaster and unnecessary loss of life over Rabaul against a Japanese Air Force with their vastly superior and more modern war planes. No Spitfires were made available to Australia. Wirraways were designed largely for training, but were not efficient fighter planes. At Rabaul, the Wirraways were shot from the sky or crashed landed with loss of most of their crews and a depleted squadron (less than half). They were against a naval air armada of over one hundred Japanese war aircraft.

Despite the intensity of the Australian propaganda machine at the time, most of the hidden reality went over the youthful Paul Brickhill's head. His dream of joining the RAAF was glamorous and appropriately patriotic. It was anything but as he was to discover. Flying obsolete aircrafts against overwhelming odds, being burnt alive, maimed or killed in training or in action was often the fate of young Australian aircrews. And yet the RAAF poster went on: 'APPLY' and, in smaller print, 'RAAF Recruiting Centres in capital cities, and voluntary selection committees in country centres' – thus a clean sweep of the nation.[6] After a brief consideration Paul Brickhill turned up at a Sydney recruitment centre. He was found suitable and joined up.

---

5 *First World War and Second World War. 16 Recruitment Posters from the collection of the Australian War Memorial,* AWM, Canberra, 2014, ARTV04297, ARTV04296, ARTV07256, ARTV04283, unpaginated.
6 Rorrison, 'The political decisions', 238.

At the time Australia was impersonating in its RAAF recruitment drive a defensive system without substance. The British were actually siphoning Australia's military resources for its own ends in Europe, the Mediterranean and North Africa while offering a high-risk strategic alliance that 'helped to bring Australia to the brink of disaster'.[7]

Narrandera and Acceptance

After enlistment in early January and by 1 September 1941, Paul opened the gate on acceptance as an officer in the RAAF. He had demonstrated more than sufficient potential as a flyer to be commissioned. At first he had spent the required time in No 2 Initial Training School at Bradfield Park, Sydney, in basic training where some others were declared unfit for further service – their enlistment was discontinued.

On 6 March 1941, Paul was posted to the No 8 Initial (Elementary) Flying Training School in the country town of Narrandera on the Murrumbidgee River in the south (locally called the Narrandera Flying School as signposted on the outskirts of the town at the local air strip). Even the local newspaper announced his arrival as being late of the 'Sydney "Sun" literary staff'.[8] Thus his early training as a pilot achieved some local press publicity. His air force career was on its way and his newspaper one left behind for more than five long years.

Paul Brickhill found Narrandera with a population a little less than 5,000 to be perhaps the town on the Riverina of the most importance. It was a place where the railway had been opened in 1881 as an important railway junction for the

7 Rorrison, 'The political decisions', ii.

8 *Albury Banner, Wodonga Express and Riverina Stock Journal*, 11 April 1941.

Riverina. No doubt Paul had travelled there by train in uniform on a railway permit. As only the second New South Wales country town to receive sewerage, Narrandera was proud of the recent establishment of an air training school in 1939 for the Australian Air Force that brought employment and air force personnel to the town. Thus it was considered a town of high prestige. The local economy expanded with the influx of personnel.

What was known as No 8 Elementary Flying Training School (EFTS) at Narrandera could be a highly dangerous place for trainee pilots and their instructors. While Paul Brickhill arrived there in early April 1941, a tragedy had occurred a few months earlier. In January that year an instructor in a Tiger Moth with his trainee swung low to "buzz" illegally an outdoor table beside a sidelight air strip near the village of Grong Grong. The prank went fatally wrong. The pilot hit the table killing himself, injuring his trainee and the two airmen innocently relaxing beside the table in the open air.

In travelling to Narrandera, Brickhill was entering a different world to that of journalism – the world of the Australian Air Force which had humble beginnings in the Great War of 1914-1918 as the Australian Flying Corps of the 1st AIF. The RAAF was formally established in 1921 and was at first simply known as the Australian Air Force. The RAAF was one of Australia's three armed forces along with the Australian Army and the Royal Australian Navy. But the RAAF was relatively more poorly equipped in its early years in comparison with the other two services having only 128 aircraft donated by the British government. Its strength did not exceed 1,200 men until the mid-1920s. During its first decade, the RAAF was under threat of being shut down and divided between the army and the navy. It only began to expand painfully and modernise its aircraft in the early 1930s and then only slowly.[9] This was, in part, due to the Great Depression and partly due to the incompetence of the Federal government about the need for a self-sufficient air force. Its expansion was during World War II where it served in every theatre of war, having 114,000 personnel, including Paul Brickhill in 1942.

On 10 and 11 March 1943, after Brickhill was captured and held in Stalag Luft III as a POW having been shot down over Tunisia, six airmen were killed in two accidents at the Narrandera Flying School. They were given a military funeral at Narrandera cemetery. Another was killed on 24 March that year and fourteen on 2 February 1944. On 3 September the following year, the day after the war officially ended, a Beaufighter hit a high tension wire just west of Narrandera and crashed into the canal killing its seven occupants.[10] Nevertheless, Paul Brickhill successfully survived such a dangerous training venue. At the school there, he mainly did his training in obsolete Tiger Moths. Despite this, he succeeded magnificently.

When he arrived in Narrandera, the town had already experienced a surge in population from the No 8 Elementary Training School having been established in 1938 at the local airport. The narrow aim of the School was to train pilots to fly Tiger Moths, then obsolete, and precious little else. The School, however, trained thousands of men in the long run of the war until at least 1945.

By the time Paul Brickhill was engaged in learning to fly Tiger Moths at No 8 EFTS, he was part of the Empire Air Training Scheme (EATS), although he may not have realised it.

---

9 'Royal Australian Air Force', Graeme Aplin, SG Foster, Michael McKernan & Ian Howie-Willis (eds), *Australians A Historical Dictionary*, Fairfax, Syme & Weldon Associates, Broadway, 1987, 355.

10 Bill Gammage, *Narrandera a Shire*, Bill Gammage & Narrandera Shire, Narrandera, 1986, 209.

Peter Finch in Charles Chauvel's Rats of Tobruk

The War for Peter Finch

Paul's friend Peter Finch, after a particularly promising, but financially unrewarding career as an actor in theatre, radio and feature film in Australia, joined up too. When war broke out in 1939, Peter had already established himself as most certainly the best young actor in Australia.

The sinking of HMAS *Waterhen* near Tobruk harbour affected him profoundly. He enlisted in the army on 2 June 1941 aged twenty-four and became Gunner Finch NX26035 in the Light Australian Artillery Anti-Aircraft.[11] He served with the Australian Division in the Middle East. In May 1942, Finch was shipped back to Adelaide with his battalion. From Adelaide they moved to Darwin up the Centre and then he

11 Dundy, *Finch, Bloody Finch*, 96.

found himself manning a Bofors quick firing anti-aircraft gun trying to shoot down Japanese Zeros and the bombers that rained down their weapons on the town during the concerted raid on Darwin.

At the end of July 1942, Finch was granted leave for duty in the Department of Information because of his film experience to make several propaganda films directed by Ken Hall and Charles Chauvel. During the rest of the war, he produced live shows, like "Finch's Follies" to entertain the troops. He used amateur actors from the services in various parts. He also worked as a director and actor in the Army Amenities Unit 12 for two years and was appointed artistic director of the Army Theatre.[12] This work included directing and acting in two popular plays written by Terence Rattigan, *French Without Tears* and *While the Sun Shines*. These plays toured the military hospitals and base camps playing to the troops.[13]

* * *

Meanwhile back to the wartime experiences of Paul Brickhill.

The Empire Air Training Scheme was initiated by leading British air marshals and politicians to concentrate on training aircrews from Britain's dominions and colonies for the war against Nazi Germany and Fascist Italy in Europe, the Mediterranean and North Africa and to a great extent ignoring the crisis in Asia and the South Pacific. So much so that in 1946 the RAAF Chief of Air Staff noted for the Australian Minister of Defence that: '[t]he major RAAF effort during the war was the training of aircrew for the European theatre. Based on a casualty basis, the RAAF effort in Europe was four times as [great as] that in the South

12 Dundy, *Finch, Bloody Finch.*

13 Faulkner, *Peter Finch,* 90-4, 291.

West Pacific Area'.[14] He was right. A large number of the RAAF dead are listed on the walls outside the Hall of Memory at the Australian War Memorial. Why was this so?

Paul & the Empire Air Training Scheme

Part of the answer lies in the function of the Empire Air Training Scheme (EATS). From April 1940 (Paul Brickhill volunteered in January 1941) to June 1944, 37,037Australian aircrew, like Brickhill, had been initially trained in Australia and in Ottawa, Canada (or later in Rhodesia and South Africa) largely for service with the Royal Air Force for the European and Mediterranean (including North Africa) theatres of war. They were slung and dispersed in squadrons across Great Britain throughout the service's lines of battle. More rarely, some were grouped together in RAAF designated squadrons numbered 450 to 467 and a Royal Canadian one as a concession to Dominion sensitivities. As such, they still operated as part of the larger RAF controlled formations. As Liberal Prime Minister RG Menzies later put it, they were 'surrendered' to the United Kingdom.[15] Paul Brickhill was one of those 'surrendered'.

There is some debate over who thought up the EATS. Vincent Massey, the Canadian High Commissioner in London and his Australian counterpart Stanley Bruce are the two main contestants.[16] Bruce and Massey were certainly the

---

14 Chief of Air Staff to Minister for Air, undated c. September 1946, Jones Papers, DRL 3414, AWM; also cited in John McCarthy, 'The "surrender" of aircrew to Britain 1939-45', *Journal of the Australian War Memorial,* no 5, October 1984, 3.

15 McCarthy, 'The "surrender" of aircrew', 3.

16 See FJ Hatch, *The Aerodrome of Democracy: Canada and British Commonwealth Air Training Plan 1939-45,* Department of National Defence, Ottawa, 1983, 13-14.

main movers and shakers to establish the scheme in Ottawa where Paul Brickhill was to travel after his initial training in Narrandera in country New South Wales.

The main issue in 1939 was that the British High Command in the air force and politicians realised that only a 'massive contribution by aircrew by the dominions could hope to turn the Royal Air Force from being a select flying club into a viable fighting service' that would compete with the strength of the German Luftwaffe. The evidence is plentiful: by September United Kingdom aircraft production had risen to 2,250 aeroplanes per month. Someone had to man these. Such a vast air force was expected if the high rate of production continued to 'consume' more than 1,500 pilots alone each year. But Britain had neither the eligible population of well-educated mathematically literate men, or anything like the training capacity required to reach this figure. Thus, the Royal Air Force seemed in a desperate position lacking the necessity of highly trained and skilled aircrew.[17] But the Dominions could provide them!

In *The Dam Busters* published in 1951, Paul Brickhill was to characterise acutely in a sophisticated manner the relationship that became pronounced during the war in the battle for air superiority over Germany:

> The Australian, the American and the New Zealander, each in some way typifying their national characters, led by the subtle and audacious Englishman, a strong combination of leaders in a squadron that ever was an oligarchy, but a respected and revered one.[18]

17 McCarthy, 'The "surrender" of aircrew', 3.

18 Paul Brickhill, *The Dam Busters*, Evans Brothers Ltd, London, 1951, 164-5.

The phrase 'that ever was an oligarchy' shows in the chain of command who really was ultimately in charge of what became the multinational character of the RAF – the Englishmen – but revered and respected by the Dominion men.

The declaration of war was only five days old when the United Kingdom asked Australia to delay its local defence program so it could supply the missing aircrew for the so-called home country and its desperate defence needs. The same was demanded of other dominions and colonies that made up the British Empire: Canada, New Zealand, South Africa, Rhodesia, India and so on. In London, Stanley Bruce saw it as a particularly urgent matter. He told Australia's Prime Minister RG Menzies that within months – if not sooner – there would be a crisis in the air over Britain. Dominion personnel initially in Australia, Canada and New Zealand could be trained in Canada to create an agreed number of squadrons for the home country in twelve months.

Anthony Eden, the British Secretary of State, wrote to Menzies on 26 September 1939 that the British Air Force was at a grave disability. The invasion of Poland by the Germans, he said, had shown the decisive nature and necessity of air power. Local personnel and training facilities in Britain could only produce about half of the aircrew needed each year (which was estimated at 50,000). Eden's message was clear. The British call proved irresistible to the Menzies conservative government. Menzies spoke on radio to the nation: 'It is no wonder that at this hour of suspense, or of real peril, and of supreme effort, Great Britain should have turned to her children, the Dominions and to us [Australia] not least of all'.[19]

Menzies pointed out that Australia must play her part in

19 Cited in McCarthy, 'The "surrender" of aircrew', 4; RG Menzies, 'Empire Air Force: Australia Plays Her Part', Melbourne, 11 October 1939, broadcast to the nation.

the Empire's endeavours. The Australian War Cabinet agreed to join a training scheme in principle on 5 October 1939. A full agreement was later reached to provide 26,000 aircrew for service in the Royal Air Force to the end of March 1943. This was signed in Ottawa on 27 November 1939. Paul Brickhill was but one of the trained 26,000 aircrew and he had keenly absorbed its ethics. To the politicians in power in Australia the British plea for support was entirely convincing and even considered mandatory. James Valentine Fairbairn, Australia's Minister for Air, was the chief negotiator at Ottawa. Back in Sydney at the Wesleyan Church in Sydney, he told his listeners on 4 February 1940:

> ... for the first time in her history [Australia has undertaken] something in which failure could mean complete disaster for the British peoples throughout the world and in which success can make victory and security against aggression certain.[20]

The Air Board of the Royal Australian Air Force had, at the same time, meekly accepted the British viewpoint. They argued that Australia's success in the Ottawa Scheme had to be one hundred percent. Therefore, virtually the whole of the RAAF became merely a training organisation for the RAF. The development also implied that many of the causes of Australia's failure in fighting the superior Japanese Air Force during the war in 1941 and 1942 could be traced 'to the ready acceptance of the Empire Training Scheme'.[21]

By the Ottawa agreement, Britain had secured unfettered

---

20 Cited in McCarthy, 'The "surrender" of aircrew'.

21 John McCarthy, 'The Defence of Australia and the Empire Air Training Scheme 1939-42', *Australian Journal of Politics and History*, vol. XX, no 3, December 1974, 326-34.

control over trained dominion personnel. As Peter Rees pointed out in a recent publication, *Lancaster Men: The Aussie Heroes of Bomber Command*, statistics for Australians who served in the RAF in Bomber and Fighter Command are difficult to pin down entirely. Under EATS, however, Australia sent 2,671 men to England in 1942 and Paul Brickhill most certainly was one of them. In the following year, EATS sent another 8,249; in 1944, 6,386 and 195 in 1945, a total of 17,301 in raw terms.

The High Commissioner Lord Bruce wrote to the Australian Prime Minister John Curtin on 3 April 1945 stating that there were 1,488 Australian aircrew alone serving with the RAAF Article V Squadron in England and another 10,532 attached directly to the RAF, but this was likely to be more than 12,000 in the European, Mediterranean and North African theatres of war. We may, however, never know the exact figure,[22] because it would be required to go through every single set of enlistment papers to tabulate exact numbers.

Be that as it may, Paul Brickhill was one of the combined total of 189,000 men and 27,000 women who volunteered and enlisted in the RAAF in the Second World War to fight in Europe, the Mediterranean, North Africa or in the South Pacific and Australia. He had decided in quite definite terms that he wanted to do his part for the home country of the Empire. He was obviously influenced by a recruitment drive for the Volunteer Air Force: 'Make them mightier yet'.[23]

At first he attended the Elementary Flying School. By 1 September 1941 he had demonstrated sufficient potential and skill in training to be appointed to a commission in the RAAF after his achievements at No 8 Initial or Elementary

---

22 Peter Rees, *Lancaster Men. The Aussie Heroes of Bomber Command*, Allen & Unwin, Crows Nest, 2015, 389.
23 Cited in Mooney, *A Powerhouse of a Man*, 15.

Flying School at Narrandera. There he had shown outstanding capability in flying Tiger Moths with great skill. The course lasted twelve weeks and gave recruits up to seventy-five hours of basic aviation instruction on a simpler trainer, the Tiger Moth. More theoretical subjects included Mathematics, Navigation and Aerodynamics. By 2 May that year, he had been returned to Sydney under orders to wait anxiously at Sydney No 2 Embarkation Depot. He was now at the end of his training in Australia and was provided with a kit and given a final medical examination which he passed.

War propaganda in Australia strongly supported the position of support for EATS and the appointment of RAAF staff in England. The *R.A.F. Bulletin* reported that during the enemy advance into Cyrenaica a fighter RAAF squadron shot down eighteen German planes in two days. The 'bag' included five Messerschmitts 110s (a very prestigious 'kill') and three Junker 87s on one day with two more Junkers two days later.

In that so-called 'simple factual message' that had been published in the 'Empire and neutral Press' in April 1941, it was confidently claimed that Australia 'sprung' into the world's consciousness as – according to the propaganda – a 'fully fledged Air Power' capable of showing 'unexpected and disconcerting pugnacity' in the grim and dangerous business of aerial combat. Later, such 'pugnacity' was to be heavily underlined in the prose publications of Paul Brickhill after the war.

It was claimed in the early 1940s that hundreds of young Australian airmen trained at Ottawa 'to such a pitch of perfection that man for man they are more than a match for the enemy'. And now they were to go into action against the much-vaulted Luftwaffe over England and Germany. Hundreds more, it was claimed, were to go to battle stations in the Far East. Paul Brickhill was to experience both theatres of war before he was shot down. Edward Axford, in a highly-charged propaganda piece in *The Home*, an Australian Quarterly, underlined that:

> More than 50,000 men have already joined the R.A.A.F. [as Brickhill had done], both as air crew personnel and ground staff, and that is only the beginning. Under the accelerated schedule of the Empire Air Scheme this country [Australia] has undertaken to train 12,000 pilots, observers and air gunners a year.

The training of pilots and other air crew was highly expensive. Yet this expenditure in manpower and money was considered justified as it might tip the scales against the Nazi Air Force. It was emphasised heavily that it would give sorely needed relief to the airmen of the RAF and save the British from having a drain on her air force in other theatres of war – especially the Far East.[24]

As the propagandist put it, all eyes were on the 'Glamour Boys' of the RAAF and Paul Brickhill was one of them.

Canada and Advanced Training

On 20 May 1941, Paul Brickhill, with the service number of 403313, embarked by transport ship to Canada to undertake in full EATS and receive more advanced flight training using more modern American planes.

He disembarked in Canada on 13 June.[25] He had originally enlisted on 6 January that year. He had left behind a highly promising career as an aviation and defence journalist. Later

---

24 Edward Axford, 'Eyes on the Glamour Boys', *The Home*, June 1941, 16-17, 60.

25 Service Record, WWII, Brickhill, F/Lt PCJ, 403313, NAA.

in January 1942, he was assigned to fly Spitfires with the No 74 RAF Squadron.

In Ottawa, Brickhill was especially successful in the training course. He topped the EATS course examinations with distinction in his cohort. While in Canada, he was ranked as Leading-Aircraftsman. He was awarded his so-called wings even before 8 September, as reported in the Australian news media.[26]

* * *

The Empire Training Scheme was indeed a vast enterprise along with the army and navy that demanded much of the so-called British Empire, the British Commonwealth of Nations or Dominions. The British Empire and Dominions raised a total of 8,586,000 men for service, but more than five million came from the British Isles; 1,440,500 came from India; 136,000

Paul Brickhill, RAAF (Elliott & Fry, © National Portrait Gallery, London)

26 'With the Force', *Daily Advertiser*, Wagga Wagga, 8 September 1941.

came from South Africa; 629,000 from Canada; 413,000 from Australia (including Paul Brickhill and Peter Finch); 128,500 from New Zealand,; 10,000 from the Caribbean and 124,000 from other British colonies.[27]

England and the RAF

After EATS in Ottawa, Brickhill went to Y Depot in Halifax where he boarded another transport ship, this time bound for the United Kingdom. He arrived there on 25 September 1941 at the Personnel Reception Centre.

Even more training was to follow in England. He was posted to No 53 Operational Training Unit on 1 October. Early the following year on 17 January, he was moved into action against the enemy on several missions in the famous 74th Squadron RAF.[28] He was considered very useful as a fighter pilot against Nazi Germany at a time when the death rate for RAF fighter pilots was extraordinarily high.

When Brickhill was finishing his training in Ottawa, Japan had not entered the war officially or outright and seemed much less of a threat than Germany. In all accounts, the threats to the British Empire in South East Asia were not considered by the British politicians a high priority or a high price to pay. To the British military and government, Germany was obviously the immediate compelling threat and trained Dominion men like Brickhill were considered sorely needed purely to protect England. The key zones where Commonwealth men were to be used were Europe, the Mediterranean and adjacent North Africa against the Luftwaffe and Regio Aeronautica, the Italian Air Force as part of the Axis.

---

27 'Who fought for Britain during World War II?', <www.aircrewremembered.com/list-of-pages-relating-to-1939-1945.html>.

28 Service Record.

Brickhill flew both against the Luftwaffe and Regio Aeronautica in Europe and North Africa before being shot down. By the war's end, the Dominions were supplying roughly half of the bomber and fighter pilots of the RAF.

As with the Great War of 1914-18, most British politicians and many British people saw the larger world in imperial terms as was aptly demonstrated by the formation of the complete EATS. They remained secure in the belief that Britain knew best that the Dominions were merely there to serve the cause of the home country as the centre of British civilisation.

The struggle and ultimate, but costly success in achieving the required number of pilots for war aircraft production is one of the frequently overlooked "battles" of World War II by military historians. By 1945 an amazing 110,000 pilots, including Paul Brickhill, had been trained for the RAF on behalf of nine different countries as well as colonies that were part of, or heavily connected with the British Empire and its war effort in the air. Airmen in the RAAF in the war were 'drawn inexorably to Britain'. Two out of every three RAAF recruits served in the European and Mediterranean/ North African theatres of war.

Flying conditions, as Paul found, were different. In Narrandera, it was over dry open land and familiar landscape with no heavy fogs during the day in antiquated Tiger Moths. Some of the flying training in England was over the foreboding Irish Sea. In Australia the sparse settlement made navigation a reasonably simple, straightforward matter; in England the countryside was much more difficult to interpret because the web of surface communication was complex. Night flying was also a new aspect of the training.[29] And British weather – the rain and fog – was noticeably different from the flying conditions in general in Australia.

29 Dyer, 'Training the RAAF', 12-13.

It has to be recognised of course that the emotional gap between Britain and Australia was much less than the vast geographic separation in the era under consideration. Australians were considered British subjects in a faraway land. Many like Brickhill were thrilled and highly motivated to go. Although they were overwhelmingly Australian-born RAAF crewmen, they came from strong British backgrounds, heritage, connections and traditions. Many of their fathers had fought in the First World War. The United Kingdom was far from being a foreign country and culturally it had a familiarity. Some of the UK families were relatives who could be either revisited or met socially for the first time – the brothers and sisters and cousins of parents. Some of the RAAF men in England carried letters of introduction to family members they had never met.

Life for a pilot trainee like Paul Brickhill in England was, nevertheless, different to his experience in Australia and Canada. Such Australians had to adapt to 'a routine acceptance of danger, to a strange environment and a different social system.'[30] The social class system was also different and more rigid for Paul Brickhill. He was to gain first-hand experience of the unfamiliar, but frequently dreamed-of society while on leave. There was, however, the social security blanket of Australia House and there were plenty of families in country areas and provincial towns to welcome and provide generous hospitality to the impressive young man in the air force uniform who was fighting to preserve English freedom. Sometimes, they were made part of the family and attended birthday parties and other celebrations. In general terms, the British people welcomed Australian trainee pilots very warmly and made them feel comfortably at home.

---

30 Steve Dyer, 'Training the RAAF in Britain', *Journal of the Australian War Memorial,* no 8, April 1986, 11.

The way members of the RAAF were welcomed by English families showed great hospitality and appreciation of the valued work they were doing to preserve freedom. They understood that such uniformed young men, usually in their early twenties, were a long way from home and their families of orientation, close relatives, other loved ones and close friends in Australia. Their home must have seemed to them like a world away.

Like Paul Brickhill they had been suddenly taken out of familiar surroundings and thrown into a new and sometimes emotionally restricted and dangerous environmental conditions alien to them. Many English families were well-aware of how they must have felt and thus some were even drawn into the very heart of generous, friendly family life.

This was the case with Ronald George Fleming, a photographer/leading aircraftsman (sergeant) in the RAAF who had been posted by military authorities to Plymouth, a port that suffered heavy bombing.[31] He was particularly well received when on leave in the home of Mr and Mrs Lumsden who even provided a special party in their living-room for his twenty-second birthday. Fleming spent the majority of the war years in Plymouth, the seaport city in the southwest corner of Devon. Under the Blitz, because of its military capabilities, the city was heavily bombed during the war and much had to be rebuilt. Bombed-out buildings would have been a common sight to Fleming as he made his way back to his base.

Fleming wrote in his diary on Saturday, 20 February 1943 – the evening the party was held – that it was a great success at which a number of his other friends had been invited. He was so touched by this gesture that he wrote: 'I shall not soon forget it'. And he never did.

---

31 Service Record, no 36306; date of birth: 20 February 1921, born in Manly NSW. Next of kin: Eric Fleming (father); Methodist. Address: 42 Frances St; enlisted 29 April 1941 aged 20; previous employment, Clerk, Sydney City Council. Discharged 15 February 1945, NAA.

Ronald Fleming, photographer/leading Airman, RAAF – 22nd birthday (Head of table; courtesy of Richard Fleming)

Later on Sunday, 17 September 1944, Fleming had started on leave for the first time in six months with his friend Arthur, another RAAF man in the squadron. Together, they cycled joyously for fifty-one miles from the RAAF camp to Polzeath to stay with another English family on holidays, Mr and Mrs Stephens, their children and their dog Peter. The Stephens had a stationary holiday caravan and camping area on a block where they stayed for a few weeks swimming and recreating themselves on the sand.

Polzeath was a tiny village on the north coast of Cornwall at the mouth of the River Camel and opposite Padslow. Its beach has remained a magnet for English holidaymakers intent on surfing and wind-surfing. Such a place was close to Fleming's heart as he had grown up in the seaside and harbourside suburb of Manly in Sydney. He was an excellent swimmer who loved the surf.

On their scenic bike ride to Polzeath, the two Australians passed through Wadebridge, Bodmin and Newquay, famous traditional Cornish townships. At Wadebridge, a prominent Cornish town also on the River Camel, upstream about five miles from Polzeath to the east, they would have ridden their bicycles over a remarkable bridge, medieval in nature, and one of the finest surviving in England. Bodmin was a traditional market town in Cornwall once the county town of Cornwell. In riding through here, the two young men would have admired St Petroc Church, the largest in the whole of Cornwall. They also rode past Newquay, a small resort town that the great Welsh poet Dylan Thomas immortalised in his famous radio verse play *Under Milkwood*. When the two men rode by, Thomas was actually living in the town and writing some of his best poetry.[32]

Ron Fleming had an eventful, challenging war in the United Kingdom, apart from his adventures on leave and the friendships he was able to develop with English families primarily through the local Methodist church. He was considered by RAAF authorities as an airman of very good character, 'keen and assiduous in attention to duties'. In his initial training as photographer, he passed all subjects and played a vital part in the war effort gaining the rank of Leading Aircraftsman.[33]

Many other RAAF men posted to the United Kingdom during the Second World War have fond memories of friendships made within the context of a violent, difficult world

32 Personal Diary of Ron Fleming, held by his son Richard.

33 In 1943 Ron was on the seriously-ill list for a week in the Royal Naval Hospital, Plymouth, after a motor accident. His father as next-of-kin was notified that his son had concussion and lacerations to the scalp. Ron married an Englishwoman Elsie Hogg, at Hall Place, Scal, Kent on 29 August 1945. When she came to Australia as a war bride, Ron was on the wharf in Sydney to meet her. They began married life in the family home in Manly where they stayed raising a family until Ron retired. They then moved to Katoomba in the Blue Mountains.

of international war. Such leave provided some relief from the many tensions, restrictions and constant fear of bombing.

Ronald Fleming (standing left; courtesy of Richard Fleming)

The 92 Squadron and North Africa

After serving in the RAF's 74 Squadron that, as part of No 12 Group, had previously seen combat first during the evacuation of the British Expeditionary Force from Dunkirk and in the Battle of Britain, Paul Brickhill was transferred as a replacement for a lost pilot into the famous 92 Squadron RAF. This squadron had also seen action first on 15 September 1940 in the Battle of Britain before Brickhill arrived in England.

In February 1942 with Brickhill now on board, the No 92 was posted to Egypt by sea transport, arriving on 1 March, to join Air Headquarters, Western Desert. They were needed to provide air support for the Allies on the ground against Rommel's Afrika Korps and the Italian Army. But when the 92 and Brickhill first arrived, no aircraft was available for them:

their Spitfires were still being manufactured in factories in England, but were nearing completion. Brickhill, like some other pilots of the 92, flew operations with the Hurricane Light bombers of No 80 Squadron on loan (which had also been previously posted to the Western Desert). The Spitfires finally arrived for the 92 in August 1942 and Brickhill climbed eagerly into one to commence operations from RAF Heliopolis base that provided air cover for the Battle of El Alamein.

Paul Brickhill first flew several missions in Hurricane bombers at El Alamein before being placed on a new Spitfire out of Cairo (RAF Heliopolis). By then he had flown over forty missions. He was shot down over the Tunisian desert by an Italian fighter. It came unexpectedly from behind and blew up both of Brickhill's cannon magazines in the wings of his Spitfire, smashing its wings and controls and, in the process, wounded Brickhill in the head and back. In later life, these injuries were to affect his health. He struggled to bail out of the stricken plane as it rapidly headed earthwards, spinning violently as it did. His parachute got caught and he was able to wriggle clear of the cockpit only at the last moment.

Parachuting down through the short distance, he realised suddenly that he was about to land in the middle of a minefield in the desert and was being closely observed by a group of armed Italian soldiers of the Fascist forces. Ironically on the ground the desert wind had filled his parachute dragging him closer to the enemy barbed wire. He was bleeding freely from the wounds he had received, but he was still conscious and alert. He was dragged from the minefield by two strong armed Italian soldiers using the billowing parachute. As he struggled up to his feet, he found himself surrounded by the enemy with guns pointed at him and, thus, captured. This occurred on 17 March 1943.

Paul Brickhill had loved flying the Spitfire despite having

to leave it desperately and hurriedly over the Tunisian Desert as it had sensitive, docile characteristics in handling as well as deadly qualities as a fighting machine for a lone pilot. Its small cockpit was set right back above the wing trailing edge. Taller pilots found the headroom restrictive, but this was not the case for Paul. The Spitfire's airframe was completely streamlined. The wings were elliptical in plan and tapered in thickness making the plane very manoeuvrable. The high performance of the Spitfire came from the low drag on the thin elliptical wings. The engine was a Rolls-Royce Merlin, a 12-cylinder V-type engine of 1,030 hp. The armaments were machine guns and cannons; the flight range 395 miles.

The Spitfire achieved a legendary status during the Battle of Britain. Those of No 74 Squadron, just before Paul Brickhill arrived in England, were able to claim to have shot down thirty-eight aircraft in the Battle of Britain in interception raids over Dover on 11 August 1941. Under the leadership of South African ace Adolph Gysbert "Sailor" Malan DSO & Bar, DFC & Bar, No 74 Squadron became one of the best RAF units. And it had that reputation when Paul Brickhill arrived on the scene. Malan was Paul's first commanding officer. Malan scored twenty-seven 'kills' during his war career.

The Spitfire flew on every operational front in the Second World War including Germany, Italy, Malta, the Middle East and Australia. Apart from being a standard fighter in the RAF and the Commonwealth including Australia, it was used by France, Poland, Norway, the Netherlands, Yugoslavia, Belgium, Portugal, Russia and the United States. 22,758 Spitfires were build during and slightly after World War II.[34]

---

34 Allan Burney (ed.), *Famous Fighters of World War 2*, Coxy Media, Midlands, 2015, 30-34.

Shot down in the Tunisian Desert

Paul Brickhill explained this situation succinctly much later in his official report written after he was released at the end of the war from Stalag Luft III:

> I was shot down by enemy fighters while on interception patrol, landed by parachute in a minefield nr [near] flank of Italian positions was pulled by parachute to edge of minefield & immediately captured by Italian front line troops.[35]

Brickhill made this official statement in 1945 to RAAF authorities in Brighton where he was recuperating after the war with other ex-POWs. It appeared in his Service Record in his own identifiable handwriting. Later in a newspaper interview, he elaborated on his experience of being shot down twenty-four years before in 1943:

> I nearly didn't parachute out in time. I had been shot in the back and I couldn't move one arm. I was stuck for a while. The man [an Italian pilot] that got me was a good shot. I heard that he was going to come and visit me, but I was moved away [to Germany incarcerated in Stalag Luft III] before he did.

Thus pilots traditionally regarded each other as gentlemen of honour and Brickhill was a believer in such a value that he maintained for the remainder of his life. He went on: 'That's

---

35 Service Record; Statements by Repatriated or released RAAF Prisoners of War taken at No 11 PDRS Brighton, England, 1945, 408513, AWM, Canberra.

how it was then and I don't think it could ever be the same again. There were no hard feelings. It was done without anger. There was just a job to do'.[36]

Being shot down and parachuting into a desert minefield near Italian frontline positions, Flight Lieutenant Paul Chester Jerome Brickhill, in peacetime a leading journalist for the Sydney *Sun*, became one of 'some 100,000 young men' who 'fell with their aircraft over hostile soil'. Of these, about 10,000 survived. In other words, there was a ten-to-one chance of getting through alive in the airborne battles of the Second World War. The remains of his Spitfire are rusting away, perhaps hidden by shifting sand, somewhere in the Tunisian Desert.

Brickhill, while his psychological and physical wounds frequently ensured a fragile health profile throughout the rest of his life after the war, was favoured by 'some fabulously slim chance [in the war zone sky of the Tunisian desert] that came off!' Nevertheless, he was subsequently forced to face years of dreary and restrictive imprisonment behind the barbed wire in Stalag Luft III in a barren cramped compound amongst hundreds of pilot officer comrades, some of whom became close friends and associates. Others were difficult to live with. But as Brickhill was to reflect, in the closed communal environment in the sternly managed Luftwaffe prison which at its height in 1943 held ten thousand captured airmen: 'Life marked time but despair and emotion didn't'.[37]

Soon after Paul was shot down over Tunisia, his father George received the dreaded letter from the military authorities informing him that his son was officially missing in action and thus feared dead. This disturbing correspondence was dated 10 April 1943, some three weeks after Paul had been shot out of

---

36 'Author: Golden Days Over', *West Australian*, Perth, 2 December 1969.
37 Brickhill and Norton, *Escape to Danger*, 5.

the sky in his Spitfire by the enemy plane. Sounding close to being an obituary, the disturbing news was widely reported in the Australian press. As far away from Sydney as Perth, Western Australia, under the by-line 'Pressman Flyer Missing', the *Daily News* reported that 'Paul Brickhill *was* a member of the *Sun* editorial staff and *was* considered one of the most promising young Sydney newspaper men'. This was published on the same day as George Brickhill received the official letter.

Such immediate publicity can only be explained by the prominence of father and son in the Australian newspaper world, partly as George Brickhill was a founding member of the Australian Journalist Association which had a powerful national membership. George Brickhill had been a prominent, well-regarded editor of newspapers in Victoria, South Australia and more recently in New South Wales when he had settled his family in Greenwich Point, Sydney.

In Paul's war record papers, George Brickhill was noted as 'next-of-kin'. He was later informed of the relieving news that his son had been located and had survived being shot down in North Africa and after being captured was taken to Germany as a prisoner-of-war. At least the father now knew that his son was substantially out of harm's way if the Geneva Convention was properly applied.

Brickhill's official casualty report of the RAF read with some precision of detail:

> At 1243 hours on 17 March 43, 12 aircraft of the 92 Sqdn [Squadron] took off from Bu [Bou] Grara [military airport, Cairo]. The incident concerning F/O [Flight Officer] Brickhill occurred at approx. 1305 hours. Map Ref. Pisida, Libya 1/500000 Z.6109. P/O Bruckshaw was at about 9000' about 2 miles out to sea when he saw three aircraft in line astern coming

> towards him about a mile away from the South, and about 500' above him. The leading aircraft, a Spitfire, when at the above position from P/O Bruckshaw [the witness of the report] turned about rate two to port and was closely followed by his No. 2 (50 yards behind) into the turn. As the third aircraft turned P/O Bruckshaw identified it as a Machi 202 and as it was only about 50 yards behind the No. 2 (F/O Brickhill), he called up on the R/T [Radio Transmission] to try to warn him. Simultaneously with his transmission P/O Bruckshaw saw the enemy aircraft fire while in the turn and immediately F/O Brickhill's aircraft flicked into a turn the opposite way, and the ammunition was seen to explode in both mainplanes. The aircraft then fell down appar[e]ntly out of control, and as P/O Bruckshaw was then himself being attacked, he lost sight of the a/craft. When next he saw the aircraft it was about 2000' [from the ground] and a parachute was just opening. The aircraft crashed and burst into flames at Z.6109 [map reading]; and when the parachute was last seen it was drifting slightly to the S.W. [South-West] of the burning aircraft. Aircraft Cat. 111. F/O believed to have been admitted to a M.R.S. Efforts are being made to confirm and to ascertain whether injured and to what extent.
>
> – Peter Harper O.O. S2 (E.I.) Sqdn RAF Me.

As an eye-witness and observer, Pilot Officer Bruckshaw – a companion to Brickhill on the raid – would have made an immediate verbal report on Brickhill's crash as soon as he returned to base and, at the same time, the base officer Peter Harper would have compiled his report that Brickhill was now shot down and missing. All pilots in the RAF on missions were required to report what happened immediately on returning to base – a long-standing protocol.

Cutting through RAF jargon in the report, it is crystal clear that Brickhill was flying a Spitfire on a mission over Tunisia in the 92 Squadron and shot down by an Italian Macchi 2 – not a Messerschmitt as later reported elsewhere in popular press reports and depicted on the dustcover of most of Brickhill's war books. Earlier on 8 December Brickhill had been transferred to the Middle East at El Alamein in the 92 Squadron where he had at first flown Hurricanes, the light fighter bomber, in reconnaissance for the landed Allied army. He was first reported as missing and then as captured by the enemy.

After six days of medical treatment for his wounds in an Italian military field hospital, he was transported and transferred as a prisoner-of-war to Dulag Luft Germany, a holding prison, for a further seven days. According to his war record, he eventually ended up in Stalag Luft III when he was incarcerated for 600 days (26 months).[38] Apparently he was considered fit enough to travel to Germany under guard after being shot down and captured at gun point despite wounds to his head, back and leg.

In typical fashion, Brickhill minimised his wounds when interviewed by the RAAF in Brighton after he had been released: 'Slightly wounded by cannon shell splinters in back, and back of head. Also contusion to left leg'. He remembered being treated in an army cot in the tented Italian field hospital Sfax, Sousse and Tunis, behind the Italian front line in Tunisia. He thought he was fairly treated by the hospital personnel with immediate treatment.

When he was shot down, Brickhill was twenty-six years old and relatively experienced as a RAF pilot having clocked up

38 Statements by Repatriated or released RAAF.

fifty-five hours against the enemy in Europe and the North African war zones. He had served in the 34, 451, 127, 274 squadrons and, after some months, the 92 squadron which was part of the Desert Air Force in North Africa.

His Spitfire had been shot down over the Mareth front line by a nimble Italian Macchi 202. (Often in popular literature this plane was erroneously described as a Messerschmitt which seemed to be more glamorous.) The blurb on the back dustcover of *The Dam Busters* is typical: 'Paul Brickhill owes the start of his career as an author to the fact that he, like Douglas Bader, was shot down by a Messerschmitt.'[39] The blurb about the author had already appeared on the inside flap of the back dustcover of an earlier book. It continued: 'A Messerschmidt 109 blew up both cannon magazines in the wings of his aircraft, smashed wings, tail and controls and wounded Brickhill in the head and back.'[40]

All this is substantially true other than the enemy plane which was a Macchi 2 flown by an Italian pilot. The editors of the two books regarded the famous German plane to be much more glamorous for readers to swallow. Aside from this manipulation by publishers, Paul Brickhill was to spend six hundred dreary days in Stalag Luft III – the main concentration camp for captured Allied air force officers.

* * *

Some days after Brickhill was shot down on the Mareth Line guarded by Italian frontline soldiers of Axis defence, they were outflanked by the Allied attack by late March and started to withdraw hurriedly in vehicles to Wadi Akarit with the

---

39 See also Paul Brickhill, *Reach for the Sky. The Story of Douglas Bader D.S.O., D.F.C.*, Collins, London 1954, back dustcover.

40 Brickhill, *Escape – or Die*, dustcover.

wounded Brickhill as a POW on board one of them. On a single day Australian squadrons flew eighty-three low-level attacks on the desert roads following and harassing the convoy of vehicles moving north from Crabes, but Brickhill survived in the truck he was in. Nevertheless, it was obviously an uncomfortable experience to be shafted by your own.

Not long after, the liberation of French North Africa, including Tunisia, was successfully accomplished.[41] By this time Brickhill was being placed in his quarters in the North Compound of Stalag Luft III at Sagan on the Polish border.

* * *

In action Paul Brickhill had served bravely in a famous 'Spitfire Abroad' in North Africa – one of fifteen planes delivered from England – when Rommel's Afrika Korps came to the aid of the defeated Italian army and the elite German Panzers pushed the British and Commonwealth troops, including the Australians, back through Libya and threatened Egypt. Flying over the Western Desert, as Brickhill had done, was to fly over the most inhospitable areas in the world. Brickhill's encounter in the Spitfire with the nippy Italian fighter plane gave the distinct impression that it was a re-enactment of a Dogfight in the First World War with our valiant protagonist, as it happened, on the losing end. Brickhill's Spitfire was one of fifteen Mk VBs shipped out to Egypt on HMS *Eagle* across the hazardous Mediterranean, arriving safely on 7 March 1942[42] and he was immensely proud of flying her – even briefly.

---

41 John Herington, *Air War Against Germany and Italy 1939-1943*, Australian War Memorial, Canberra, 1962, 339, 405, 414.

42 John Vader, *Spitfire*, Purcell's History of the Second World War. Weapons book, no 6, London, 1970, 103, 108.

* * *

Tunisia, where Brickhill was shot down in the desert, was a French protectorate from 1881 until 1956, interrupted by a period of Nazi German /Italian Fascist rule during the Second World War campaign between 1942 and 1943. The Tunisian Campaign had been the final campaign of the war in Africa. Field Marshal Rommel's army had retreated towards Tunisia pursued by the British 8th Army under General Montgomery (referred to commonly by historians as the Desert War). The British 8th Army was supported by the Desert Air Force whose Spitfire pilot Paul Brickhill had been part of in No 92 Squadron until his capture, ironically, towards the end of the campaign that proved highly successful for the British.

Spitfires

CHAPTER 4

INSIDE STALAG LUFT III

Many families also wrote to their sons in the camp strongly discouraging them from any escape attempts, as a result of the Stalag Luft III (Sagan) experience when fifty of the men who had taken part in the 'Great Escape' in March 1944 were executed on being recaptured.

– Barbara A Bond, *The Times Great Escapes*, 30

Stalag Luft III in the outskirts of the town and railway junction of Sagan, near what was the German-Polish border in the east, was about halfway between Berlin and Breslau. Paul Brickhill appears to have arrived there at the beginning of April 1943 after being shot down in Tunisia on 17 March. This was just after prisoners-of-war, incarcerated originally in the older South Compound or in other POW camps to the west, were moved into the newly-built North Compound. The new population in the North Compound was about seven hundred when Brickhill joined them until the end of the war. The composition was cosmopolitan in nature. About five hundred men were RAF and Dominion Air Force officers. There were a few score Poles, some Norwegians and some from other European countries who had flown into enemy territory as part of the RAF and had been shot down and captured. In the mix, there were Czechs, Scots, Welsh, Irish, Canadians, Australians, South Africans, Americans and New Zealanders. There were about one hundred other ranks of prisoners who were to act as orderlies (or servants to the officers) for camp maintenance and labour, in the cookhouse and so on.

By this time, there were about a hundred USA Air Force officers from a wide range of places in the American Republic. Soon more USA pilot officers began to arrive in numbers from the USA Air Force stationed in Britain and the Middle East (as Brickhill had been). Most of the population of the North Camp were already planning escape and this was the cultural community that became stronger as time went on.[1] Already, prisoners in the working parties who helped build the compound had studied its layout and paced off its relative distances – with tunnels in mind.[2] The multi-cultural

---

1 Brickhill and Norton, *Escape to Danger*, 221.

2 F/Lt Paul Brickhill RAAF as told to Allan A Michie, 'Tunnel to Freedom', in Charles S Verral (ed.), *True Stories of Great Escapes*, vol.1, Reader's Digest Services, Surry Hills, 1983.

nature of the compound's population became much more than a mere melting pot when it became highly organised as an escape organisation called "X".

The opening of the North Compound about the time Paul was placed there marked the beginning of what some commentators regarded as 'the Golden Era' of Stalag Luft III's history and created an extraordinary escaping enterprise and strict organisation rarely before witnessed in modern warfare. One POW reported on the place in the early months of its opening: 'there was plenty of living space, plenty of food, [and] plenty of recreation and athletic activity'. The situation was like this only at first; as time went on conditions began to worsen, especially in the case of food. Despite the circumstances of total war, it was occasionally characterised in this manner – almost everything a POW could want or expect, and yet the need to escape back into harm's way in the service of their country became paramount in the minds of most of the men.

The North Compound

The North Compound was larger than the rest of the compounds (East, Centre and South) put together. Provisions were better than elsewhere in German concentration camps. There were sick quarters; solitary cells (called by the prisoners the "Cooler") and a large storage area in a well-designed prison structure that rivalled most traditional European criminal prisons.

Inside the new compound were fifteen large timber barracks, subdivided into several bedrooms, a large cookhouse, a large well-designed theatre built by the prisoners and a huge sporting field. With German approval, the POWs began with the early building of barracks to work on the theatre as well as to clear the stumps out of the athletic area even before the compound was opened for occupancy. A perimeter exercise trail was also established near the warning wires to provide a circuit for something to do in terms of gentle outdoors exercise. But it provided the opportunity for private and secret conversation. It became a safe place to plan escapes.

The wooden barracks of the compound had a central corridor flanked by seventeen rooms, each designed to bed and house four to eight officers in wooden bunks. Unlike most of the POW accommodation in the rest of Germany, the one room comfortably accommodated about eight men and the entire new North Compound potentially could hold 1,200 men. The barracks were more self-contained than those in the East and Centre Compounds. Each had its own tea kitchen, washing and toilet facilities, a dayroom and a recreation room for orderlies and batmen who were culturally separated from aircrews on a social class basis.

In each room there were several timber wardrobes which the prisoners could use to store food and private or personal items. Each prisoner had only a very small number of personal possessions anyway which were on them when they arrived on enemy territory, commonly by parachute like Brickhill. The washroom with twelve to sixteen faucets in each building was used for cold water showers of a temporary nature that became permanent due to worsening economic conditions in Germany. The prisoners attached hoses to some of the faucets directed into a tin can with punched holes in it[3] – an example of the inventiveness that became part and parcel of the prisoners' lives, especially in their escape attempts in designing makeshift tools, equipment and so on. Red Cross parcels were a rich source of materials that could be re-cycled. They had plenty of time to innovate and create useful objects from scrap materials.

---

3 Arthur A Durand, *Stalag Luft III. The Secret Story*, Simon & Schuster, New York, 1988, 110-11.

Some of the prisoners Paul met when he first arrived had already been making plans for a well-organised escape for at least four months before they were actually marched into the new compound. He immediately joined in and took part in the highly creative and inventive work where he could that kept up the individual's morale in a complex communal context.

"X" Escape Organisation and Roger Bushell

Already some of the new inmates of the North Compound had dug escape tunnels at other prisoner-of-war camps in Germany and, although ultimately unsuccessful as they were still imprisoned, they had gained plenty of experience and know-how. All of this was to be brought together brilliantly in the North Compound.

A multi-cultural escape secret organisation, which Brickhill joined, became known simply as "X". Roger Bushell, a tall South African pilot who had been a prominent lawyer prior to the war and in his spare time a dare-devil British ski champion, was elected head of "X" – the supremo of the whole organisation. As someone who had lived successfully in two distinct cultures, he had an ability in abundance to draw the threads together. Paul Brickhill described him thus:

> ... a fighter pilot until shot down over Dunkirk. Bushell had already made two remarkable escapes and once had got almost to Switzerland before he was caught.[4]
>
> Roger was an unusual-looking chap in an impressive way that accorded well with his unusual personality.

4 Brickhill, 'Tunnel to Freedom', 167.

> He was tall, nearly six feet, and well built, but it was his eyes that were so remarkable. They were a light grey-blue, with heavy rings under them and in some uncanny way they seemed to probe right through you. One couldn't analyse the reason but got the impression there was a terrific amount of thinking going on behind that penetrating, almost lowering and sinister look.[5]

A natural charismatic leader of men in simple terms.

As a rising barrister in London when the Second World War began, the South African-born Bushell was an Auxiliary Air Force squadron leader in charge of veterans of the Great War who was, as the war progressed, to lead the RAF score of 'kills'. Roger, however, was soon shot down over the beaches of Dunkirk and captured by German soldiers. The incisive character sketch of Bushell by Brickhill was to be the hallmark of his writing style that makes it so evocative and memorable. He understood how to write biography for popular rather than academic consumption.

Most importantly for the inmates of the North Compound, Roger Bushell was an 'escape genius' with brilliant organisational and leadership powers and skills and had the ability to make urgent decisions. He was known as "Big X" and the absolute boss of "X" organisation. His word would become law. He was, as Brickhill consistently portrayed him in *The Great Escape*, 'a big tempestuous man with broad shoulders and the most chilling pale blue eyes'.

In his early twenties, Bushell had been British ski champion. In an international race in Canada, he had a bad accident over a boulder. The tip of one of his skis caught him in the inner

5 Brickhill and Norton, *Escape to Danger*, 222.

corner of his right eye and gashed it. After it had been sewn up, the corner of his eye drooped permanently and the effect 'on his look was strangely sinister and brooding' as Brickhill aptly put it.[6] Brickhill's portrayal made Bushell one of the famous personalities of the Second World War as he did for Squadron Leader Guy Gibson in *The Dam Busters* and for Douglas Bader in his biography of the legless pilot in *Reach for the Sky*. Brickhill created the fame of these men of war that soon became legend.

Roger Joyce Bushell was born on 30 August 1910 in Cape Province, South Africa. He attended Wellington Public School in England as a boarder in the 1920s. He was a good student well-admired by his teachers. Even at school he organised other boys and showed natural potential as a leader. He took being beaten at sports well and was liked and admired by all. He graduated from Wellington to study law at Brasenose College, Oxford, and then began practice eventually becoming a well-regarded barrister. As recounted, after learning to fly in the RAF's Auxiliary Reserve Volunteers, he became a member of No 601 "County of London" Fighter Squadron that trained on weekends and annual holidays. He flew solo on 6 August 1932 and obtained his pilot's licence three days later. He was flying twin-engine Bristol Blenheim Mk 1 fighters from Biggin Hill RAF Station on 1 September 1939 when the Second World War broke out.

About a month later, he was given command of No 92 Squadron based at Tangmere. He welded the squadron into a first-class fighting unit showing the great leadership qualities he was to show again in Stalag Luft III. In March 1942, No 92 Squadron moved to Croydon Airfield near London where they exchanged their Blenheims for the glamorous single-engine Supermarine Spitfire Mk 1 fighters. In April and May

---

6 Brickhill, *The Great Escape*, 1.

1942 the squadron flew around London mastering their new fighters. They were then sent on a dangerous mission to patrol the Dunkirk beaches where the French and English armies anxiously awaited rescue.

Bushell was shot down on a second sortie to Dunkirk by German Messerschmitt Me-109 fighters that had attacked out of the sun. He was taken prisoner and after several exploits in other concentration camps was sent to Sagan.[7]

Paul Brickhill accurately described the North Compound of Stalag Luft III in dimension as a square. Each side was one thousand feet long, enclosed by two tall barbed-wire fences, parallel and five feet apart. The space between them was crammed with barbed-wire coils. Ten yards inside this formidable barrier was the warning wire lowly slung. If a POW stepped across it, he could be shot. There were numerous sentry towers of fifteen feet high, each with a searchlight for night surveillance of both the barracks inside and the exterior beyond the wire. A manned machine-gun was maintained twenty-four hours a day.

Twenty-five yards outside the exterior on all four sides of the square were dense pine woods that almost entirely cut off the prisoners' view of the outside world. But such woods would help cover up an escape attempt. Nevertheless, the purpose was to completely isolate those in captivity from the local German community to prevent any interaction whatsoever.

Stalag Luft III in its formation, and in Brickhill's vivid and accurate memory, concentrated all the 'coercive technologies of behaviour' to totally control the lives of the unfortunate prisoners-of-war.[8] Such coercive technologies of behaviour –

---

7 William B Allmon, 'The Man Behind the Great Escape', *World War II*, vol.17, issue 3, 2002, 1-6.

8 See Michel Foucault, *Discipline and Punish: The Birth of the Prison*, trans. by Alan Sheridan, Pantheon, New York, 1977.

the barbed wire, the total incarceration, the danger of machine-gun bullets, the isolation – all led to post-traumatic stress in ex-POWs, like and including Paul Brickhill: nightmares, loss of identity, emotional depression and so on. Such factors were to affect the health status of Paul Brickhill after the war for the rest of his life.

It is clear Paul Brickhill in *The Great Escape* was intent on painting a realistic portrait, on the one hand, of the harsh destructiveness of life in a POW camp at a time when the public had become aware of the tens of thousands of men who had seen out the remainder of the war incarcerated and had returned home. Their participation in the war, in the minds of the public, was frequently considered to be non-existent – a mindset Brickhill was intent on changing.

He was well aware of the tendency to dismiss the wartime experiences of the POWs. It was believed they had not seen action since they were captured. They were not likely to have won any more battle honours than they had before being captured. They had no further combat to be proud of, no further combat or campaign medals to show off. In popular culture of the day in the late 1940s, it was not difficult to imagine quite wrongly that they had an easy time of it, loafing around in a camp, while others fought and won the war. In general, POWs were not viewed in the public mind as heroes and their efforts had not been widely recognised. Brickhill's purpose then was to show factually the extent of loss suffered and the sacrifices made by such men.

On the other hand, he wished to commemorate the comradeship that developed in Stalag Luft III with the escape plans and the organisation especially, but also the other camp social activities and rituals. As well, there was the sheer inventiveness of the freedom of mind behind barbed wire and the inspirational moments of the community spirit. Brickhill's memory was alive with the physical and emotional images of the Stalag that he needed and was compelled to convey to his reader.

German authorities believed that the North Compound, as a maximum security prison camp, would hold even the craftiest escape artists amongst the Allied captured pilots and thus permanently remove their influence over the outcome of the war. In concentrating so many able and intelligent officers in the one place, however, the Nazis unwittingly assembled what could probably be known as the finest escape team in military history. Underneath the 'coercive technologies' of a controlling behaviour was an oppositional subculture of rebellion.[9]

All the skills and expertise the men in the camp had before the war in their different occupations and even in their hobbies were put to use: tailors mended or converted garments; photographers made passport photos; tradesmen made their own tools; teachers organised libraries; engineers invented gadgets and so on.

As soon as the men moved into their new barracks quarters, "X" organisation placed a notice on the noticeboard of the recreation room in a secret code that all POWs were well aware of. On the surface, the notice called for volunteers to play cricket and softball on the big athletic ground in front of the barracks buildings, but inside the wire. Paul Brickhill and many others immediately volunteered knowing what it was all about as the word had quickly passed around the sub-culture of the compound. The unspoken but understood message was that volunteers were needed to work on all aspects of a massive

---

9 See a similar Foucauldian coercive structure in John Ramsland, 'The agricultural colony of Mettray. A 19th century approach to the institutionalisation of delinquent boys', in David Stockley, *Melbourne Studies in Education, 1987-88*, La Trobe University Press, Bundoora, 1988, 64-80.

Colonel Friedrich-Wilhelm von Lindeiner, Luftwaffe Commandant Stalag Luft III

highly co-ordinated escape strategy, primarily by building in secret escape tunnels for "X". Men passed on the word quietly to their trusted comrades as they walked the perimeter for exercise out of earshot of the guards and "ferrets".

The recruitment drive was signed by "Big X" (Roger Bushell, the supremo) and responded eagerly by prisoners who wanted and needed to do something constructive and positive, something that would boost their morale in the most depressing and desperate of circumstances. They clearly missed their dangerous, but thrilling busy experiences as bomber or fighter pilots and their loyal crews as well as the close comradeship and especially the prestige that their former role as 'glamour boys' in warfare had brought them. They were young, full of life and energy that could not be expended. It had to be contained within the boredom of the routine of the concentration camp that was thoroughly efficient in the German rigid authoritarian manner. The very dullness of the routine of daily existence bred rebellious invention and innovation.

Such men were to become an essential part of an exciting, quietly rebellious secret group born of the very notion of incarceration in oppositional terms. They were ready to resist the nature of Stalag Luft III's structural architecture that palpably aided the maintenance of a fixed, rigid approach to the control and discipline of largely youthful inmates throughout the war.

"Tom", "Dick" and "Harry"

Five hundred of the prisoners-of-war signed up for the so-called sports teams. Enthusiasm was infectious as the undercover it was for tunnelling out to freedom – no matter what the cost. These men had signed the pledge of secret rebellion against absolute authority. More and more joined in.

The "X" governing committee had decided to start three long tunnels simultaneously: "Tom", "Dick" and "Harry", in the grand hope that at least one would get through undetected.[10] The very notion of these three names together was to take on a legendary character. The POWs never used the word 'tunnel' in any of the conversations for obvious security reasons – they were simply "Tom", "Dick" and "Harry" and were personified into human beings, as there were too many guards in Stalag Luft III who understood English and they were always on the alert, listening in where they could to conversations. Hence the privacy of the perimeter walk was frequently used to avoid

10 Brickhill, 'Tunnel to Freedom', 167-8.

being overheard especially when extensive plans were being formulated.

"Tom" was to be dug from Block 123 to the wire, 150 feet away and then on to the shelter of the woods which surrounded the camp. "Dick" was to be dug from Block 122 towards "Tom" so that it could either be joined with the shaft of "Tom" or be dug all the way. "Harry" was to begin from Block 104 and driven to the woods on the north.

The tunnels had to start from within the huts or barracks buildings. Each hut was one hundred feet long with sleeping quarters in rooms, washrooms and small tea kitchens as already described. The huts had been built about a foot from the ground so that the special investigators (called "ferrets" by the prisoners) could look underneath to see whether the POWs were up to 'any funny business'. The so-called "ferrets" could be easily spotted by the prisoners as they wore special bright blue overalls when on duty. They used torches and long steel probes to identify tunnelling efforts by the prisoners. They looked for evidence of tunnel trapdoors or distinctive coloured soil spread from the underground – a different colour to the surface soil of the open quadrangle of the compound. The escapees needed to fool them consistently and put them off the scent.

"Big X" organised three efficient teams each under a veteran tunneller. Every volunteer was interviewed by the "X" chief of his block. Miners, carpenters, engineers were assigned to each of the three tunnels. Much of the North Compound became an escape factory. "Big X" wanted each potential escapee to be equipped with a full set of forged documents to fool the German police and civilians in the perilous journey to the German border. They needed a set of convincing civilian clothes or fake German military uniforms to impersonate soldiers. They were to be equipped with accurate maps and compasses to help them reach the border of a neutral country of their choice.

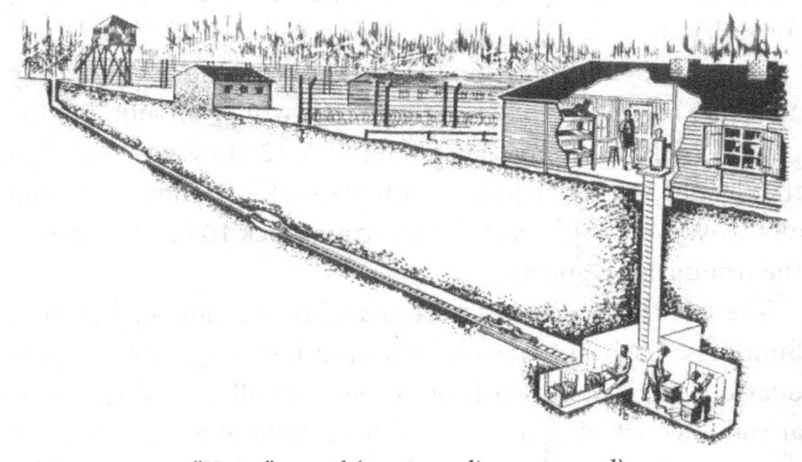

"Harry" tunnel (museum.eline.serwery.pl)

The "X" organisation spotted human weaknesses and frailties in the "ferrets" and bribed them with chocolates, coffee and cigarettes from the Red Cross aid packets. Such items were in increasing short supply in the German civilian society and hence very tempting. Soon they had ink and pens, a camera and a set of official documents to copy. A forging factory that Paul Brickhill participated in ran day and night. Each product was carefully inspected to ensure its quality. In other huts, prisoner-tailors made convincing versions of civilian clothes by cutting and reshaping military uniforms worn by the POWs as well as the linings of winter coats and other pieces of cloth. An Australian inmate ran a factory that made two hundred compasses out of melted phonograph records with compass needles made of slices of magnetised razor blades.[11]

Thus tailors were organised to turn out disguises; artists and navigators were to set up a forgery shop to fake papers that

11 Thomas Fleming, *The Great Escape*, EBSCO Publishing, 2002, 25.

each escapee would need to carry with them. Any man who spoke fluent German was assigned to making friends with a "ferret", keep him always in sight, cultivate him and eventually bribe him to bring an item for the enterprise from the outside in exchange for chocolates and cigarettes.[12] They also gave lessons in fundamental German to non-German speakers.

The escape factory made rubber stamps from the heels of wellington boots; paper was stained to make it look authentically aged using cold tea and drying it; and the vital eagle-and-swastika embossing forging tool was made from melted-down silver paper from cigarette and chocolate packages and then cast in a soap mould.

Extending "Harry" at the working face Stalag Luft III. The air pipe is made from Klim milk containers (drawing by Albert Comber, 1945)

12 Brickhill, 'Tunnel to Freedom', 167-8.

In Stalag Luft III, there was no newspaper for Paul Brickhill to use his expert journalistic skills. But he spent six hundred days there. Some part of every day was expended on working quietly for "X" organisation, but the other part of the time was used by him to collect stories about the POWs earlier experiences of war or their experiences in earlier attempted but unsuccessful escapes from Germany. In other words, he was developing a dossier through a series of interviews that could form the basis of a history of the concentration camp and the people inside it – a preliminary manuscript to base his future books on. The prisoners, however, began to print their own newsletters and small occasional papers. To provide copy and collect material, Paul and a South African, Conrad Norton, began interviews with inmates. Brickhill with the aid of Norton became their secret chroniclers, carefully recording what they observed on scraps of paper which they hid in safe places from the "ferrets" and more elaborate search parties by the Gestapo.

Thanks to the Regio Aeronautica and its fighter planes, Brickhill had found himself in Stalag Luft III. To keep sane, he did two things to make the days shorter: worked for "X" and collected war stories with Norton. These he secreted away as something for the future, part of a dream of eventual release.[13] Otherwise his time in the prison camp would have been rudderless and depressing.

It was even a question of staying alive by purposeful activity. In this situation, he became the biographer of Stalag Luft III as well as of individual contributions to warfare. There were, hidden away on the pages being written, 'stories of men who had fantastic escapes from death'. For instance, there was a story of the pilot of a burning bomber who jumped from certain death, but without a parachute. On his way down through the

13 Brickhill, *Reach for the Sky*, back dustcover.

sky, he caught hold of the legs of another member of the crew who was in his parachute and the two men floated safely to the ground together in the one parachute.[14]

Despite the many true life adventurous and heroic stories, those of escape that could excite the imagination, Brickhill was well aware of what he termed 'the atrophied stagnation of a prisoner of war's life'. He pointed out that it was something that had to be experienced to be believed or understood at the emotional level. It was even not so much the physical hardships like hunger, recognising that the Red Cross ameliorated a certain amount of that, one could put up with what was left 'equably' enough in a concentration camp.

He argued that it was not so much the negative features of prisoner life, but 'the complete lack of positive elements': the demoralising monotony of life that 'did not vary one iota' from day to day for years, a life that lacked any 'spot of colour or brightness', just drab existence that 'went from a ramshackle hut to a small sandy desert of compound' enclosed 'with barbed wire'. And back to the hut at evening.[15] As another POW once put, in full agreement with Brickhill's position:

> We will remember the comradeship, the freedom of mind, the rare moments of community spirit; we will forget the wet days, the wet weeks, the days when it was an effort to do anything, the days when it was an effort to do nothing, and our bunks seemed the only escape.
>
> – Guy Morgan, *Only Ghosts Can Live*, 1945[16]

14 Craig Wilcox, 'Fall from the Sky', *Wartime*, Issue 58, 2012, 30.
15 Brickhill and Norton, *Escape to Danger*, 113.
16 Cited by Taylor Downing, 'War on Film: The Captive Heart', *Military History Monthly*, Issue 67, April 2016, 60.

Nevertheless, for Brickhill and many others, the work of "X" organisation provided colour and brightness and, frequently, a touch of excitement and danger within the borders of the barbed wire. The "ferrets" were omnipresent in a game of hide-and-seek. For Brickhill and his friend Norton as well, recording stories was an all-absorbing process that wiped away a dull existence providing another positive element in their daily life.

The activity of the "X" organisation of the North Compound of Stalag Luft III culminated in what soon after became known as The Great Escape. Paul Brickhill had worked hard with his many comrades in "X"'s underground and above the ground workshops, tunnel railway, the air pumps and innovative electric lighting and as 'penguins' distributing soil taken from the tunnels carried in sausage-shaped bags under their trousers. Because of his writing ability, Paul tended to specialise in writing preliminary texts for the variety of forged papers that the escapists would use. He was a master of characterisation in a small space that was convincing.

Claustrophobia, however, prevented Brickhill from entering the narrow escape tunnel. His main contribution to the enterprise was above the ground not down in the confined tunnels. But in a real sense, he was fortunate not to have escaped as the end-game became more than grim – a tragedy of major dimensions.

Gardening

Typical room

The Break-out!

The famous mass escape occurred at night. It was the culmination of a brilliantly conceived scheme of events over nearly two years. At half-past ten, the man lying flat on the trolley at the base of the tunnel felt the rope tug as the hauler-in at Piccadilly station signalled to begin moving up the line. Piccadilly was the first change-over station on the tunnel railway. He tugged back at a positive signal and went rolling softly up to Piccadilly over 'blanket-deadened rail'. The trolley then went back in a minute and another POW lay his belly on it and waited for the signal.

As each hauler pulled ten people past him, the eleventh took over. This action was repeated allowing the ex-haulers to proceed down the tunnel and out to freedom. This action was repeated allowing the ex-haulers to proceed down the tunnel and out to freedom. The controller outside the hole behind the 'ferret fence' got twenty men out and then the twenty-first relieved him in turn and so on through the whole process, again and again.

It was not long, however, before they were falling behind schedule. Bushell's planning had aimed at getting a man out every three of four minutes. Larger suitcases as part of the men's disguises were the main trouble, frequently getting stuck or partly caught temporarily on the sides of the tunnel. This made the hauling difficult and there were many interruptions which slowed the process down as well as heightening the gut-wrenching tension.

A few minutes after midnight, sirens in the compound went off for an Allied air-raid and all the lights in the tunnel switched off automatically with the rest of the Stalag's electric system that they were secretly connected to. In the tunnel was 'terrifying blackness' and the whole process of movement out came to a full stop. Nerves were at snapping point. Eventually the sirens sounded the all-clear and the electric current was switched on again. But too many stoppages continued. At about four o'clock, number sixty went through the tunnel. Two more men were signalled out of the exit, but another hold up was caused by German guards marching down the nearby road and another passed close to the hole without noticing it. The exit had not reached the woods through a miscalculation and escapees had to crawl over the last twenty feet in the snow before reaching the woods for shelter.

Back at 103 hut (Brickhill's hut) the controller ticked off the 83rd down the shaft. But it could not last much longer. The tunnel was crammed. Finally, a guard noticed a slushy trail through the snow from the hole to the woods and the game was up. The tunnel was identified by the guards and an alarm was sounded bringing other guards to the spot.

Morning soon came and the hue and cry erupted spreading rapidly throughout Germany like a tidal wave. Thousands of German troops and auxiliaries were turned out to search for the would-be escapees. Border control was tightened. Gestapo and secret police worked through all the passenger trains inspecting papers, searching vehicles on the roads, checking hotels, houses and farms.

The warning went to all SS Army and Luftwaffe troops, in the neighbourhood at first, and then further out to the whole of Germany. Old men and adolescent underage boys of the Landwehr and Landwacht (a sort of Home Guard) searched across the landscape of the fields and country lanes. Far away ports like Stettin and Danzig were more heavily guarded and searched. Around various borders (Czech, Swiss, Danish, Dutch and French), Grenzpolizei were alerted. For hundreds of miles around the small town of Sagan, the countryside was thick with enthusiastic searching Germans. In fact, it became the greatest search in Germany of the war and probably of any war.

The Great Escape lead to the Great Search. German efficiency was shown at its ruthless best even though at first it was sorely tested. One by one the escapees from the Sagan concentration camp were rounded up as the coercive technologies tightened the net by a co-ordinated variety of means.

A fortnight after the breakout of the seventy-six men who had got clear of the tunnel and made some distance away in the misty dark, only three were still free. They were never found; two were already in England; the third was on his way there through Belgium, France and Spain, but Paul Brickhill was still in the North Compound of Stalag Luft III and it could even be said, much safer out of harm's way where he was.

Murder of the Fifty Escapees

Adolf Hitler at his heavily-guarded retreat Berchtesgaden eyrie had received a report from the Gestapo on Sunday morning, twenty-four hours after the breakout in the North Compound of Stalag Luft III.[17] It was fairly detailed and accurate in nature and the dictator flew into a wild rage. Heinrich Himmler, chief of the Gestapo, Reich Master Hermann Göring, head of the Luftwaffe, and General Wilhelm Keitel, Supreme Commander of the Armed Forces (OKW), were also staying at Berchtesgaden at the time and witnessed Hitler's bizarre behaviour, but were accustomed to it.

The Fuhrer summoned an immediate conference, ordering that no minutes be taken of the secret meeting. He had reached a state of mind in his anger that there was only one method he

---

17 Hitler had been vacationing in the Berchtesgaden area since the 1920s. By this time, it served as an outpost of the Imperial Chancellery with an expansion of offices, security and support services. Goering (Göring), Joseph Goebbels and Albert Speer were frequently in attendance when Hitler was present.

would use to counter the seventy-six POWs who had dared to escape and who were still at large at the time. Keitel later admitted that at the meeting Hitler was 'very excited' – very much a bland understatement – as he told the three prominent Nazi leaders what had happened in ferocious detail.

Himmler immediately and smoothly blamed Keitel for the outbreak. It would take, he said bitterly, 'seventy thousand police and God knows how many working hours to recapture the escapees'. In his turn, Göring blamed Keitel as well. But Keitel then blamed Himmler and Göring; the situation was becoming particularly tense and heated. Keitel argued that Stalag Luft III was an Air Force camp and therefore Göring had the ultimate responsibility. He also claimed passionately that he would not endure any more reproaches and accusations in front of the Fuhrer. And so a three-cornered overlapping argument developed before the even more angry Fuhrer put a stop to it with a sensational statement.

Suddenly, Hitler squashed the lively dispute and brought them all to silence. He ordered that *all* the escapees from the North Compound be shot immediately on recapture. Göring protested as tactfully as he could, but only on the grounds of practical political strategy. To shoot all of them would be, he claimed, murder. It would have the effect of encouraging reprisals that may be taken out on Germany POWs in Allied hands.

Hitler accepted part of the logic of Göring's viewpoint. So he stated that half of them should be shot; he considered this a more reasonable reprisal. Afterwards, Keitel and Himmler held a private meeting to plan the executions. Later, Keitel saw Generalmajor von Graenitz, his staff officer, to put the Fuhrer's command into obedient practice. When Keitel was challenged about the proposed executions by Graenitz who argued: 'We cannot just shoot these officers [without a trial]', referring to the escapees, Keitel shouted: 'The time has come for an example to be made or we will not be able to cope with escapes. This ought to be such a shock that the prisoners won't escape any more. Every prisoner must be told about it'. Thereafter, a text was issued which has since become known as the "Sagan Order", named after the town where Stalag Luft III is found. In part it read in translation:

> The increase of escapes by officer prisoners of war is a menace to international security... As a deterrent the Fuehrer has ordered that more than half the escaped officers are to be shot... I order that Kriminalpolizei are to hand over for interrogation to the Gestapo more than half of the recaptured officers. After interrogation the officers are to be taken in the direction of their original camp [Stalag Luft III], and *shot en route*. The shootings will be explained by the fact that the recaptured officers were shot whilst trying to escape, or because they offered resistance, so that nothing can be proved later.[18]

This direct and recorded order was carried out to the letter.

The commandant of Stalag Luft III von Lindeiner was removed from his post by the Gestapo. Slightly before this, however, the ashes of the fifty men had arrived at the North Compound to reinforce the fact that the same fate would be in store for anyone else intending to escape. Engraved on each urn was the location where death had occurred. Four were engraved 'Danzig'; four were marked 'Hirschberg'; two more with the name of a town near the French border. There were some from Liegnitz and many from Breslau.

Five million Germans had spent time looking for the escapees:

---

18 Brickhill, *The Great Escape*, 140.

'That meant that the break was some sort of success, if one could overlook the heavy cost', wrote Brickhill optimistically soon after the war. Before Commandant von Lindeiner left, he obtained some suitable stone and let a working party of POWs go to a nearby local Sagan cemetery and build a vault in which to place the urns that had been received. This provided some sort of dignity of ceremony for the POWs before the commandant disappeared from the camp. He too was executed after a military court trial (tribunal).

Fifty men were dead, but fifteen others were caught and returned to the compound. The POWs wondered what had become of the other eleven.[19] Fear entered the hearts of the men in the compound. As Anthony Eden said in the House of Commons in May 1944: 'It was cold-blooded butchery and we are resolved that the foul criminals shall be tracked down'.

Two Norwegians and a Dutchman

In June, the POWs left in the compound received a coded letter that indicated Per Bergsland – known by Brickhill as "Rocky" Rockland – and Jens Müller (Muller to Brickhill) had made it back to England via Sweden. Before entering the concentration camp, Bergsland had deliberately anglicised his name to Peter Rockland to protect his family in occupied Norway. Even his fellow POWs did not know his real name.

Bergsland and Müller had travelled audaciously in disguise as Swedish labourers by train to Stettin where they eventually met some Swedish sailors who smuggled them aboard their ship and then set sail for home – Stockholm.

The Norwegian aviators of the RAF, Per Bergsland and Jens Müller, both in the North Compound, had decided to work

---

19 Brickhill, *The Great Escape*, 153.

together in their escape plan. On the night of the escape, they lined up as numbers 43 and 44 out of the tunnel. Then out through the woods successfully. They had straightened their makeshift civilian garb which needed attention from the rigours of the tunnel and headed straight for Sagan railway station. Bergsland was wearing a civilian suit he had made from a Royal Marine uniform together with a RAF overcoat slightly and subtly altered with brown leather sewn over the buttons.

They both spoke perfect Swedish and German and had well-designed fake papers identifying them as Swedish electricians ordered to relocate in Stettin. After escaping to Sweden by ship, they reached Britain in just a few weeks. From there they sent a coded postcard to Stalag Luft III to indicate to their POW comrades that they had reached England safely. This information lifted morale a little in the compound.

After the war, Jens Müller wrote a book in 1946 about his war experiences, *Tre kom tilbake* (*Three Returned*). Per Bergsland stayed in aviation and became an executive CEO for Fred Olsen Air Transport (1968) and later Widerøe aviation from 1970 to 1981.[20]

Bram (Bob according to Brickhill) van der Stok, a Dutch pilot in the RAF, was the third success story wearing a dark-blue Australian Air Force greatcoat, Dutch naval trousers and a jaunty beret. He was number 18 of the seventy-six men who managed to crawl out of the escape tunnel. He posed as a Spanish labourer according to Brickhill, but in reality he posed as a Dutch labourer which made his disguise more authentic. At Breslau station, he obtained a ticket that took him all the way through to the Netherlands. His forged papers passed the test on a number of occasions when examined by railway guards or Gestapo.

20 <http://spotlightsfolder3com/2013/08/23escaping-luftIII>.

IN MEMORIAM

F/Lt. Henry Birkland, R.C.A.F.
F/Lt. Edward Brettell, D.F.C., R.A.F.
F/Lt. Leslie Bull, D.F.C., R.A.F.
S/Ldr. Roger Bushell, R.A.F.
F/Lt. Michael Casey, R.A.F.
S/Ldr. James Catanach, D.F.C. R.A.A.F.
F/O Arnold Christenson, R.N.Z.A.F.
F/O Dennis Cochran, R.A.F.
S/Ldr. Ian Cross, D.F.C., R.A.F.
F/O Haldo Espelid, R.A.F. (Norway)
F/Lt. Brian Evans, R.A.F.
F/O Nils Fugelsang, R.A.F. (Norway)
Lt. Johannes Gouws, S.A.A.F.
F/Lt. Alastair Gunn, R.A.F.
F/Lt. William Grisman, R.A.F.
F/Lt. Charles Hall, R.A.F.
F/Lt. Albert Hake, R.A.A.F.
F/Lt. Anthony Hayter, R.A.F.
F/Lt. Edgar Humphries, R.A.F.
F/Lt. Gordon Kidder, R.C.A.F.
F/O Reginald Kierath, R.A.A.F.
F/Lt. Anthony Kiewnarski, R.A.F. (Poland)
S/Ldr. Tom Kirby-Green, R.A.F.
F/O W. Kolanowski, R.A.F. (Poland)
F/O S. Z. Krol, R.A.F. (Poland)
F/Lt. Patrick Langford, R.C.A.F.
F/Lt. Tom Leigh, R.A.F.
F/Lt. J. L. Long, R.A.F.
Lt. Neville McGarr, S.A.A.F.
F/Lt. George McGill, R.C.A.F.
F/Lt. Romas Marcinkus, R.A.F. (Lithuania)
F/Lt. Harold Milford, R.A.F.
F/O Jerzy Mondschein, R.A.F. (Poland)
F/O K. Pawluk, R.A.F. (Poland)
F/Lt. Henri Picard, C. DE G., R.A.F. (Belgium)
F/O P. P. J. Pohé, R.N.Z.A.F.
Lt. Bernard Scheidhower (France)
F/O S. Skanziklas, R.A.F. (Greece)
F/Lt. Cyril Swain, R.A.F.
Lt. Rupert Stevens, S.A.A.F.
F/O Robert Stewart, R.A.F.
F/O Denys Street, R.A.F.
F/Lt. John Stower, R.A.F.
F/O P. Tobolski, R.A.F. (Poland)
F/Lt. Ernest Valenta, R.A.F. (Czechoslovakia)
F/Lt. G. W. Walenn, R.A.F.
F/Lt. James Wernham, R.C.A.F.
F/Lt. George Wiley, R.C.A.F.
S/Ldr. J. E. A. Williams, R.A.A.F.
F/Lt. J. F. Williams, R.A.F.

21

Eventually, the Dutch Underground were able to get him to England via Belgium, then France with the support of the French Resistance network and across the mountainous border to Spain. A few days later, van der Stok reached Madrid successfully. The British Consul had him taken to Gibraltar where he was flown to England. 'It was just four months since he had crawled out of the tunnel', wrote Brickhill.[22]

The fifty murdered pilots from the North Compound became a *cause célèbre* when the foreign secretary Anthony Eden, as related, addressed the House of Commons in London on 19 May 1944 giving the Members of Parliament the news of the escapees and the atrocities ordered by Hitler which followed.

Memorial to "The Fifty" down the road toward Żagań (en.wikipedia.org/wiki/Stalag_Luft_III#/media/File:The50Memorial.jpg)

21 Brickhill and Conrad, *Escape to Danger*, In Memoriam, (courtesy of the National Gallery), 220.

22 Brickhill, *The Great Escape*, 154-6.

For seven decades the 'Great Escape' tunnel "Harry" at Sagan, which was used for the famous but tragic mass escape of air force officers, lay relatively untouched in the grounds of what had been Stalag Luft III that had been entirely demolished.

The 111-yard passage named "Harry" had been sealed off by German authorities after the audacious breakout. The place of the former prison camp is now part of Western Poland in what is now known as Zagan (formerly Sagan on the German side of the former German-Polish border). For decades the former Soviet authorities in Poland had or showed no interest in its significance as it was a British affair.

At last British archaeologists were given permission to have "Harry" and the surrounding grounds excavated so as to discover its remarkable secrets so accurately described by Paul Brickhill in *The Great Escape* published as far back as 1951. He described how "Harry" had been concealed under an iron stove in hut or barracks 104. "Gordie" King, a RAF radio operator of 91 years of age, watched the archaeologists working steadily and carefully on the excavation site. He had been 140th in line to go out and therefore missed leaving the tunnel which was discovered by the German guards before he got to it. It brought back bitter-sweet memories for the elderly man. For him, it was a heavily emotional return to the site of Stalag Luft III where he had spent many days in both winter and summer.

It was soon discovered in excavating "Harry" that many of the bed-boards joined together to stop the tunnel collapsing were still in place. Amazingly, the ventilation shaft that had been ingeniously crafted from used powdered milk containers (Klim tins) had remained in working order. Scattered throughout the tunnel and other parts of the ground were bits of old metal buckets as well as hammers and crowbars which were used to hollow out the route within the tunnel.

On the three tunnels ("Tom", "Dick" and "Harry") an amazing

six hundred prisoners-of-war worked. The archaeologists found that the tunnels for most of their lengths were measured at two square foot each. The tunnel reconstruction revealed the trolley system on rails. In all and broadly speaking, the 'dig' uncovered on the entire site 90 wooden boards from the bunk beds; 62 tables; 34 chairs and 76 benches as well as thousands of other items like knives, spoons, forks, towels and blankets that had apparently been squirreled away on the site by the Allied prisoners to aid in some way the escape plan in terms of manufacture under the very noses of their captors.[23]

The several sketches of artist Ley Kenyon made on-site in Stalag Luft III during the war provided invaluable aids to the researchers at the 'dig' including his picture of the air-conditioning plant, the tunnel workshop thirty feet below the surface, the tunnel exit and the section drawing of the escape tunnel "Harry" with its wonderful detail.[24]

Anzac Day, 25 April 1944, Stalag Luft III (Paul Brickhill second right front) (AWM, P00270.027)

---

23 Andrew Levy, 'Tunnel back in time: Revealed after 67 years, the passage used in Great Escape', 21 November 2011, <www.dailymail.co.uk/news/article-2064068/Tunnel-time-Revealed-67-years-passage-used-Great-Escape.html>.

24 See Brickhill and Conrad, *Escape to Danger* and Brickhill, *The Great Escape*, various illustrations as listed.

CHAPTER 5

THE LONG MARCH TO FREEDOM

AUSTRALIAN WAR MEMORIAL ART34781.027

The shapeless ghosts leave camp (Albert Comber)

At 3pm on 17 January 1945, the German news broadcast announced unprecedented Russian military advances toward the German border town of Sagan and, therefore, to Stalag Luft III. That same day inmates heard that a large shipment of Red Cross food parcels had arrived by truck at the camp from Lübeck. For four and a half months the POWs in the North Compound had been placed on half rations and their physical condition had been considerably weakened by a poorer diet.

The senior camp controllers decided it was time to put the half-starved prisoners back on full rations. Word spread amongst the men that they were to be fattened up in readiness for any eventuality – probably to convince the Allies that they had been well cared for. The news spread quickly and electrified the men – they had much to think about. Would they soon be released?

The Stalag Luft III inmates had already heard the news that prisoner-of-war camps further east had been evacuated and on very short notice. Word had travelled through the mouths of the more compliant ordinary "ferrets" and guards whose seeming friendliness was increasing daily. In response, many of the more thoughtful of the POWs were extending their walking circuits around the perimeter to get in better physical shape for the possibility of an arduous forced march through the snow drifts at the height of a severely cold winter of what was to become the final brutal winter of World War II. The men began to make containers for carrying their few personal belongings and supplies. They realised that they would not be able to carry much weight over long uncertain distances.[1] They began to prepare their bedrolls.

Paul Brickhill assembled his manuscript together from the various hidden places in the barracks to bunch under his shirt and to help keep him warm in the sub-zero temperatures which could drop to minus 20 degrees. It was, after all to him, the most valuable record and possession of their experience up to the Great Escape. Indeed a unique document that does not seem to have survived today.

By 12 January 1945, the Russian winter offensive started and, as Brickhill put it, the Russian Eastern Front 'came sweeping' towards Sagan 'like a hurricane'. The POWs thought that, in a few days hopefully, they would be evacuated or perhaps freed by the Russian troops in their rapid advance. But they feared in

1 Durand, *Stalag Luft III*, 326.

their darkest of thoughts that, before the Russians arrived, they could all be summarily executed as had been their comrades who had escaped through the "Harry" tunnel only to be recaptured in the freezing cold of the European winter.[2] Fear and tension began to dominate the atmosphere in the camp. The prisoners tried to keep everything in perspective, but it was an impossible task in the innate culture of a prison camp. Speculation and rumour spread endlessly and frequently every day. The example of the murder of the fifty pilots following the Great Escape was central to their thoughts. In real terms, they were about to face the grimmest episode of their captivity. In the prison camps as a whole across the eastern front of Germany, 100,000 Allied prisoners-of-war were to be forced under Hitler's orders to march under heavily guarded surveillance away from the liberating Russian forces to the West.

On 27 and 28 March, the Germans marched the POWs in Stalag Luft III out of the concentration camp into a foot of snow for several miles. As Brickhill jocularly put it, it was to be 'a fairly grim trip' – not a piece of cake, in RAF jargon.[3]

The marching prisoners were still in poor physical condition after the long months of being allowed only half the food in their Red Cross parcels per week, supplemented by other fairly insignificant German rations. The total was just above starvation level. On the route march, of the 10,000 about 2,000 men were from the North Compound – the previous scene of *The Great Escape*. In different large groups, they filled the main roads and byways of eastern Germany at first heading west away from the Russian advance.

---

2 Brickhill and Norton, *Escape to Danger*, 340.

3 Brickhill, *The Great Escape*, 164; see illustration opposite title page in Brickhill and Norton, *Escape to Danger*.

The March Begins

When the order came to evacuate, many of the thespians in the North Compound were rehearsing a play, *The Wind and the Rain* by Merton Hodge (1934). Suddenly, the curtains were drawn and the adjutant called: 'All pack up and be ready to move out in an hour'. At the same time, the prisoners in the South Compound were watching the American hit play *You Can't Take It With You* by George Kaufman and Moss Hart (1936). Colonel Goodrich walked on to the stage and announced: 'The goons have just come and given us thirty minutes to be at the front gate' ready to march away.

There was a mad rush back to their rooms to get ready for the march through the snow; then some unnerving delay and confusion. A few optimistic POWs felt that the stalling by the concentration camp authorities to begin the march might allow the Russian advance to overtake them. It was now close to the camp. Others simply had a lot to do before they departed as it had been their home for up to nearly five years.

In the North Compound, Brickhill was frantically but systematically putting the pieces of his manuscript on the history of the place together page by page from his secret hiding places around the hut. Bedrolls had to be repacked to accommodate some available food from Red Cross parcels. As well, they tried to eat as much food as possible before they left to provide them with enough energy for the tough march that might lay ahead.

They also destroyed anything they had to leave behind that might be of value to the Germans or reveal too much about their former secret escape plans and factories within their huts. They lit bonfires of old clothes, furniture and other items. Brickhill's old home of barracks 104 from where the Great Escape tunnel had been dug suddenly went up in flames. Not until 11pm did the last lingering prisoner leave the South Compound of the partly deserted Stalag Luft III with its many empty wooden buildings. The prisoners from various compounds departed at different times and throughout the night of the next day. North Compound, with Brickhill, cleared the camp at 3.45am in below zero temperature. Centre Compound followed soon after and the East Compound brought up the rear at about 6am Sunday morning.

A lot had to be left behind – mainly sport equipment, theatre make-up and costumes and musical instruments that symbolised the main pastimes of the camp over its years of existence. It is estimated that between 25,000 and 55,000 Red Cross parcels had to be left. Prisoners who passed by the Red Cross store skilfully pilfered mainly gathering up cigarettes and chocolates and other small goods that were valuable for barter purposes with local German country folk they passed by on the march.

After they all passed by the Red Cross store, thousands of unwanted cans from the parcels littered the ground, almost covering it. One million books from the libraries and personal collections had to be left behind. About 500 prisoners in hospital too sick to be moved were left behind in the camp with a few medical personnel, clergymen and healthy volunteer prisoners to care for them. They found plenty to eat from what had been left behind in the compound barracks. Finally, on 6 February 1945 the sick were removed in boxcars to Nuremberg. Stalag Luft III then ceased to exist as a Luftwaffe prisoner-of-war camp.[4]

The men who left on the march were very much a mixed lot nationally: Americans, British (English, Scottish, Welsh and Irish), Canadians, South Africans, Indians, Australians, New Zealanders, Dutch, Belgians, Poles, Norwegians,

---

4 Durand, *Stalag Luft III*, 328-9.

Czechoslovakians and Russians. In *The Great Escape* Paul Brickhill took care to define the nationality of each of the real characters he portrays in the narrative. The men on the march had a huge variety of pre-war civilian occupations that sometimes helped to define their social class background and cultural values, interests and pursuits. Apart from career soldiers and pilots there were journalists like Brickhill, tramway conductors, bus and buggy drivers, sons of millionaires, waiters, English lords, Hindu princes, horse trainers, racing car drivers, professional dancers, professional hockey and football players, cowboys, farmers, artists and photographers like Ley Kenyon, actors, policemen, travelling salesmen, movie house operators, veterinarians, missionaries, private detectives, singers, diamond and coal miners, lawyers, engineers, organists, jockeys, plantation owners, scientists, hotel managers, porters, cardsharps, chauffeurs, band leaders, firemen, pianists and school teachers. Colonel von Lindeiner, the commandant of Stalag Luft III, earlier had found this mixture of men a most interesting and intriguing phenomenon. He was once reported as having remarked: 'A budding diplomat could have received excellent schooling here [at Stalag Luft III] studying the mentality of all the peoples of the globe'.[5] He was no less intrigued by their skills and backgrounds and so could list their occupations fluently on demand.

Brickhill narrates how the prisoners of the North Compound were forced to march under German guard one hundred kilometres for days and nights to Spremberg where they were loaded onto cattle trucks packed closely together. On the march they were on half issue of food parcels. Only one other meal was provided on the way: barley soup.

---

5 Durand, *Stalag Luft III,* 303.

The March continues (courtesy Bob Neary, 070101-F-1111Z-001)

They were two full days on the cattle trucks. As Brickhill described it:

> There was just room to sit, but not to move, and after thirty-six hours they *did* give us each a cup of water drained off the engine. They let us out of the trucks near Bremen and we marched to an old condemned camp and waited seven hours outside in the rain to be searched before we entered. A lot of men collapsed at that point. About seventy-five were already missing – about half left at various places through illness and the rest just 'missing', maybe escaped, maybe shot. Of the rest of us, seventy per cent were sick and everyone had lost more weight, up to thirty pounds. We really hadn't had that much to spare and most of us were looking a little bony.[6]

6 Brickhill, *The Great Escape*, 164.

In his published narrative in *Escape to Danger* and *The Great Escape*, Brickhill was still too close emotionally to the event of the Long March to Freedom of 1945 as it was named. The trauma of the darkest side of the forced march made it too much for him to write about in the fullest of horrific detail which he merely touches on lightly. While describing it in short hand as a 'fairly grim trip', the experience he probably felt was too much to burden readers with so early after the war.

Roadside rest: the winter march from Sagan (Albert Comber)

He did not evoke completely the 'savage landscape of a bitter winter'; that winter of 1945 was close to the coldest one on record. He did not dwell too much on the many deaths from exhaustion and exposure that occurred during the night when the men were sleeping or trying to in the coldest of draughty farm barns amongst pigs and cattle; the unwashed men smothered with lice and the 'terrible pain of hunger'; the desperate scavenging for food; and the huge problem of dysentery that took the lives of many – and so painfully.[7]

Indeed, it was more than 'fairly grim'. The march must have affected Brickhill's physical and emotional health and remained with him throughout the rest of his life. And yet in his writing, he found he was not able to talk about it much. He could not even dare to contemplate it.

Instead, in a typical RAF light-hearted manner, Paul Brickhill played down the very grimness and hardships of the Long March to Freedom in his written accounts. One of the frequent stories he told about it, however, was humorous in nature.

He recounted how one day on the march a suspicious German guard demanded to know what was in the bundle he was carrying (which was his secret manuscript about his time in Stalag Luft III). Cheekily and defiantly, he replied: 'a tommy gun to shoot you with'. He got away with the quick-minded quip and his POW independence of spirit – he could have been shot down on the spot, but the guard just shrugged his shoulders in a frustrated way and stormed off. Paul's family were later well aware of this incident since he recounted it on a number of occasions after the war. So well known was the story that his brother Lloyd told it again as part of his eulogy at Paul's funeral service at St Clement's, Mosman, on 24 April 1991.

From the west, the Allied armies had crossed the Rhine River. They surged toward Berlin and the marching POWs, but 'the rosy dream of liberation [that dominated the prisoners' thoughts] didn't come off'. They were marched off again, this time heading north. Those who could not keep up were shot or thrown into a wagon at the rear.

The Germans were reluctant to let them go to any sort of liberation. According to Brickhill, a few were killed by 'trigger-

---

7 *The Long March to Freedom,* DVD 3-part documentary film, produced and directed by Stephen Saunders, 2012.

happy' guards and a few more were killed ironically by straffing Allied war planes. This threat was not an uncommon feature of their march and numbers were killed. Nevertheless, when they turned north the weather was better than at the start of the march. The milder weather restored their spirits – the spirits of those who had survived thus far. The POWs traded Red Cross coffee and chocolates for eggs and bread with the locals they passed. At night they stole from the fields 'bushels and bushels of potatoes'.[8]

The prisoners in the march were not aware that their guards had been issued with direct orders to execute all of them if they did not reach the Elbe River on a particular day. But that day had already passed. They were late. The guards, however, were prudent in their belief that the war was already lost to them and the Allies' rapid advance guaranteed the sure defeat of Germany. They decided to disobey their masters for the first time.

The POWs were sheltering in barns near Lübeck when they heard the barrage as the British 1st Army crossed the Elbe. Two days later, on 2 May 1945, they heard gunshots nearby on the road and two British tanks rumbled through the trees from the south, appearing suddenly. Brickhill reported that 'the nerves [were] sticking out of everyone's skin' as they were not sure whether they were British tanks or the massive German Tiger tanks that could blow to small fragments all the barns where the POWs were quartered.

Luckily, it was the former – free at last! The hatch from the front tank opened and two Tommies stuck their heads out. 'We ran up to them', wrote Brickhill, 'screaming at the top of our voices'.[9]

Today, the Long March is commemorated by an annual three-

8 Brickhill, *The Great Escape.*
9 Brickhill, *The Great Escape,* 165.

day sixty-mile route march by fit young British army trainees in uniform, starting from the actual site of the exit tunnel of the North Compound of Stalag Luft III now demolished and wiped off the face of the earth. On the way, the eager troops are provided with a serialised narration of the original event. At night, they are fed and housed much better, of course, than the original participants of the march – the prisoners-of-war.

A memorial for the original POWs who went on the Long March to Freedom has been established.[10] This recognises the many POW camps that the Nazis spread all over eastern Germany and into modern Poland and the battle for survival the prisoners all experienced. The legend of the Long March is now well established and remembered in British folklore. Families are full of pride if they happened to have relatives who took part in the first Long March – now acknowledged as a heroic undertaking.

The Long March Ends

The march ended not with a massacre as the prisoners expected, even predicted and feared every night of their ordeal, but in liberation by the Allies in April 1945.

* * *

The freed men were taken to Brighton for a thoroughly but superficially organised rehabilitation. While Brickhill was still in the RAF at Brighton, he began to regain his physical health slowly and put his journalistic writing skills back in practice. As the war ended, brief but exciting narratives of the great escape from the North Compound began appearing in British

10 *The Long March to Freedom*, DVD.

newspapers and popular magazines around the English-speaking world under his steady and prolific pen. These featured Flight Lieutenant P.C.J. Brickhill, as author, before the by-line of each story.

A lot was based on a talk Paul Brickhill gave for the armed services radio station in full-dress uniform even though the audience were not physically present, but sitting around the wireless in the kitchen or living room of their homes. In mid-September 1945, Brickhill gave the talk again, this time from the prestigious BBC studio in London. Then he and Conrad Norton turned their carefully preserved manuscripts written in Stalag Luft III into *Escape to Danger.*[11] The book breathed authenticity and the reading public hungered for more true stories.

* * *

Back in Australia briefly, Paul Brickhill was still suffering from post-traumatic stress and was bored with the routine of ordinary work on the Sydney newspaper, the *Sun*, that further stressed him. He found out from some associate that his girlfriend at the time of his enlistment had not waited faithfully for him to return during his years overseas both in the RAF and in the six hundred days spent in Stalag Luft III. All of which helped him decide to take a ship back to England and to write *The Great Escape.*[12] *Escape – or Die*, *The Dam Busters* and *Reach for the Sky* followed swiftly and he took on the mantle of the celebrated author by the mid-1950s. His books sold in their millions.

11 Wilcox, 'Fall from the Sky', 31.
12 Wilcox, 'Fall from the Sky'.

Australian P.O.W.s on the march through Germany (Alan Moore)

FAME IS THE SPUR

CHAPTER 6

FOREIGN CORRESPONDENT: TRAUMATIC WAR MEMORIES

Such was the pattern of life after the years at the North Compound of Stalag Luft III that Paul Brickhill and his fellow inmates could hardly remember any other life. Just as Brickhill did frequently in prose, another Stalag Luft III POW Joe Boyle examined and expressed the feelings about what existence was really like behind barbed wire, but in verse:

Guard Tower
(Bob Neary, 070101-F111Z-003)

The fate we share as prisoners
Is drab and often grim.
Existing on such scanty fare
As Reich-bread, spuds and klim.
Beds and books and little else
To fill Time's flapping sail,
She makes or loses headway all
Depending on the mail.
Oh! Drab the days and slow to pass
Within this barbed-wire fence,
When all the joys of living are
Still in the future tense.
So here's to happy days ahead
When you and I are free,

To look back on this interlude
And call it history.
"The Fate We Share as Prisoners" [1]

Paul put it more succinctly: 'time hung heavily but with a persistent undertone of fear that never quite left them [the POWs]'. [2]

In barrack block 103 next to block 104 from where the successful tunnel "Harry" was dug, Brickhill and Conrad Norton spent their empty days of incarceration busily preparing the first account in manuscript form of that 'strange and dramatic affair' that later became known as the Great Escape – coined by Brickhill himself. As a trained experienced journalist, Brickhill interviewed many of fellow inmates, carefully recording their various experiences of escape in enemy territory. Both Brickhill and Norton were alert to the hard, bare uncompromising facts of life for the inmates of the German concentration camp. But much of the story of work building up to the mass escape through "Harry" they dared not write about directly while they were incarcerated in the North Compound at Sagan. As the more minor co-author, Conrad Norton had collected of few of the stories of previous individual escapes and their degrees of success or failure in enemy territory.

Instead, they committed the details and major incidents to their memory that they then later added to their manuscript while they were still in uniform in Brighton undergoing an emotionally inadequate rehabilitation to allow them to rejoin a much freer civilian world. They had to remember it all till they 'got back' to England and freedom. That was not so difficult for them as the 'incidents of those days' were still vividly etched in

1 Durand, *Stalag Luft III*, 363; 'klim' was powdered milk.
2 Brickhill, *Escape – or Die*, 59.

their minds not merely as memories, but as nightmares in the mental realm. The rewriting of the manuscript while they were still getting back on their feet was, by accident, the best therapy of all. This was especially so as the repatriation program they received at Brighton was poor in terms of psychological treatment and support.

With their sole joint venture *Escape to Danger,* Norton and Brickhill carefully avoided including strong elements of personal memoir and tried, mainly successfully, to stand at a distance. They told the story of life in Stalag Luft III and the mass escape objectively as a form of public history to reach a wide audience, that is for the general interested reader. Brickhill adhered to this policy in all his other books. He does not write memoir, but investigative journalism or accessible history. References to himself in his published book texts are indeed rare, but this is not quite the same with his despatches of foreign correspondence from Europe to Australia.

While in the German prison compound, they had hidden their ever-growing manuscript of raw material for nearly two years from the German "ferrets", sometimes behind a secret wooden wall panel in their room, sometimes down another tunnel called "Dick" and sometimes by 'the simple expedient' of putting it in the barracks block the German "ferrets" had last searched, knowing that it would wait its turn before being searched again under the systematic schedule of the administrators of the concentration camp. They depended on the rigidity of the methodical German approach to surveillance and, as events turned out, they were correct in their estimation. Not one part of their manuscript was located by the "ferrets".

Eventually, they lugged their precious manuscript on the route marches in the snow at the height of the winter across Germany to the east in the middle of a most severe winter recorded – eventually to freedom. During those hard days they cursed the weight of it on their frail, underfed bodies. It made them throw away precious food from Red Cross parcels as they tramped along the snow-ridden roads from daylight to dark.

At night they used the manuscript as a pillow. While the march went on seemingly endlessly, there was always the undertone fear of death by execution, so much so that liberation 'seemed like a lovely dream that never could come true'. But one day it did and they found themselves by the seaside in the rundown, but lively resort of Brighton.[3] And yet their fear of death on the Long March had been real enough. They knew of the fifty executions of escaped prisoners that had recently taken place before the enforced long march.

They swiftly revised, checked and expanded the narrative reportage of the combined manuscript and it was published as *Escape to Danger* by the prestigious publisher Faber and Faber of London to instant acclaim in 1946 while they were still in uniform. Significantly, the frontispiece displayed a fine visual evocation as a grey-washed sketch of the long march in the snow by fellow POW Ley Kenyon. The caption – equally evocative – read:

> A rest in the blizzard. Some of the 10,000 allied Air Force prisoners-of-war from Stalag Luft 3 sink exhausted in the snow during the ninety-five kilometre forced march following the evacuation of the camp in the face of the oncoming Russian army in January, [12] 1945. For the ill-nourished and half-frozen prisoners the march was one of the grimmest episodes of their captivity.

It was a miracle that Norton, Brickhill and their manuscripts

3 Brickhill and Norton, 'Preface', *Escape to Danger,* 5-6.

survived it all to tell their tale of adventure, suspense, fear, captivity, deprivation, escape and survival or death during the Second World War to an ever-eager public.

Donald Bain's logo for the Sydney Sun *newspaper*

Becoming a Journalist again

It was while the ineffective process of rehabilitation was going on at the run-down pleasure resort of Brighton that Brickhill came to the realisation that he could return to his profession of journalism. His RAAF appointment was terminated on 8 April 1946. He had arrived in the United Kingdom as an ex-prisoner-of-war on 8 May 1945. While the rehabilitation had lasted eleven months, it achieved little other than restoring some physical fitness and providing cursory health checks. To many, Brighton appeared like a more pleasant concentration camp by the sea.

At the same time as Brickhill's demobbing, the Sydney *Sun* – where he had served his apprenticeship as a cadet in the early 1930s – appointed him as their foreign correspondent in Europe and later in the United States of America before he returned more permanently to Sydney in 1958.[4] The *Sun* ceased its daily

4 Craig Wilcox, 'Brickhill, Paul Chester (1916-1991)', *Australian Dictionary of Biography*, Australian National University, <http://adb.anu.edu.au/biography/brickhill-paul-chester-14647/text25780>, published online 2014; Service Record: Brickhill.

afternoon newspaper in 1957 and his journalistic career drew to a close soon after. The *Sun*, however, had remained intensely loyal to Brickhill as their star reporter and fully restored his appointment as soon as he was officially demobbed. He had even started supplying the newspaper with despatches before he was out of uniform and they were very pleased with his efforts that made good copy in their network of Australian urban and rural newspapers emanating from the Elizabeth Street headquarters in Sydney.

From 1946 Brickhill – *Sun* journalist extraordinaire – was using the official correspondence paper to type on with his old friend Donald Sackville Bain's familiar and famous elaborate headpiece with the logo of the Roman chariot of fire drawn by several horses charging forward from the sun. Bain's logo for the *Sun* was patriotically endorsed: 'Above all for Australia'.[5] The paper was a central part of Associated Newspapers with a wider distribution and syndication beyond Sydney to Associated Newspapers other provincial newspapers. Thus, Foreign Correspondent Paul Brickhill's despatches and articles had a comprehensive distribution around the country. His fame in the Australian newspaper world had taken off again.

From late 1945 while still in a Flight Lieutenant's uniform, Paul Brickhill wrote many despatches on a variety of subjects and themes that began to appear prominently under his name as a by-line in the city and country town newspapers under the control of Associated Newspapers.

Battle in Berlin--To Save Europe From
Disaster Worse Than War

5 Paul Brickhill to Mr Long, *Sun* editor, 7 January 1948, Service Record: Brickhill.

As Foreign Correspondent in Berlin

In the Adelaide *News* on Monday, 24 December 1945 appeared one of his first despatches to Australia to be published under the banner 'POW Goes Back --- How the Germans Have Changed' 'From Paul Brickhill'. The article carried a handsome portrait of the smiling foreign correspondent in a smart RAF uniform. Image was important. The melodramatic lead-in ran:

> In "Escape to Danger" Flight-Lieutenant Brickhill, in "The News" recently of his life as a Nazi [*sic*] P.O.W. Now he is back in Germany – and his former guards are on the other side of the barbed wire. Here he tells what it was like to go back and see how his erstwhile enemies are behaving now they are the underdogs.

In his despatch which followed, he described a hungry dream he had while an inmate at Sagan's concentration camp and his initial personal view was: 'if only the positions were reversed'. He flew to Berlin by US Dakota. On the flight he noticed the green fields sliding under the plane's wing. Suddenly they were 'pockmarked with old black bomb craters', vivid reminders of the grim and brutal total war which had just finished.

The Canadian navigator remarked to Paul: 'There you are… You're back here. It's Sausage Land.' So Paul was on his pilgrimage of 'The Man Who Came Back', as the well-known correspondent had depicted it – after 'two years of starvation and misery as a prisoner of war in Stalag Luft 3'. He reminded his readers that he had never intended to return: 'They shot 50 of my friends for escaping, and would have shot me too if I'd have drawn an early ticket for the escape tunnel. So I didn't exactly acquire a love for them [the German military]'.

He had arrived back in Germany on the third consecutive

winter since; the first two had been spent in the North Compound, but now he was on the other side of the track, as it were, and in 'a strange new world' for him.

His descriptions of this world brought back many bitter memories of his wartime experiences behind the barbed wire that were still startlingly vivid and disturbing. But he was there primarily to cover the Nuremberg Trials. Nonetheless, the shadows of the past haunted him and revealed themselves from time to time in his journalistic accounts.

As his Dakota from London touched down on Berlin's Gatow airport and taxied in, eager young ex-Wermacht soldiers dashed out, picked up his bags, bowed and trotted alongside him. He then thought of his last welcome into the country that was with the 'hollow end of a sub-machine-gun' poked into his ribs.

This time, however, he was taken to the airport's control tower with great courtesy for refreshments and handed tea cakes by a bevy of 'attractive frauleins in diaphanous dresses – and ye gods! silk stockings'. He noted wryly that he had never seen silk stockings on London waitresses since his return from the prison camp and certainly not wearing 'diaphanous' dresses.

In the drive along the frosty roads towards the 'jagged' Berlin skyline, he tried to adjust to the situation. The taxi from the airport passed the once fashionable Kurfurstendamm sector that 'resembled the ugly smile of an old beggar showing a mouthful of broken or blackened teeth'. In the so-called pressmen's hotel, all was 'sweetness and light'. The 'pink-faced' German porter could not debase himself enough at Brickhill's arrival. In four minutes, Brickhill noted, he called him 'sir' as many times as he had been called 'sir' in the four years he has spent as an air force pilot in the RAAF and RAF. His remark was bitter. On this occasion, he was offered several 'jerky' bows and 'sir' kept popping out 'like a chronic hiccup', he told his Australian newspaper readers.

But then his mind went back to the previous April when a 'surly German policeman' had pushed him off the footpath: 'Other policemen kicked and clouted with rifle butts several of my friends and called them "bandits, gangsters, murderers"'. Again, it was an intensely bitter tone. It was one of several flashes of memory he was to relay to his avid readers in Australia.

He noticed in the hotel dining room that no sooner had a diner stubbed a cigarette in an ashtray than the ashtray was whisked away and returned clean after a few seconds. Commenting on this to his army officer colleagues – all the Allied journalists were still in military uniform – he was told that, for each table thus served, each waiter was paid a retainer of about 200 marks (£5) a week by a black-marketeer to hand over all the cigarette butts customers left. Then the tobacco extracted from these was sold for a so-called 'fat' profit as individual cigarettes remade cost about seven marks (3s 6p) each.

Brickhill was always brilliant at harmonising the particular with the general – a detail that would symbolise broader social concerns, in this case the huge shortages that existed in Berlin that stimulated an undercover black market.

Social Conditions in Post-War Berlin

At Berlin's exclusive Royal Club when he was there, Brickhill found what he labelled 'the sordid soul' of the new Berlin aristocrats. They were Berlin's 'new kings' – the black-marketeers, 'rolling in money, plump, impeccably dressed'. He found the city a crazy blend of opulence coupled with obsequiousness. Drinks were hugely expensive and smart women ate sardines from a tin for meals, 'garnished with dry bread'. Brickhill's article as a whole was made up of his fast impressions of Berlin as he found it. Thus his early despatches were extremely impressionistic and emotionally-charged.

At the Royal Club he met an attractive, smartly-dressed woman, Gertrude – 'blond, shapely, throaty voiced'. She sighed that she hoped he would like the German people and their country. This comment made him recall vividly 'the foam-flecked mouth of the Stalag Luft commandant as he fulminated last year at four Air Force prisoners who had tried to escape. "So, gangsters, you do not like my camp. I will hand you over to the Gestapo. They will finish you all"'. Brickhill was to make further literary use of this recalled scene in *The Great Escape.* It was as if he found his articles had to contain his own vivid, haunting memories of being so recently behind barbed-wire. His despatches tended to take on a highly personal tone.

In reaction to this situation, Gertrude continued: 'You think I am a Nazi? I am not. No! No!' She went on to claim that very few Germans were actually Nazis, but they could not fight them as the Nazis had the power – they were cruel, brutal murderers – no one would know how not to bow to them in the same situation. Thus she justified her position emotionally to Brickhill and he was swift to include it in his despatches. Her comment triggered another emotive memory for him that he shared with his readers: 'Last year a German guard said to me, "You understand not? To be Germans we must be Nazis. I know that the whole country is ardently behind the Fuhrer"'.

Then Gertrude went on wistfully; she was always hungry. She had to live for the day she could get a real meal again. 'Life is very bad'. To Brickhill, Gertrude looked plump and healthy enough, although slightly 'pasty' – a typical comment of his. He made the comparison that she was not nearly so thin as he and his POW companions were ten months before, 'after the Germans had marched us 100 kilometres through a blizzard on half a loaf of black bread and one bowl of soup for the whole eight days'. The recent wartime events for him and other ex-POWs were clearly playing heavily on his mind. Such stark memories continued to tumble out in his despatches. For Brickhill, the recent past remained raw and cruel. He was not surprised, however, at Gertrude's line of conversation except for one issue: she hadn't heard about the Nuremberg trial he was about to attend and cover as one of Australia's leading foreign correspondents in Europe.

As he was about to leave, Gertrude softly made known 'the considerable extent of her immoral amenability for a pack of 20 cigarettes'. She was making an overt sexual proposition. He looked at her briefly with surprise and left the Club alone. This triggered yet another painful memory he relayed to his reader: 'Said a German guard suggestively, fingering a machine-gun, when our party arrived at prison camp two years ago: "If ever you are found with a German girl, you will pay for it with your life"'. Paul Brickhill left Gertrude and the Royal Club behind at the same time receiving a barrage of bows and "Sirs", but with some discreet scowls which he astutely observed in the mirror by the cloakroom door. He was not fooled.

The night of his arrival, he slept in what he regarded as a luxurious bed at the 'pressmen's' hotel. He unsentimentally thought of his former guards, probably now in a concentration camp trying to sleep on hard wooden boards on 'the wrong side of the wire'. A personal note is expressed when he writes that he was not 'so maliciously glad' as he thought he might be, but he was not sorry either for the situation faced by a former enemy.

His suspicious, perhaps biased, first impression was that the Germans, since their defeat, were not so badly off 'as they would have us believe'. He gained the impression 'that even the battle of winter horrors will be a minor shadow of their former fears' unlike his own experiences as a POW.[6] He was soon to revise his

---

6 'POW Goes Back --- How the Germans Have Changed', *News* (Adelaide), 24 December 1945.

thoughts about the living conditions that prevailed in Germany.

Four days later Brickhill reported on the social situation and conditions in Berlin in a more nuanced, less personalised manner. He described the place as a 'Dazed City'. A lamentably large portion of the population seemed 'glassy-eyed' and indifferent – they couldn't care for anything. Most Berliners were ignoring celebrating Christmas, not just because of the lack of food and warmth. They had no enthusiasm for such a cosy celebration. They were a bitterly defected people. His arrival in Berlin happened to be the Christmas season.

Few people ventured into the streets apart from necessity; there was no sound of revelry or the spirit of Christmas joy, naturally enough of course. The houses of ordinary people were battered and broken and he repeated his black-market theme of earlier – the wealthier, still functioning quarters of the city were being supplied with black-market goods and services at exorbitant prices. He noticed that the few people who were on the streets walked aimlessly, even in front of moving cars in a dazed condition.

One dramatic detail of the post-war German capital's apathy, Brickhill pounced upon for his readers:

> One of the nastiest examples ... was a gaunt old man, so thin that he was like a walking skeleton who collapsed on the pavement in Bulowstrasse.
> He was too weak to get up again and just feebly worked arms and legs like an overturned beetle.
> **German men and women passed him by with scarcely a sideways glance.**

He stayed there until Brickhill helped him up, steadied him and offered him some chocolate 'while he wiped blood from his streaming nose'.

Brickhill saw several reasons for such apathy. Many people were still undoubtedly 'bomb-happy' (shell shocked). Everyone was too preoccupied with the 'exacting business of maintaining life from day to day' to worry about anything or anyone else. He concluded: 'Malnutrition is slowing up their mental and physical reactions'.[7]

In the same month in yet another of his frequent despatches, he described Berlin as a 'gaunt city' that had become the centre of a battle against the spread of a 'virulent' influenza epidemic similar in potential, he thought, to the epidemic that killed millions immediately after the Great War in 1919. A medical expert feared the winter in Europe causing a decimation of the population. Brickhill went on to describe the fate of three million people living in Berlin's ruins – 'the blackened shell of a city' – at the hands of the occupying Allies. The battle for winter had already begun in another sense – the imminent danger of a flu epidemic.

A small bright spot Brickhill noticed was that some Berliners had picked up a little in health – they looked plumper (a favourite word of his), but their resistance to disease was dangerously low. Food was not the only problem. Tens of thousands were living in 'tumble-down, bitterly cold rooms' in danger of collapsing altogether.

A changeable winter with mugginess, mild then cold, fog and slush was the most dangerous. A steady crisp, cold winter was considerably better. At that time the average Berliner was getting barely 1,260 calories a day – if that – amounting to four slices of bread, about five medium-sized potatoes, the 'merest smear of margarine' and a 'tiny token' of sugar. In comparison, Londoners who were not particularly well fed on restrictive rations were

---

7 'Glassy-Eyed People of Berlin Have Now Ceased to Care', *Newcastle Sun*, 28 December 1945.

receiving on the average nearly 3,000 calories a day.[8]

In another despatch at the end of December 1945, Brickhill continued to discuss melodramatically the health dangers of Berlin, with three million 'shivering people in the ruins ... waiting in dread for death to sweep through them like wildfire'. They had only an even chance to avoid it, he claimed, but the battle of winter had already begun with Berlin as the centre of it all, at least in terms of population.[9]

Christmas that year, therefore, was a drab affair for Berlin families, as Brickhill constantly highlighted: 'Frau Grades and her six children' will have for the Christmas dinner potato and barley soup, dry bread, a little jam or ersatz honey thinly spread on the bread.[10] This specific example was meant to capture the general condition more vividly.

The Jewish Situation

Paul Brickhill was visiting Berlin and Germany at a tumultuous complex time. He discovered that Jewish refugees were 'seeping out' of Poland in search of a new safe home since the Soviet takeover of that country. They were moving in desperation to the Jewish relief committee's transit camp in Berlin's Russian sector, about 1,700 of them all Polish-born Jews. Brickhill was sure there were dangerous cases of violence towards them although no one was prepared to speak when he visited the camp to interview willing families. Fear was in the air.

The Russian authorities were warning nearly two thousand

8 Paul Brickhill, 'Doctors Fight To Save Europe From 'Flu', *Newcastle Sun*, 22 December 1945.

9 Paul Brickhill, 'Battle in Berlin – To Save Europe From Disaster Worse Than War', *News* (Adelaide), 29 December 1945.

10 Paul Brickhill, 'Berlin Family's Drab Xmas Outlook', *Mail* (Adelaide), 22 December 1945.

Jews already in the transit camp that they would take them back to another camp on the Polish frontier in two days. Overnight, the whole camp vanished. People fled in desperation. Some tried to take refuge in the British sector of Berlin; others tried American and French camps in their respective sectors of the city. Few were accommodated. Harsh barriers remained in place on the borders of each of the Berlin sectors. No one was prepared to resolve the desperate situation. Not the French, not the English or the Americans.

Most people were missing and it was expected they would try to 'seep' through the Russian sector to the American one.

Brickhill suspected a secret Jewish exodus to the Middle East, but he didn't express this directly.[11] He noticed that there had been recent reports of parties of Polish Jews arriving at refugee camps in southern Germany in 'mysteriously acquired trucks'.[12]

Dresden and the Russian Zone

From Dresden, Brickhill reported that the Russian Zone of Germany was making a comparatively rapid recovery after the war. He was with the first party of British and American journalists allowed to visit on a strictly guided tour of the so-

Russian Zone Of Germany Is
Making Speedy
Recovery

From PAUL BRICKHILL, "The Newcastle Sun" Correspondent.

11 Paul Brickhill, 'Jewish Exodus Organised', *Telegraph* (Brisbane), 10 January 1946.

12 Paul Brickhill, 'Do "Jungle Drums" Guide Jews?', *Mail* (Adelaide), 12 January 1946.

called forbidden territory about which there were ugly rumours in the British, French and American zones of Berlin, a much divided city. While it was obviously a 'shop-window tour', as Brickhill defined it, and they were conducted everywhere suitable by polite Russian officers who had strict control, real advances in post-war restoration had taken place especially in accommodation and transport for city populations.

Dresden with a population of almost a million had suffered badly towards the end of the war. On 14 February 1945 in a night and day nightmare of relentless bombing by the RAF and then the US Air Force, Dresden was reduced to a smoking ruin of rubble. Between 60,000 and 180,000 people were estimated to have been killed (the total casualties could have been as high as 400,000 according to some estimates). The restoration of such devastation in terms of buildings dramatically surprised Paul Brickhill when he visited Dresden on the guided tour of January 1946.

While the German population were still 'pasty-looking', they appeared healthier than those elsewhere; they were often lean, but not starving. Most seemed adequately dressed for the prevailing weather. Trams ran frequently and train services seemed to Paul to be sound enough and well restored from the relentless bombing.

From a few hundred there were now twelve thousand factories operating in the Saxony Russian Zone. Nearly two million of Saxony's 5,200,000 were working on a full-time basis. Unemployment was no longer regarded too serious a problem in the zone. Ten per cent of the State's budget was being spent on the restoration of buildings. At the same time the Russians had smashed the militaristic Prussian Junker, which had been in absolute power, with one blow by a radical and controversial land reform scheme.

In summing up the situation in the Russian Zone which

was to become East Germany, Brickhill noticed that the two peoples – the Russians and the Germans – did not seem to be relating well to one another. 'The gap between the two peoples is so large', according to Brickhill, 'that it will be a long time for real friendship to be established'.[13]

Returning to London for a few days later, he wrote on the same subject of the Russian Zone more directly on the political level that the Communists and the Socialists were engaged in a neck-to-neck struggle for supremacy in the whole of the Russian-occupied Germany. It was an area where there were some twenty million Germans and which was about half the land mass of what had been Germany before the war. Brickhill was also more explicit about land reform. Estates of 750 acres of land that supported about eleven extremely wealthy families were split up between seventy families (about three hundred people). Thus former peasants under feudalism became landowners. Some were refugees from elsewhere in Saxony with an original family background. They were given ten-year loans to pay off the land.

Brickhill was well aware of the huge political struggle taking place throughout the zone at the time. Saxony's new government election in the following summer would probably give the answer to the struggle. The Social Democrats had 121,000 members at that time and had a slight edge over the Communist Party with its 117,000 members. But forty per cent of the population of Saxony belonged to no political party. With such figures and circumstances, it was anybody's race. Two other splinter parties, the Liberal Democrats and the Christian Democrats or Democratic Union, with about twenty thousand members complicated matters. Both splinter parties

13 Paul Brickhill, 'Russian Zone of Germany is Making Speedy Recovery', *Newcastle Sun*, 22 January 1946.

stood a little further to the right.

All four political parties in Saxony, however, were united on one issue: restoration of the damaged built environment and reconstruction of society after what turned out to be a disastrous war for them. Brickhill predicted they would all drift apart in time. The aim of all parties was communal cooperation of one sort or another, increased and restored industry, social insurance and the re-education of the German population into being a political responsible anti-Nazi community.

Agriculture in the future was to have an 'increasingly loud political voice throughout Russian-controlled Germany', Brickhill opined. He had made this claim earlier and later elaborated on the same topic in a second article. In Saxony, political authorities led by the Soviets had smashed the power of the former militaristic overlords of 1,200 Junker providing an economic base for four times as many people in the countryside. He claimed that throughout the Russian Zone more land was being cultivated than before providing a substantially increased yield. The acute food shortage was thus being addressed. He found in the case of certain former estates that they looked like yielding twice as much as before. The Russian methods of reorganisation were, however, more compulsory than those of the Allied zones of Germany that were more orthodox. The great agricultural problem overall was the lack of the availability of fertilizer.

The refugees entering the Russian Zone permanently were, on the main, peasants from Sudentenland, Silesia and German Poland – few had owned land before. Each refugee family received ten acres or more on a fixed price they could pay off over a period of ten years (if they worked hard enough). Livestock and agricultural implements were split up among all these people on the subdivided land. One man told Brickhill that he had moved from one village to another under the Nazi regime like a beggar. Now he had received some good land and a four-roomed dwelling for his family. He felt much better, but expressed an emotional desire to go back to his homeland in Silesia, now part of Poland.

His basic attitude was that, in his mind, his original country was still part of Germany despite the political changes. Using this example, Brickhill neatly defines one of the key social tensions he found in the Russian Zone. He could not see such an attitude changing and believed it could be one of the ingredients of the next war. He took it very seriously as an investigating journalist.

He concluded on a broader front. Without sufficient fertilizer the economic prospects for Germany were not particularly bright in the immediate future. Nevertheless, he thought the land reforms seemed to bid fair towards helping the situation in the long run. As well, he noted that the thirty-two castles in the Russian Zone seized from the Junkers were being turned into orphanages, schools, hospitals, homes for the needy and workers' holiday accommodation.[14]

The Ruhr

Brickhill's next despatch focussed on the Ruhr Valley of Germany. He claimed that the people in that rich agricultural district were well fed 'throughout the war'. When he visited the area he noted that many people were still in better condition to withstand disease than some of the ill-nourished people of London, especially in the East End where poverty was widespread and had been since the nineteenth century. He was paraphrasing the words of one of the senior British health officers in the

---

14 Paul Brickhill, 'Russians Watch Germans In Big Political Struggle', *Telegraph* (Brisbane), 24 January 1946.

district that confirmed his own impressions that sympathy could be better placed elsewhere in other parts of Germany.

As Brickhill saw it, the coming of the winter on the Ruhr was a matter of 'tolerable hardships' as the German people were in 'surprisingly reasonable condition'. Some even looked 'fairly plump' and none seemed too lean in appearance or too haggard. All were well enough dressed. While there were privations to be noted, they were nothing like the conditions the Third Reich had imposed on millions in slavery or in prison concentration camps for Jews, Allied military prisoners-of-war and other groups.

In the Ruhr, Brickhill believed, British authorities had already done a magnificent job in restoring bridges and transport communication. They had even imported one hundred thousand tons of wheat, but he thought the Germans would never appreciate it as their country was heavily occupied. He claimed that the basic rations of the area were as high as anywhere in Germany. While the diet of Londoners was better balanced with more variety, they were only getting three thousand calories a day. The German diet was not ideal, he concluded. Nevertheless, they were not starving. He thus believed that Germany would be able to weather the harsh winter that was expected.[15]

The Nuremberg Trials

By mid-February 1946, Paul Brickhill began to report as foreign correspondent on the Nuremberg Trial where the surviving Nazi leaders, apart from those not yet captured, were sitting in the war crimes dock.

The chaos that prevailed in Germany in the final months

---

15 Paul Brickhill, 'Germans Do Well For Food', *Telegraph* (Brisbane), 4 February 1946.

of the war did not end with the unconditional surrender of the Third Reich. The men responsible for the chaos, for the devastation of Europe, for the extermination of millions, the plunder of entire nations had to be brought to trial. Some, however, had disappeared.

The Nuremberg Trial had begun its work in November1945. Hitler, Goebbels and Himmler had already committed suicide. Göring, who Hitler had wanted to execute a few days before his own end for the attempt to negotiate with the Allies, surrendered to the Americans on 7 May 1945 and was detained with full military honours for the trial.

Wilhelm Keitel was arrested on 13 May 1945 in Flensburg. On 17 May, Karl Dönitz, Alfred Jodl and Albert Speer were also arrested in the same place. Franz von Papen was seized in Westphalia where he sought refuge with his relatives. The Americans got hold of Hans Frank in Berchtesgaden where he cut the veins of his wrist with a razor blade, but the injury was not critical and he survived.

Hjalmar Schacht, who had been interned by Hitler in a concentration camp, was captured by the Americans. The French had arrested Konstantin von Neurath on 6 May. Hans Frank was captured on the 11th in Berlin. On 15 May the Americans seized Ernst Kaltenbrunner in Austria and the Canadians detained Arthur Seyss-Inquart in Flensburg. Fritz Sauckel was arrested at the same time. Robert Ley was hiding in the mountains near Berchtesgaden and was located by the Americans on 15 May. Four days later Alfred Rosenberg was arrested by the British in a military hospital at Flensburg and the Americans detained Julius Streicher in a village near Berchtesgaden on 23 May.

Joachim von Ribbentrop, hiding in Hamburg, was identified by the British on 14 June. Baldur von Schirach was likewise in hiding in the Tyrol. He was captured by the Americans on 5 June.

The Soviets also arrested several others and brought them in.

The tribunal received a massive pile of documentation from its special commission and took the testimony of twenty-two witnesses on the matter of the criminal organisations.[16] In February 1946, Paul Brickhill was present at the Nuremberg Trial as the *Sun*'s foreign correspondent. The trial concentrated on two men: Hjalmar Schacht, the former Nazi finance minister, and Albert Speer, 'Hitler's key munitions man'. Brickhill noticed these two men were in a huddle for days plotting together 'To Rat on Mates', as the headline of his despatch colourfully put it the on the second page of the Adelaide *Mail* of 16 February. The complete headline was 'Nazi Leaders Plotting to Rat on Mates from Paul Brickhill [Nuremberg, Saturday]'.

Albert Speer had been a member of the Nazi party since 1932. As well as Minister for Armaments and Ammunition, he was 'Hitler's court architect. He was the only defendant deserving a little respect'. Brickhill pointed out that Speer might get away with his life, but he would have to fight hard. He pronounced the current tip in the press gallery about those defendants who would be found innocent or get a sentence other than the death penalty: 'Schacht, Baldur von Schirach (Hitler's Youth Leader) and Hans Fritarche (radio propaganda director)'. It was predicted with confidence that they would at least get away with their lives.

Of the rest, Brickhill provided his favourite colourful pen portraits. Göring was still in his 'pearl grey uniform with brass buttons, a red silk scarf around his neck'. He had an American blanket wrapped around his 'Falstaffian' middle. He still has 'an aura of cruel strength' as he continually gestured and posed during the proceedings.

---

16 Tadeusz Cyprian and Jerzy Sawicki, *Nuremberg in Retrospect. People and Issues of the Trial,* Western Press Agency, Warsaw, 1967, 40-43.

There were heavy bags under von Ribbentrop's eyes which seemed to worsen as each day of the trial passed. He was following the trial carefully according to Brickhill's keen observation – 'he is a very worried, frightened man, as he follows the trial' constantly communicating with his lawyer close by.

While there in the last few days, Brickhill noted that there had been talk of an attempt by Nazi sympathisers to raid the Palace of Justice and rescue 'Goering and Co'. There were signs a plenty that rumours were taken seriously with extra well-armed American soldiers on duty. Machine-guns had been installed along the hundreds of yards of the rambling corridors of the building. Brickhill noted a Sherman tank being installed outside beside one of the entrance gates.

According to him, there were only flashes of drama in the trial. The British President Lord Justice Lawrence as the tribunal went on seemed a most impressive figure. The shortest of the eight judges, thick-set, peering constantly over his spectacles, had a voice as thin as reed – 'as hard as a razor-blade, but twice as cutting'. He rules the court on occasions and stiffens the defendants 'like an electric shock'.[17]

The main point Brickhill was making was that Schacht and Speer were plotting against the others, getting ready to 'spill the beans' to save themselves. The rest of the defendants at the time were not on speaking terms with the two men. They had not addressed a single word to them during the whole time Brickhill had observed them, over several days sitting in the press gallery of the crowded court.

* * *

---

17 Paul Brickhill, 'Nazi Leaders Plotting To Rat on Mates', *Mail* (Adelaide), 16 February 1946.

On 16 October 1946, ten Nazi war criminals mounted the gallows erected in the prison gymnasium at the Palace of Justice in Nuremberg early that day. Two others were missing: Hitler's deputy Martin Borman, believed to be already dead, and Hermann Göring who had committed suicide a few hours earlier with a cyanide pill. There were three black-painted wooden scaffolds in the long room. Two were used alternatively, one was kept in reserve in case the others malfunctioned.

The first to be executed at 1.11am was Joachim von Ribbentrop, Foreign Minister in the Nazi regime. Before execution took place, he gave his name in a loud voice. As the black hood was placed over his head, he said: 'I wish peace to the world'. The trap sprung and he fell from view behind a dark curtain.

Field Marshal Wilhelm Keitel was executed next. The others were Ernst Kaltenbrunner, Alfred Rosenberg, Hans Frank, Wilhelm Frick, Julius Streicher (who screamed 'Heil Hitler'), Fritz Sauckel, General Alfred Todl in his Wehrmacht uniform and the last to die was Arthur Seyss-Inquart. Between the executions hangmen and guards were allowed to light up cigarettes to ease their tension.[18]

* * *

While Paul Brickhill was working flat out as a prolific and intrepid foreign correspondent for the *Sun* in Sydney and the syndication of his despatches throughout Australia by Associated Newspapers immediately after the Second World War, he had also started to pave the way to eventually becoming a fulltime bestselling author of wartime non-fiction. His own war experiences in the RAAF/ RAF as a fighter pilot and the

---

18 John Ross (ed.-in-chief), *Chronicles of the Twentieth Century*, Viking, Ringwood, 1999, 656.

two years or so he spent as a prisoner-of-war at Stalag Luft III provided colourful material for his stories. As well as working for the "X" escape organisation in the camp, he recorded the experiences of the men around him for future use, when and if he survived the ordeal. While imprisoned his dream for the future sustained him and gave him a purpose in life.

As foreign correspondent at the war's end, he began as early as 1945, soon after arriving in Brighton for rehabilitation, writing in his despatches about such wartime experiences that were published in newspapers around Australia. In some cases they were the first drafts of pieces he would revise and place in *Escape to Danger, Escape – or Die, The Great Escape* and even *Reach for the Sky.* Thus newspaper despatches were neatly blended with his ambitions as a fulltime author. They provided him with rehearsal time, as well as making his name widely known throughout Australia. His various books then appeared to an eager public who already knew him.

The Bomber Fought for The
Lives of Its
Crew, and Won

One of his first attempts in late 1945 in a despatch was headlined rather ambiguously as 'The Bomber Fought for The Lives of Its Crew, and Won'.[19] It appeared prominently on the second page of the Adelaide *News* as well as in several other Australian newspapers. In it he talks about pure aerodynamics coupled with 'uncanny precision' that saved the life – 'the day' – for Squadron Leader Bren Hooper and some of the crew of his Wellington in June 1942.

19 *News* (Adelaide), 3 December 1945.

On Hooper, he provided his usual signature pen-portrait, his shadow biography in a few concise words: 'stocky, solid Dublin-born Irishman … Bren already had 63 bombing trips to his credit and a D.F.C. when he went on the last trip … after which he was listed for a delightful trip to the U.S.A. as an instructor'. On this occasion, Hooper and his crew had dropped 'their cargo' of bombs on the German industrial city of Bremen and were on their way back to England and safety flying at about twelve thousand feet. They had almost reached the Dutch coast and had passed the worst of the dangers of the heavily armed enemy night flight belt when a sudden sharp warning from the rear-gunner was 'blotted out' by a 'hellish explosion'.

Cannon shells 'slammed' into the Wellington. Inside the 'battered fuselage' Hooper's instrument panel was blown into pieces 'in front of his nose, spraying him with sharp fragments'. The glow of a fire appeared under the port engine and suddenly burst into flames. Brickhill continued the exciting narrative: 'Bren shoved stick and rudder into the same corner, and the lumbering bomber hoisted her tail and peeled off in a screaming vertical dive to evade the enemy night-fighter and (they hoped) put out the flames'. Such a colourful narrative style was to make Brickhill a fortune in a few years.

Hooper saw a layer of cloud far below him and was able to hold the plane in a headlong dive seeking the cover it would provide. The aircraft reached its maximum speed ever flown and they successfully lost the night-fighter in the process. But 'long banners' of flame stretched out from the port engine and grew even longer.

Brickhill told his readers that Hooper decided it was 'time to pull out' so he eased back on the stick, but nothing happened. He pulled harder. Still nothing happened. The controls had 'packed in' altogether. 'It was the last straw'. Hooper, badly injured and shaken, lost consciousness. The plane rocketed out of the cloud cover, 'like a comet' and at about 300mph headed towards the ground. Brickhill then tells his reader that aerodynamics came to the rescue. Increased speed will make an aircraft lift its nose. The hurtling Wellington did exactly that. Slowly it began to pull out of the headlong dive.

But the ground was 'mighty close' – less than one thousand feet below. Yet the nose lifted faster and faster. It was going to be very close. The front gunner had a paralysing, terrifying view of it all. In the end, it was a dead-heat. At about 300mph the heavy bomber just got her nose up to hit flat fields near Groningen in a screaming skid that 'ripped up her belly like a gutted fish', as Brickhill graphically put it. The plane slapped her tail on the ground and the rear turret with the gunner still inside snapped off and went somersaulting over the fields at an erratic tangent. The rest of the aircraft went 'charging on as only a 20-ton amorphous mass of battered, blazing, uncontrollable bulk can charge'.

Twice the aircraft lifted and hit the ground. Both wings ripped off. It went for half a mile before it skidded to a 'crumpled, smoking stop.' The crew scrambled out quickly mostly unhurt dragging Hooper with them. He had suffered almost no further injury after the initial attack of the night-fighter. Even the rear-gunner scrambled free from his turret several hundred yards away. He was also relatively unhurt. He was dazed, however, and accidently fell into a nearby canal and was nearly drowned. All of these men soon joined Paul Brickhill in the 'barren backwater of Stalag Luft III' in the North Compound.

In the same newspaper despatch, Brickhill referred to another pilot officer, "Freddy" Bist who also joined him in the concentration camp. Bist too had had a lucky escape. He was blown out of his aircraft at about five hundred feet minus his parachute and yet survived the free fall, landing in a large crater full of water softening the fall. The incident is followed immediately by a typical Brickhill concise pen portrait. Bist was an American theological student studying in Montreal. He was overage for air crew. Nevertheless, he had volunteered well before his country 'entered the turmoil' to become a wireless operator/ gunner in the Royal Canadian Air Force.

In yet another despatch to Australia, he worked out the draft version of his book with Conrad Norton *Escape to Danger* in a deliberate attempt to turn the wartime non-fiction into foreign correspondent journalism, probably with the intention to spread the word in Australia about their soon-to-be-published bestseller. The by-line used in the second of the series of newspaper articles of this kind by Paul Brickhill was in the Adelaide *News*: 'At Last the Night Came For A Dash To Freedom.'[20] The newspaper's introduction to the article read excitedly:

> Continuing Flight Lieutenant Paul Brickhill's story of the airmen who planned a mass escape from their prison camp in Germany, as told in his book, "Escape to Danger." Brickhill, an Australian, was a member of "X Organisation" which planned the escape.

It is noticeable that Brickhill is identified to the newspaper's readership as an Australian and no mention is made of the co-author Conrad Norton – who seems to disappear from fame as a writer of wartime non-fiction fairly quickly, unlike Brickhill. What follows in the article is the exciting episode extracted from the text of the book starting: 'As 1944 dawned, Squadron Leader Roger Bushell and the Big Four began to plan a "blitz" campaign to finish the tunnel and break clear from Stalag Luft III'. It ends in bold with: 'Each man had a particular room to go

20 *News* (Adelaide), 5 December 1945.

to, where he was to sit or lie down, keep quiet, and wait till his turn to leave'.

A cliff-hanger indeed! And the episodes continued in the Adelaide *News* sporadically, but was eventually serialised elsewhere in other newspapers. It is obvious that Brickhill well understood the power of book serialisation in the newspapers to achieve fame in Australia. And he did! Newspapers frequently ended wrapped up with the fish-and-chips and thus disappearing – that is newspapers were ephemeral, but books have a more lasting valued quality.

In his despatch published a day after the episode from *Escape to Danger* was one of Brickhill's favourite miracle stories he told as a master storyteller of wartime non-fiction. In 'He Joined His Friend On a Parachute', he introduced Joe Herman who walked into Stalag Luft III, the 'latest and greatest, the brass-bound ultimate among all the people who should have died but didn't'. Thus Brickhill enthused and then told the story of his remarkable adventure:

> He was blown out of his Halifax about 17,000 ft without a parachute; fell about two miles in darkness and distress, then met a friend with a parachute about a mile above the ground, and joined forces with him. They came down safely together.

This concise exciting episode is followed by one of Brickhill's swift biographical portraits. Joe Herman was depicted as a twenty-two-year-old flight lieutenant from Hughenden, North Queensland, who 'used to be a miner before the war'. He was a 'good-looking lad, tallish and slim, with a dimple-cleft chin'. He had taken off from Driffield airfield in England on 4 November 1944 in a Halifax bound for Bochum in the Ruhr. It was his thirty-third mission.

The plane was 'coned' by searchlights as soon as they arrived over their target. He dived and twisted to get away, but he was 'coned again' in the 'blinding rays'. Herman told his crew to clip their parachutes on. He was too occupied to do so himself as he piloted the Halifax with great difficulty. They had already dropped their bombs and were practically clear when they received a direct hit on the fuselage – a 'shattering explosion'. Through his Perspex window, Joe Herman saw the fire leap up 'just behind the mainspar of the wing'.

After an effort by the flight engineer Sergeant Harry Knott – 'stocky, unemotional' – to put out the fire with an extinguisher, but two more explosions shook the aircraft. One shell 'smacked' behind the port engine and the other exploded into the starboard outer. The wing's petrol tanks burst and exploded into flames. In seconds the aircraft seemed 'to be a mass of fire'. Then Brickhill introduces some dialogue: '"Hell's bells!" shouted Joe into the intercom.

"We've copped it in the wings", and then three times, "Bail out! Bail out! Bail out!'

Flying Officer "Irish" Vivash mid-upper-gunner from Tamworth, New South Wales, after being hit thought his leg was broken. He eventually got out by crawling along the fuselage while Herman tried to keep the plane straight and as level as possible. When Herman realised that the crew had got clear he jumped out of his seat and went back to get his parachute and to see if Vivash was 'OK'. The starboard wing then folded back suddenly before coming away entirely.

In a flash, the bomber whipped on her back and started to spin. The roof disappeared as it blew up. Brickhill, then, in his prose, reconstructed his emotions by using his imagination as in fiction. Without a parachute Herman found himself 'falling and falling'. A 'horrible piercing chill' went through him. Then the crisis passed and 'strangely' enough he felt almost calm descending towards the earth. Brickhill adds more dialogue: "God don't let me die like this!" and then, "If this is death, it can't be so bad".

Joe Herman was to come out of his 'mental void' to find himself 'fiercely clinging' to Vivash's legs with both arms wrapped tenaciously around them. To which Vivash said: "Be careful of my right leg, Joe … I think it's broken". As it turned out it wasn't broken, but had several nasty flak wounds. His legs were 'quite numb' which explains why he did not at first realise that Herman was hanging onto them and struggled to get him off.

He Joined His Friend On a Parachute

Brickhill relentlessly adds more exciting detail to his discourse on the event. And then: 'They brushed treetops and then hit hard, Vivash collapsing on top of Joe. They rolled apart and lay gasping until Joe staggered to his feet with sharp pains in his chest'. He later discovered he had two broken ribs. Vivash stood up in pain as feeling had returned to his legs, but he was able to 'hobble along'. Herman's left boot was missing, but when they later stumbled across the wreckage of the plane, he found a boot standing upright by itself. It was the dead navigator's left boot, but fitted Herman perfectly.

The two men then hobbled toward the River Rhine and kept on going for a few days. The winter cold, however, beat them. They were captured at a farmhouse trying desperately to obtain food, shelter and warmth.[21]

---

21 'He Joined his Friend On a Parachute', *News* (Adelaide), 6 December 1945.

Brickhill justified the veracity of this incredible, almost unbelievable yet true story of two men coming to earth together with only one parachute on personal and official grounds. He pointed out that the story was officially verified later by RAAF interrogators and investigators. They believed the story to be absolutely true even though it was a freak happening. Brickhill also believed it on personal grounds as he knew Joe Herman particularly well having lived with him and thousands of POW colleagues at Stalag Luft III, the concentration camp for Allied officers run by the Luftwaffe. Having interviewed Herman, Vivash and many others he believed 'that these things do happen'. He knew Herman was completely honest. This story of Herman and Vivash was extracted from the written account of interviews Brickhill kept compiling while incarcerated in the camp at Sagan. At the end of the article it was announced that it was the final – and most astonishing – instalment of extracts from the Flight Lieutenant's book *Escape to Danger*. Again no mention of Brickhill's co-author Conrad Norton.

* * *

Douglas Bader (SA Devon, RAF official photographer)

In his many despatches as foreign correspondent to the *Sun* between late 1945 and about 1955, Brickhill explored a broad range of social, economic and political subjects in Europe and later in the United States of America. In doing so, he achieved a fair degree of fame, especially amongst newspaper readers of the Associated Press throughout Australia. Even in 1954 he was promoting his his new book *Reach for the Sky*, the story of Group Captain Douglas Bader, the RAF legless air ace in articles sent to Australia as foreign correspondent.

At the end of the author's research and publication of this biographical study, his subject's response was an uneasy one – he felt 'too ruddy naked'. For eight months Brickhill, amongst other research, recorded very detailed interviews with Bader. The project had been originally launched over dinner with Bader at the Belfry Club in London in 1951, but had some stops and starts. Brickhill and Bader bonded and became good friends – both had flown Spitfires and Hurricanes during the war and both had spent time in Stalag Luft III.

In his article '"Getting to Grips" With Amazing Bader', Brickhill claimed that they both used rude language and disliked 'pompous officials'. With that much in common, at the Belfry dinner the celebrated Bader suggested over cigars that, as a biographer, Brickhill might not make too abominable a mess of his life story. As things worked out, Brickhill was given about 100,000 words in which Bader, he claimed, had recorded the momentous things that had happened to him. This manuscript may have been written by someone else other than Bader. As well there were provided for his free use, Bader's flying log book, combat reports, over two thousand letters, press clippings, photographs and other memorabilia and oddments.

'To put meat on these solid bones', Bader submitted to more than 123 hour sessions of interviews with Brickhill which were recorded by Brickhill on a tape-recorder, a fairly new technology for writers in gathering information to distil. These interviews were later typed in manuscript form by a paid professional typist in London. Brickhill called it an exhausting process, but seldom dull because Douglas Bader was to Brickhill 'an unpredictable mixture of public school and uninhibited pirate'.

It had become an intimate relationship as it would usually do in such a circumstance.

Mostly the two met at night in Bader's London flat – Brickhill in an armchair, beer in one hand, microphone in the other. Bader was opposite on a sofa, 'puffing a cigar and persistently trying to cross his legs that would not cross easily, and Thelma, his wife, sewing in another chair unobtrusive and an unruffled and effective referee when needed'.

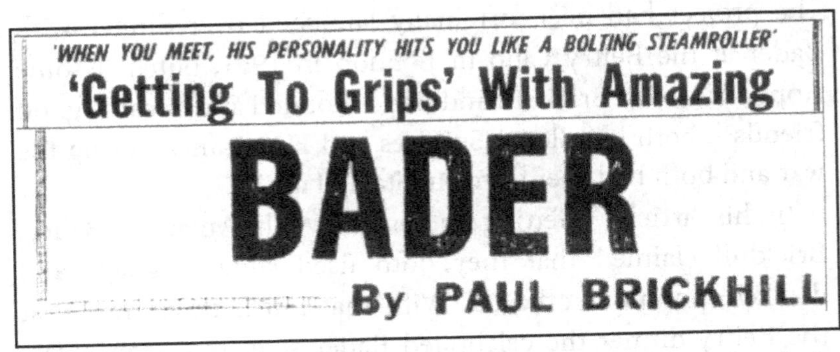
'WHEN YOU MEET, HIS PERSONALITY HITS YOU LIKE A BOLTING STEAMROLLER'

'Getting To Grips' With Amazing

BADER

By PAUL BRICKHILL

Brickhill noted that there was no gradual revelation of Bader's personality because he was like 'a bolting steamroller'. To him, Bader had a 'glowing dominating charm that could change to a disconcerting brusqueness'. At first, Brickhill admitted that he was uncertain how to act toward Bader as a man with no legs: 'did one refer to them casually or not at all?'. Fortunately, Bader settled that matter the first time they met. Brickhill related how, when they sat down to dinner together, Bader exclaimed: 'Just a minute while I fiddle these ruddy legs under the table. He grabbed his right thigh, dropped his leg with a thump in the right spot and relaxed as though it was the most natural thing in the world'.

Later, the famous air ace removed his trousers and demonstrated to Brickill how he moved around on his rivet-studded yellow-painted artificial legs, with his shirt-tail flapping behind. Brickhill was careful to point out that this was not performed as a party trick. He began to realise certain things such as how essential ankles are. 'Try walking with rigid ankles and I'll bet you won't move one pace'. Bader demonstrated how he had solved this problem.

In his extended article Brickhill takes the reader back to 1931, a week before Bader's crash, to how he was chosen to play rugby for England – 'the peak of his ambition'. Brickhill then claimed that he had become fascinated at the thought of writing the feelings of an athlete who wakes up in hospital to find both his legs cut off. Between the lines Brickhill was saying that he was turning away from the journalism of a foreign correspondent to the fascinating work of a fulltime author, a creative producer of books rather than articles. He felt his hopes were felled when Bader remarked: "My dear chap, I didn't mind a bit". But Brickhill was able to hold his ground. His training of professional patience helped with Bader and he continued to probe about emotions and depression in the many interviews that followed – to look beyond the legend to the real emotions of the man.

He began to read between the lines of Bader's clipped fighter pilot speak of understatement fitting together pieces of the 'jigsaw of a very complex character'. He studied the background context assiduously. In 1952 he even went with Douglas and Thelma Bader on their annual holidays to their holiday home in Cornwell to soak up the atmosphere and quietly observe. He also took the 'hated recording machine' with him to continue the vital interviews in a vastly different context. All of this was part of the art of becoming a writer and becoming a competent biographer.

Brickhill's powers of observation on the Cornwell holiday led to other more official perspectives and military documentation:

> One night when the research [the recorded interviews] was over, I noticed in his wardrobe his R.A.F. tunic bearing a couple of unusual ribbons that

> I recognised as well as the double D.S.O. and double D.F.C. Surprised, I asked, "What have you got the Legion of Honour and Croix de Guerre up for?"

While Bader's answer was blunt, humorous and underplayed, Brickhill did some further research into what official documentation was then available. He went on beyond the Bader documentation to explore his subject's remarkable Hurricane and Spitfire days during the war. As well, he interviewed Bader and others on these matters finding his subject 'bluntly objective' which helped in writing his biography.

After eight months Paul Brickhill had over two million words and considered this enough to write his book of 140,000 words. As Brickhill put it, he wanted to produce a biography 'with colour and intimate detail that is normally found only in a novel'. He saw that he had undertaken a massive experiment and admitted freely that 'neither Douglas not I would go through it again'. He reflected that Bader had bore the ceaseless probing into private thoughts with 'remarkable patience... Real explosions were rare' despite Bader's well-known fiery temper. There were, however, a few minor disagreements.

Bader took a while to react to the carbon-copy of the completed book manuscript Brickhill provided him with and then there followed some disagreements and 'blunt' exchanges between author and his subject. Finally, however, Brickhill got a letter from Bader saying that 'he was delighted I was so unbelievably offensive, because now that made us all square'. The two remained good, if distant friends and both of them gave credit to Bader's wife who 'nipped budding clashes with a tolerant "Now, now, you two"'. Her tact and input lead to the great success of the book. Thus Paul dedicated his book to Thelma.

* * *

Ironically, *Reach for the Sky* was to be his final great achievement and, apart from his thriller novel *The Deadline* (1962) or *War of Nerves* (1963) as it was called in the United States, Paul Brickhill had no more major successes as an author and had quietly removed himself from what had been a famed life – living a quiet, but troubled life on Balmoral Beach until his death in 1991. The question remains: Had he burnt himself entirely out as an author? By 1963 he had relapsed into a melancholy that had been triggered off in Sagan and from which he was never to recover fully.

"THE SUN" (DAILY)
"SUNDAY SUN & GUARDIAN"
"POCKET BOOK WEEKLY"
"THE WORLD'S NEWS"
"WOMAN"
"RADIO & HOBBIES"
"PIX"

ASSOCIATED NEWSPAPERS LIMITED

CABLE ADDRESS:
EDITORIAL "JAGANATHA"
BUSINESS "SUNBUSI"
TELEGRAMS "SUN" SYDNEY
CODE: "BENTLEY'S"

TELEPHONES:
GENERAL B 0333
ADVERTISING DEPT. B 6824

60-70 ELIZABETH STREET
SYDNEY, N.S.W.

ADDRESS ALL COMMUNICATIONS TO BOX 2728 C, G.P.O.

7th. January, 1948.

Dear Mr. Long,

I don't think we've ever met, but Lionel Wigmore suggested I drop you a line. He thinks a book of mine called "Escape to Danger" might contain some useful stuff for your war histories, and, as a matter of fact, it might, at that.

The book is actually two books. One part is a collection of some rather exceptional Air Force escapes, such as people who baled out without parachutes and lived through it. Several of these people were Australians. I knew them in my prison camp.

The second part is an account of the tunnel escape of 76 Air Force officers at Stalag Luft III in Germany in 1944, after which 50 were shot. Again, a lot of us working on the show were Australians, and four Australians were among the victims. The book is the only full record of the thing.

You may have come across the book, though paper shortage didn't allow many copies to reach Australia. Faber and Faber published it in London and the Reader's Digest ran a condensation of it. I've only just arrived back in Australia after seven years abroad so I don't know an awful lot about your historical set-up or how much stuff you want.

Wiggy tells me you'll probably be another couple of weeks in hospital, which is a pretty dreary business. If you're interested in the stuff in the book or if you're just bored lying in bed, drop me a brief note and I would quite cheerfully drop in on you at the hospital and perhaps relieve the boredom a little. In the meantime, I hope you get better very quickly, with the least possible discomfort, and that you don't adhere to bed too long.

Yours sincerely,

Paul Brickhill

~~Paul Brickhill~~

Answered
18th Jan 47.
Sydney.

CHAPTER 7

THE PRICE OF FAME

Paul Brickhill, portrait c. 1951
(Bulletin*)*

The famous best-selling books, *The Great Escape*, *The Dam Busters* and *Reach for the Sky*, are usually immediately recalled by people young and old. The ready remembrance is due to the lasting popularity of the three war films of the same titles. All three titles are iconic and have taken on a life of their own in popular culture. Their author Paul Brickhill, who chose these evocative titles, is, however, mainly-forgotten or only vaguely-identified. The few who recall his name as author – who rose to vast international fame in the early 1950s and then seems to have disappeared in the 1960s – rarely realise that he was a heroic RAAF fighter pilot, a prisoner-of-war in Germany and, in particular, an Australian who grew up in Sydney. After an avalanche of media publicity of the 1950s in England and Australia, he slipped from media attention in newspapers and magazines; by the 1960s he was no longer the headliner that he had been. People now wanted to forget the war and the outpouring of literature that came from it, especially in non-fictional form. Thriller adventure fiction had taken over in popular reading.

After the genre of his non-fiction books declined in popularity in the 1960s and was part of the past of the preceding decade, it is natural enough that the author became largely forgotten. He lived out the rest of his life seemingly as a recluse at scenic harbourside Balmoral Beach, Mosman, in a fifth floor apartment overlooking Middle Harbour and the famed Sydney Heads with ships passing in and out. He died without the usual fanfare given to notable Australian writers at the age of seventy-four on 21 April 1991 shortly before Anzac Day.

But how did he come to fame as a best-selling writer whose books were translated into more than fifty languages?

As soon as the war was over, Paul Brickhill, still in the RAAF as seconded to the RAF, was a released POW who was relocated to the famous seaside resort of Brighton in England under medical observation and treatment as a rest cure from the rigours of the infamous Long March conducted by the Nazis from the North Compound of Stalag Luft III in the small town of Sagan. By the time he was freed and taken to Brighton, his health profile was fragile. Each night on the forced march, the POWs had been terrified by the fear of execution. They were well aware that fifty of their seventy-six comrades in the mass escape had been summarily murdered under Hitler's orders.

Brickhill, who had collapsed a couple of times on the way from exhaustion, carried with him – wrapped in his blanket or sometimes under his shirt – a grubby secret manuscript containing a series of accurately written escape stories he had carefully gathered while incarcerated in the camp. He had painstakingly collected them in his twenty-six month stay there as an Allied prisoner-of-war who had plenty of time to fill in each monotonous day. In effect, he had begun his career as a full-time author while in prison. But many of the details of the "X" organisation of the famous escape were kept in his mind alone as he realised the ramifications if the Gestapo ever got hold of his manuscript. His memory of such details was vivid and accurate and haunted his mind for the rest of his life.

* * *

During the war Paul Brickhill was accepted into the RAAF as a volunteer and had served with them from 20 May to 8 September 1941, primarily learning to be a fighter pilot skilled in the complex art of war. After Ottawa, Canada, under the regime of the Empire Air Training Scheme preparing for the European and Mediterranean theatres of air combat, he became attached to the Fighter Command of the RAF as a British Empire pilot from 9 September 1941 to 8 April 1946, twenty-six months of which were spent as a prisoner-of-war in a prison camp in the bleak eastern German frontier.

His war honours and awards include the 1939-45 Star, Aircrew Europe Star, African Star and clasp, Defence Medal, War Medal 1939-45 as well as Australian Service Medal 1939-45 and a Returned from Active Service Badge. He was then a charge of the Imperial Government due to his active service in the RAF. If, and only if in strict legal terms, his disabilities were found to have occurred between 9 September 1941 and 8 April 1946, or resulted from that period they would have been recognised. He could then have received an Imperial War Service pension. But he never made any attempt to apply for one even though he had a very solid case. Perhaps he was too proud. His service number was 403313.

The rehabilitation program provided at Brighton before

Brickhill's discharge was not adequate and failed to address health problems of post-trauma syndrome. Those in charge were merely satisfied that the body was sound and sufficiently recovered without a deep concern for the mind. Physical wounds were summarily considered to have healed and to have no lasting effect in the future.

In 1949 he received from the RAAF his Airman's Certificate of Service and official Discharge papers (No 33896). He acknowledged receipt of these on 22 March that year. He had been promoted from Pilot Officer to Flight Lieutenant just before demobilisation, no doubt as a just reward and delayed or overdue recognition of his war service, including that of an active POW in Stalag Luft III in the "X" escape organisation under South African Flight Commander Roger Bushell.[1] His first London address after discharge was 21 Bale Street, Chelsea SW 3.

In reaching England safely, the precious tattered escape stories manuscript was to form part of the first of his international bestsellers, *Escape to Danger* co-written with his friend and fellow prisoner-of-war, Conrad Norton, a South African. It was also the basis for *The Great Escape* and *Escape – or Die*. As well, there were several radio broadcasts and dramatisations and newspaper feature escape stories – all accomplished by the end of 1955.

Brickhill's work had quickly passed the appeal of John Buchan's *The Thirty-Nine Steps* and Baroness Orczy's *The Scarlet Pimpernel* as the author was now telling true life adventure stories about extraordinary escapes of wide appeal during the first half of the 1950s.

Brickhill found it simple to dramatise the real-life action and move his narratives along at a cracking pace like the earlier writers in the field of popular fiction, such as Buchan, Anthony

1 Service Record: Brickhill.

Hope and Alexander Dumas – by then all dead, but not forgotten as their works were still in print. His nearest rivals in non-fiction publications after the war were Eric Williams for *The Wooden Horse* (1949), Nicholas Monsarrat for *The Cruel Sea* (1951) and PR Reid for *The Colditz Story* (1952). Unconsciously, they supported each other's sales as cherished remembered and exciting fragments of the recent war. The general public were still obsessed with its impact as it was so close to their own individual experiences of total war and readers responded emotionally to such works.

All three books, like Brickhill's three, were made into highly popular post-war motion films further boosting sales and helping to create a distinct genre of popular wartime non-fiction – stories of breath-stopping escapes in World War II – that had burst onto the scene after 1945.[2] They provided collectively great boosts to the English publishing world of bestsellers. There were many other one-book successes in the genre during the 1950s. But Paul Brickhill was the princely doyen of them all with his episodic, brisk and tense colourful narratives that were as broken as life is broken into fragments. He was avidly read by young and old and of all social classes throughout the 1950s and 1960s. He soon became a larger-than-life legend and celebrity.

In the immediate post-war period, Brickhill resumed a frenetic journalistic career at the same time as he was writing his well-researched and well-received books. In Europe, he represented his old Sydney newspaper, the *Sun*, as a freelance foreign correspondent, covering for the *Sun* the Nuremberg

---

2 Monsarrat's *The Cruel Sea* was turned into a feature film the year after the book was released; *The Wooden Horse* was filmed in 1950 and *The Colditz Story* was filmed in 1953. Brickhill's *The Dam Busters* was filmed in 1955; the film version of *Reach for the Sky* came out in 1956 and *The Great Escape* in 1963.

trials of Nazis in Germany and other major European events. His articles commonly appeared dramatically on the front page of the Sydney *Sun* and the rest of its syndicates across regional Australia.

Some important examples under Brickhill's by-line were thus syndicated in Australia to other newspapers of Associated Newspaper Ltd, including 'Glassy-Eyed People of Berlin' (*Newcastle Sun*, 28 December 1945); 'Russian Zone of Germany is Making Speedy Recovery' (*Newcastle Sun*, 26 January 1946); 'Nazis leaders Plotting to Rat on Mates' (*Mail*, Adelaide, 16 February 1946); and 'Budapest shows you can starve on £40,000 a week' (*News*, Adelaide, 16 March 1946). The frequent appearance of his name on important articles from overseas alone made him a famous journalist across Australia.

For nearly two years after London he worked in the hectic newspaper world of New York. He returned briefly to Australia to work as a sub-editor for the *Sun*, but then returned to London to research and write *The Dam Busters* under an official commission he had won. The *Sun* ceased its operations as a daily afternoon newspaper in 1957.

His 1946 co-authored *Escape to Danger*, a selection of exciting and varied escape stories during the war which he had originally collected to maintain his sanity in the prison camp, was doing so well in the British book market that it was suggested by prominent London publishers that the story of the mass escape from Stalag Luft III which had been briefly been told as the last major chapter of *Escape to Danger* should be elaborated into a full-length book. With this urgent proposal in mind, Brickhill returned once more to London by ship. In 1951 he was able to finalise *The Great Escape* for release to worldwide acclaim.[3]

This was accomplished in a short period of time; he claimed

3 Dustcover back blurb, *Reach for the Sky.*

he had completed the manuscript for submission to the publishers in seventeen days extensively using his old battered prison manuscript which had even survived the Long March to Freedom. Through this process of outstanding publication with Faber and Faber, the distinguished London firm, he rapidly entered the London book world a much acclaimed celebrity, but not without achievement as well in radio broadcasting and foreign correspondence despatches in the press. His thought processes worked swiftly on all his projects. Heady recognition in the world of bestselling non-fiction became his, but eventually there was a serious price to pay.

Ley Kenyon, POW Artist

As a publication *The Great Escape* was considerably enhanced by the iconic line drawings of the prominent artist and leading book illustrator Ley Kenyon who had previously evocatively illustrated *Escape to Danger* for Brickhill and Conrad Norton. Ley Kenyon's artworks in these two books contributed significantly to their success with the public. As inmates of the North Compound of Stalag Luft III, Paul Brickhill, Conrad Norton and Ley Kenyon collaborated closely to make a written and visual documentation in vivid personal terms of the soon-to-be-called "Great Escape".

Several months before the mass outbreak, the senior British officer in the compound asked Kenyon to create a visual document of "Harry", the tunnel the escapees were to use on the night of 24-25 March 1944 to make the mass breakout. Kenyon rendered six drawings inside "Harry", lying face down in the two-foot square tunnel. The drawings were sealed in a watertight container made out of old milk tins from comfort Red Cross parcels and stored in "Dick", the abandoned escape tunnel.

At the height of winter when the advancing Russian army

neared the camp in January 1945, the Germans evacuated prisoners on the so-called Long March east. The departing prisoners just managed to flood "Dick" before they left in the hope of deterring a thorough search if the Germans discovered the tunnel. They never did and when the Russians seized control of Stalag Luft III to liberate the few remaining inmates, a British officer, who had stayed behind as he was too ill to evacuate earlier, recovered the drawings and brought them back to England. (They now reside in the Royal Air Force Museum, London.)

Bennett Ley Kenyon was born in London in 1913 and educated in art schools in London and Paris. He became a prominent art teacher specialising in watercolours. After volunteering for the submarine service of the Royal Navy at the outbreak of the war, he was called up as a driver for the RAF instead. He then became an air gunner and was commissioned in 1941. He went on many missions in bombers over enemy territory in Europe. After his twenty-ninth mission, he was awarded the Distinguished Flying Cross for his cool courage and determination.

Kenyon went on to survive forty-four full operations in bombers across enemy territory, including three raids on Berlin. On his forty-fifth mission his Halifax was attacked by German night fighters as it neared the English Channel on the home run. When the Halifax was set ablaze, Flight Lieutenant Ley Kenyon was the last to bale out. The French Resistance protected him in occupied France and tried to smuggle him out to Spain, but the Gestapo arrested him on a train to Bordeaux. He was placed as a POW in Stalag Luft III because of his officer rank. He soon became involved in the mass escape plans. His artistic skills were used to forge papers in the escape factory where he became a close associate and friend of Paul Brickhill. He also worked on the design for the all-important tunnel air

Paul Brickhill

pump. It was manufactured of Red Cross parcel large cocoa tins and pieces of cloth cut from inmates' uniforms.

Kenyon produced a valuable pictorial record of camp life and the escape tunnel. They were later reproduced by him for both *Escape to Danger* and *The Great Escape* and later were used in the production of the feature film of *The Great Escape* based on Brickhill's book. Like Brickhill, Kenyon's number did not come up for those inmates selected for the famous mass escape. He felt later that he was lucky not to have been selected as fifty of the escapees were executed under Adolf Hitler's express orders.

After illustrating the escape books, he went on to underwater filming for French oceanographer Jacques Cousteau and published books about underwater diving. He illustrated many books during his packed adventurous lifetime. He died on 15 November 1989 a few years before Paul Brickhill when he was visiting New Mexico.[4]

The Release of *The Great Escape*

On release as a book *The Great Escape*, in its dramatically illustrated dustcover, appeared in the window of every bookshop in the United Kingdom and elsewhere in the English-

4 'Obituary. The full life of Ley Kenyon', by Kendall McDonald, February 1991,<http://classicdivebooks.customer.netspace.net.au/Authors/Ley-Kenyon-Obituary.jpg>.

speaking world. Many copies worldwide of the book almost literally walked out of the bookshops with readers of every class and gender eager to understand the meaning behind the mass escape in Sagan – and they were not to be disappointed one little bit, with the result that it was a grand exposure of a significant event in World War II. By word of mouth, the book continued to take off and Brickhill's reputation was made. The book had become a publishing phenomenon of the first water.

The book and the earlier one were preceded and followed up by astute radio broadcasts narrated by Brickhill as well as newspaper articles and stories written by the same author. As a writer, Brickhill clearly understood the advantage of maximum exposure in all forms of the media of mass communication to ensure the success of his book and others that would rapidly follow.

The Great Escape received positive reviews across the United Kingdom, the United States of America and all parts of the British Empire and the former British Empire. By 1973 Faber and Faber had produced ten huge imprints to satisfy much of the market. Reviewers all enthusiastically claimed that Paul Brickhill had given a tragically truthful account of life in a German prison camp and of the way in which the will to escape dominated the minds of the POWs. The organisation, work, relentless determination and devious cunning involved in the heroic mass breakout from Stalag Luft III in 1944 was box-office magic as an outstanding war story, well supported by Brickhill's deft portrayals of the individual and distinctive characters of those who made up the members of the "X" escape organisation. The story of each protagonist was epic in itself. Brickhill made his account unbelievably exciting as it reached its climax. It was clear that Brickhill intended the book as a fitting tribute to those fifty executed officers who never knew defeat, 'who tried to escape a score of times and whose sense of duty and courage stayed them'.[5]

The release of *The Great Escape* simultaneously took place in the United States in New York as a Penguin paperback by WW Norton in 1950 with the cover design by A Games, artist for Faber and Faber. This cover was beautifully designed using the symbols of a machine-gun barrel, a shadow of a prisoner shot escaping, a watch tower with powerful searchlight and a red swastika with its clockwise arms, the official emblem of the fearful Nazi Party and the Third Reich arranged in a pattern.[6] These images were backgrounded in green, brown, fawn and blue in a cubist pattern. Such a cover would have caught the attention of the public.

> This is one of the most powerful and moving of all the war books. Its theme is tremendous and it reveals human nature and human conduct in their very highest and lowest aspects. It inspires one with admiration and infects one with loathing. It is not, of course, a happy story, but it is a great and powerfully dramatic one.[7]

In *The Great Escape*, as with all his other works, Paul Brickhill was centrally concerned with the old values of courage, decency, stoicism and honour in an updated form. And they permeate every paragraph of the book as a fine tribute to the men of Stalag Luft III.

---

5 *New Chronicle*, cited in Bear Alley, by Steve Holland, 'Paul Brickhill', <http://bearalley.blogspot.com/2010/09/paul-brickhill.html>.
6 Illustrated in Bear Alley.
7 'Drama And Tragedy Of Famous Escape', *Advertiser* (Adelaide), 28 April 1951, 6.

Fame is the Spur

Fame was the spur at almost the same time in the 1950s for Paul Brickhill and Peter Finch, the close friends at school and newspaper companions at the *Sun*. Finch, now in London, was powerfully developing his acting reputation and career on stage in the West End as well as in British feature films – many about the Second World War like his erstwhile friend's books. The mythology of their fame soon gathered force as was promulgated by an anonymous feature writer for *People* in 1954:

> One of their fantasies was that, one day, Peter Finch would get a cable from a West End theatre in London begging him to fly there immediately and take over the lead in a smash-hit play. No one else in the world, the cable would explain, could handle the part except Peter Finch. But how was he to get there in time? Easy. Paul Brickhill, by now a world-famous pilot, would fly him there.[8]

A childhood fantasy that could be exploited by the media as fame could always have behind it a spur of some kind in the individual's personality. Some people simply desire fame; others do not and have it thrust upon them; and others, having achieved it, eventually turn away from it after experiencing its dark side. Nevertheless, Paul was to become a more than successful writer about the war in the air and Peter Finch, the great and versatile actor, could portray more than just a war hero: the telling cameo part of an RAF officer incarcerated in Stalag Luft III in the feature film *The Wooden Horse* (1950)

---

8 'Mountain out of a Brickhill', *People*, vol.4, no 6, 20 May 1953, 20.

directed by Jack Lee and adapted by Eric Williams from his own book relating his personal wartime escape story. Finch's second British film was *Passage Home* (1955) in which he played a brave mercantile sea captain during the war; *A Town Like Alice* (1956), again directed by Jack Lee, gave Finch the lead part of a brave Australian soldier, Joe Harmon who was crucified by the Japanese – a brilliant performance that won the British Film Academy Award for best actor. And then there was *The Battle of the River Plate* (1956) with Finch playing the role of the courageous and cunning Captain Langdorff of the stranded German battleship (a Royal Film Performance in 1956);[9] in 1958 he starred in *Operation Amsterdam*, a wartime espionage thriller. There are therefore strange parallels in the careers, lives and rise to fame in the 1950s for the two Greenwich Point schoolboy friends. Finch like Brickhill was a shaper of full-throated war heroes of a diverse range for public consumption.

Enter Margot

Margot Olive Slater (dailytelegraph.com.au)

When Paul Brickhill travelled back to England by ship in April 1949, he met a beautiful young Australian woman, Margot Slater, of striking appearance who was born in New Zealand, but had come to New South Wales as an infant when her parents settled in the countryside of Narrabri.

Margaret (Margot) Olive Slater was heading for London for fame and fortune, like Paul. Both saw London

9 Dundy, *Finch, Bloody Finch*, 343-4; Faulkner, *Peter Finch*, 295-7.

as the exciting cultural centre of the world. It soon became an intense shipboard romance. Margot was later described in the press as tall, willowy and intensely attractive in an individual and stylishly independent way. Paul and Margot, who had recently trained at East Sydney Technical College (in the buildings of the former Darlinghurst Gaol) as an artist, fell heavily for one another and soon married. The wedding took place in London's fashionable Anglican St Michael's in Belgravia – a socially elite occasion, a year after they had met.

In 1914, the convict-built Darlinghurst Gaol had closed down and the inmates were transferred to the new Long Bay Gaol. By 1922, Sydney Technical College including the art department had taken over the grim sandstone premises. By 1935 the name 'National Art School' first appeared in the institution's handbook. In 1955 East Sydney Technical College formally separated from Sydney Technical College. By the early post-war period, the Art Department or School had produced many fine professional artists like William Dobell and Margaret Olley.

To gain enrolment, Margot Slater had to be a high achiever with a recognised and tested artistic talent and a good pass in the New South Wales Leaving Certificate examination. The Art School was highly selective in nature. At the Tech there was for Margot a gay social life with balls and parties in the art studios. Lunch could be had at the fashionable but cheap Rose Cafe nearby opposite the Darlinghurst Courthouse.

Margot mingled with a lot of promising artists and highly sophisticated young people. She would have studied under Jean Bellette, an inspiring art teacher who managed to make the often tedious life classes exciting. In the process, Margot would have studied the posing styles of the male and female live models like Moira Claux who became a dancer in the

Bodenwieser Ballet Company.[10] Moira's skills as a live model later influenced Margot's style as a top London fashion model.

The Dam Busters to *Reach for the Sky*

Even while Paul Brickhill was researching *The Great Escape* in London, it was suggested that he also write a third book on the story of the famous 617 Squadron, often referred to as the Suicide Squadron or even more famously as the Dam Busters. The subject was literally dumped on his lap after a couple of other writers had failed. Some considered Brickhill a lucky man, as literary critic John Hetherington suggested later in 1960; others did not as it overloaded him with a massive amount of research to be completed in haste along with the other writing tasks he was faced with.

For the subject of the 617 Squadron, two different commissioned writers tried to write the "dambusters' story" and had failed, not being able to master the technological aspects. But when Brickhill completed his manuscript *The Dam Busters* and it was released as a book to the reading public at large, it very quickly became a world bestseller and was followed by a highly popular radio serial and then a feature film starring screen idols Richard Todd and Michael Redgrave supported by

10 Deborah Beck, *Hope in Hell. A History of Darlinghurst Gaol and the National Art School,* Allen & Unwin, Sydney, 2005, 76, 83.

equally-distinguished English actors as well as a New Zealand and Australian cast of expatriates.

It wasn't long then for Douglas Bader, the famous legless RAF ace and POW to write to his former POW colleague in Stalag Luft III, Paul Brickhill who was living in the south of France with Margot in a countryside villa in early 1953. Bader suggested very forcefully that Brickhill write his biography.[11] Bader always got what he wanted. Brickhill readily accepted and went straight ahead with a prodigious amount of research required to produce *Reach for the Sky. The Story of Douglas Bader D.S.O., D.F.C.* that was soon published by the eminent London publisher, Collins – first impression in March 1954. By August of the same year it went to its sixth impression – so fast did it sell.

The book was loudly trumpeted in the media that the Australian author had 'hit the jackpot' as the most successful author in Britain after its general release. In eight months *Reach for the Sky* had sold nearly 300,000 copies. It was estimated that with film and serial rights, the book had earned nearly £70,000 for the author. Another newspaper reported with some immediacy: 'By last week-end seven months after its first publication, the 276,000th copy of "Reach for the Sky", the story of the legless wartime flying ace Douglas Bader, had been sold'. A Sunday columnist of some respect had estimated that Brickhill would have made £40,000 from the book plus £15,000 for the film rights.

Meanwhile Brickhill's so-described history *The Dam Busters* at about the same timeframe had sold 132,000 copies and yielded the author some £20,000 plus £15,000 in film rights.

---

11 John Hetherington, 'War launched an author', *Daily Telegraph*, 6 August 1960; John Hetherington, 'Paul Brickhill: The Fighter Pilot War launched as An Author', *Age*, 27 July 1960.

In the same report which carried Brickhill's side photographic portrait it was claimed *Escape – or Die* and *The Great Escape* made £25,000 each for the author.[12] Such newspaper disclosures began to cause some difficulties with both the British and the Australian taxation authorities. The *Morning Bulletin* in Rockhampton summarised it all earlier on 19 October 1954 by claiming that the author had earned £115,900 from his four books and was the biggest name in publishing.

As one of the three or four most inspiring and enthralling war books published after World War II, *The Dam Busters* had a phenomenal publishing record from when it was first published by Evans Brothers in 1951. Twelve impressions by Pan had come out even by 1956 with huge print runs with a cover by artist Carl Wilton. The 13th impression came out in 1961 with a new cover design by Pat Owen, quickly followed in 1963 with the 14th impression. The 15th followed in 1964; the 16th and the 17th in 1965; the 18th and 19th in 1967 with a newly designed cover.

Between 1951 and 1970, the royalties for Paul Brickhill rolled in abundantly. The overwhelming success of the great raid on Moehne and Eden Dams on the Ruhr also became an overwhelming success story for Brickhill, its post-war author. The book realistically portrayed all the grimness of air warfare, but also provided humorous episodes and a vivid portrayal of the disappointments when theories and plans were upset.

Escape – or Die, published in London by Evans Brothers in 1952, did well for Brickhill in the 1950s and 1960s, beit on a more modest scale. By 1965 it had had twelve impressions with changing cover designs in paperback form. A new impression was also launched in 1970.

---

12 'Big Sales of Air Ace Book', *SMH*, 22 November 1954; 'Australian Author's Big Success', *Chronicle*, Adelaide, 21 October 1954.

Reach for the Sky. The Story of Douglas Bader, D.S.O., D.F.C. followed such successes for Brickhill in 1954, this time published by Collins. It came out in paperback in Fontana Books with ten impressions by mid-1981. In addition, *The Great Escape* was adapted as a secondary school text by James Britton in 1956 for Faber & Faber. It sold like hot cakes when set as a text in school courses. In 1981 it was adapted for pre-adolescent children by Sue Gee for the publisher Hutchinson in London.

Likewise, *The Dam Busters* was adapted as a 'Cadet Edition' by Evans in 1958 for younger adolescents and adapted for smaller children by Christopher and Dorothy Welchman for Hutchinson in 1974 and in a revised edition by Evans in London in 1977. *Escape – or Die* also became an Evans 'Cadet Edition' in 1963.[13]

In short, Brickhill's publishing career was both fabulous and entirely overwhelming for a man who had once spent nearly two years in a German concentration camp during World War II. Fate had played him a most handsome card, but somewhat darker on the other side.

(Stephen McKay,
<geograph.org.uk>)

13 Bear Alley.

Margot and Paul

Both Paul and Margot Brickhill were found as early as 1953 heavily involved and sometimes swept off their feet with media publicity as celebrities in the 'jungle' of modern glamorous high fashion and 'high pressure' publishing circles. They socialised with other celebrities, novelists, literary agents, poets, artists, playwrights, film producers, stars and directors, and wealthy men and women about town. Their social life became a furious one and a requirement of their twin celebrity careers.

Brickhill was now just as suddenly the husband of a high-achieving and elegant Norman Hartnell model intent on realising her ambitions and goals of gaining a prominent place in the London world of fashion. Now he was a strongly sought after successful writer of extraordinary bestsellers. Events were moving fast, too fast probably. They always found themselves as a couple in the public arena of celebrity in London.

When they had arrived upon the London scene, Paul was freed of his sub-editor's work for the *Sun* and had taken to writing with relish and amazing energy on a full-time basis at the Chelsea flat in the fashionable London suburb. Margot was a young twenty-four-year-old: 'a tall, willowy, hazel-eyed girl with the sort of poise needed for modelling before a roomful of duchesses', after she had met Paul on the boat that took them both to London in 1949 as an unknown yet aspiring woman with dreams of fame.

Margot, one of three sisters (Jeanette 22, Margot 24 and Beth 26, in 1953), grew up in the historic town of Richmond near Sydney. The Slater parents expected their girls to grow up in Richmond, marry local men and settle quietly into family life. But not so! The year of 1953 found Margot, a professional highly-paid model with her famous husband in London's fashionable circles and her sisters in Hong Kong, then a British colony: Beth was married to a British army chaplain there and had four children and Jeanette, still single, was working there as a personal secretary to John McNeill QC. The three girls were quite markedly high achievers and highly intelligent.

Margot had spent the war years (while Paul unknown to her had become a POW) at Parramatta High School and then at Homebush High School going on to the Leaving Certificate examination. After leaving school, she immediately travelled to England in 1947 with her mother and her younger sister in a gap year. The central purpose of their visit was to see her elder sister Beth with her army chaplain husband who had been posted to the British Zone of Western Germany. This was about the time – still unknown to Margot – when Paul was frequenting Berlin as a foreign correspondent. The visit turned the youthful Margot into the beginnings of an international sophisticate.

When she returned home to Sydney with her mother, she became determined to return as soon as she could to London as the only place 'for a girl with ambition'. At the time she had no plans to become a model. Two years of study at the tertiary level in the famous East Sydney Technical School and the National Art School prepared the way for Margot 'to mount an attack on the biggest and most competitive city in the world'. Margot, twenty-one years of age, and Jeanette aged nineteen travelled together and planned a year to explore the British Isles.

But it was only a few hours after the ship departed from Sydney with the two sisters on board that Margot's plans for independence began to change. Paul Brickhill was on board. He set his sights on her; he was intensely attracted to her beauty and poise. Amongst other things, he believed he would write much better as a full-time author if he were married.[14] At the time Paul was a dapper, handsome thirty-seven year old and the twenty-one-year-old, apart from being most attractive, sparkled with a highly imaginative intelligence, grace and sophistication.

When they met, Paul had already written with Conrad Norton his first prisoner-of-war escape book, *Escape to Danger*. He considered it as a 'rush job' and believed he could do a lot better with the backing of stronger research. His second (and first as sole author) soon became an outstanding bestseller, transforming Brickhill from being a little-known Australian foreign correspondent as far as Europe was concerned into a celebrated author in the world's centre of publication, as the popular journal *People* put it crudely in 1953: 'into a man in the big money' with a 'queue of publishers asking him to write a book for them'. It was now quite different from his days as a copy-boy on the Sydney *Sun* and the terrible time he had spent in the war in Germany as a prisoner-of-war.

In the early days of their marriage, the Brickhills established a working relationship: Paul worked alone in their elegant Chelsea flat when he was writing or rather typing his manuscripts while Margot found a job modelling in London. Otherwise, he was engaged in heavy research in archives examining official reports as well as exhaustingly tracing the whereabouts of POW survivors who were spread internationally across Canada, the United States, Australia, South Africa, Rhodesia, Hong Kong and several European countries. The correspondence to such countries was prodigious and time-consuming. Some survivors were spoken to through an international hook-up by telephone. Churning out four highly-researched books in as many years began to take a heavy toll on him. His twenty-

14 'Mountain out of a Brickhill', 21.

six-month incarceration till the end of the war brought back frightening memories, nightmares and many sleepless nights. He overworked. The past seemed to haunt him. Ill health began to stalk him in his late thirties and early forties.

When Brickhill was sought after to write about the 617 Bomber Squadron – the Dambusters – he was in the middle of the most detailed research for *The Great Escape* and soon after, and at times simultaneously, researching for *Escape – or Die*. At first he refused the idea because he felt he could not cope or believed he would be under too much strain and stress. He felt he was not ready to undertake what was to be a huge, complex research project.

Margot had different ideas as she thought he was throwing up a marvellous opportunity and wanted the best for him. According to Paul: 'She told me I should take on the Dam Busters story'. She was obviously concerned to advance and enhance her husband's writing career. After all, he was ambitious as a well-recognised author. Consequently, he wrote an acceptance to Sir Ralph Cochrane, the RAF's Air Chief Marshal and constant mentor of the 617 Squadron and one of the key instigators of the plan to attack the German dams. In this sense it was to be commissioned by the RAF as a book. Paul said he had finally decided to take on the task together with its significant responsibilities. Margot was fully behind him, encouraging him all the way in this vital period of his writing career. It would establish him as a writer in a slightly different direction, away from escape stories to a fully-supported operational story of one of the greatest events in the history of the RAF – an event that was already legendary in the English-speaking world.

Meanwhile when released *The Great Escape* proved a huge success. It was broadcast on radio and it ran as a serial in newspapers and magazines all over the world. It was even televised and in shorter extracted pieces and translated into several languages. It appeared dramatised as a radio serial in a dozen countries.[15] All of this required more and more work in extra commentary by the author. Its success was surely almost overwhelming. Paul Brickhill demonstrated that he had a mastery over integrating the media in all its spots: book publication, newspapers and magazines, television and feature film production.

Nevertheless, *The Dam Busters* brought Brickhill lasting success as it is frequently quoted as an authoritative reference in the contemporary world of war history. Many books have now been written of the 617 Squadron. Many have attempted, but no one has surpassed Brickhill's concise work in terms of comprehensive completeness. After the book was accepted for publication, Brickhill moved immediately on to publishing *Escape – or Die* despite the fact he was still working on the dambusters' story in a variety of media forms, particularly as a radio serial.

15 'Mountain out of a Brickhill', 22.

Escape – or Die

The request to write *Escape – or Die* as a set of short escape stories in World War II came through a persistent approach by Sir Basil Embry, the charismatic leader of the RAF Escaping Society, a post-war charitable body that raised funds for the support of orphans and widows of the French Resistance people. Finally, Brickhill caved in and agreed to take the commission. It was a project right up his alley, despite being overloaded with work. The agreement between Brickhill and the Society was made into a limited liability company that the author devised whereby the author and the organisation took an equal share of the royalties for the sale of the proposed book. With an introduction by the eminent author HE Bates, it was advertised as 'Authentic Stories of the R.A.F. Escaping Society' on the spine of the dustcover. It was Brickhill's fourth book. And it sold well, earning money for both the Escaping Society and the author.

Basil Embry pointed out in the foreword of the book that many RAF POWs managed to escape in World War II. Many who were shot down managed to evade capture by the enemy. This was in part due to thousands of courageous civilian men and women and even children which became known as the French Resistance, as well as those civilians in other occupied countries like Norway, Holland, Belgium, Denmark and others. All developed resistance organisations.

In their respective German-occupied countries, civilians 'under a reign of terror' helped the RAF men and other stranded Allies with the most remarkable cool-blooded courage. Often they risked their lives to assist. They faced death and torture by the Gestapo on many brutal occasions. The society was, therefore, intent on providing charitable support for the orphans and widows of the underground resistance of

European occupied countries of the Second World War.[16]

The Escaping Society was founded on 18 September 1945 at the British Embassy and finally wound up its charitable work in 1995, four years after Brickhill's death. The first meeting to initiate the society's constitutional expansion occurred on the 3 May 1947 on the Strand, London, in the British House Restaurant; by late December that year a membership list of 552 aircrew 'evaders' – that is, those stranded in enemy territory trying to escape capture by the German overlords – had been gathered together as members by the founders. They also located the records of many thousands of resistance helpers from nine different occupied countries.[17]

By about 1951 Paul Brickhill had been approached and he had joined in to write the proposed money-raising book since, by this time, he was a famous bestselling author of renown in his own right. Immediately after the delivery of the manuscript of *The Dam Busters* to Evans Brothers Limited in London, he turned the *Escape – or Die* manuscript to the attention of the same publisher and they took it up. At about the same time, Evans Brothers released *The Dam Busters* to great acclaim by the British public.

As the sub-title of *Escape – or Die* directly indicated, Brickhill re-told a selection of the many real-life stories of

16 Brickhill, *Escape – or Die*, 1952.
17 <http://www.ww2escapelines.co.uk/?pageid=290>.

the RAF Escaping Society members. Clearly, the celebrated author met the distinguished Air Marshal Sir Basil Embry KBE, CB, DSO, DFC, AFC to discuss the book proposal and eventually he agreed to do it. With the approval of the Society's executive members, Brickhill selected eight stories of flying men who fought or struggled for their freedom in Germany or in German-occupied countries and even in South-East Asia. This selection was made after having to read hundreds of accounts. He had followed them up with communications by letter or telephone calls. It was overwhelming, exhausting, but fascinating work that contributed to lowering his physical well-being and mental health.

In choosing the eight stories, Brickhill skilfully selected key themes that demonstrated the rich variety of escapes. By his dramatic and spare writing style, he made each one new, fresh, immediate and different in geographical location during the war. Audacious methods of escape and the individuality of character were cleverly addressed by the author. These feats of escape were intended to fire the imagination of the prospective reader – and they did! This was Paul Brickhill's fourth venture into publishing having been written after *Escape to Danger* (with Conrad Norton), *The Great Escape* and *The Dam Busters*. With *Escape – or Die*, Brickhill was to return to the same format as his first published book – a selected collection of individual stories.

Beginning with the financial success of *Escape – or Die* which told the eight stories of its own members, the RAF Escaping Society used various other means to raise funds to fulfil its charitable purpose. These included radio and television appeals, spectacular air shows and sporting events, large and small. Even the seventy-year-old secretary of the Society, Elizabeth Harrison, undertook a sponsored tandem parachute jump as her contribution.

Society members, including Brickhill, co-operated with the production of the BBC television series *Secret Army* that raised the profile of the clandestine operations and the courage of the civilian 'helpers' of escape lines – the secret network of resistance in countries occupied during the war.

Air Field Marshal Sir Basil Edward Embry (1902-1977) in his wartime career with the No 107 Day Bomber Squadron flew many hazardous operations, was wounded, shot down over St Omer in France by anti-aircraft fire and captured. This was during a low level raid against advancing German Army columns. His aircraft crashed over Eperlecques. Two of his crew became prisoners-of-war and one was killed. Embry escaped while being marched away by rolling down a bank unnoticed when he suddenly saw a sign to a village bearing his name – what was for him a good luck charm. He evaded recapture successfully for two months in occupied France with support from the Resistance before getting back to England via Spain and Gibraltar through a secret network of safe houses organised by the Resistance. His adventures while on the run are detailed in the book *Wingless Victory* by Anthony Richardson (1950).[18]

The prolific and highly popular Northamptonshire novelist and short story writer H(erbert) E(rnest) Bates (1905-74) wrote the short overview or introduction in Brickhill's *Escape – or Die* under the simple title of 'Escape'. Like Brickhill, he was in the RAF during the war and wrote, under the pseudonym "Flying Officer X": two collections of authentic short stories, *The Greatest People in the World* (1942) and *How Sleep the Brave* (1943); the novel *Fair Stood the Wind for France* (1944) and, later, *The Jacaranda Tree* (or *The Purple Plain* (1949) –

18 *The Concise Dictionary of National Biography*, vol.1, Oxford University Press, 1992, 931.

all fictionalised stories based on factual events of World War II, especially of the RAF.[19] In his essay 'Escape', Bates at once pointed out that:

> when a member of the armed forces of this country is captured by an enemy in time of war it is his duty, by all possible and reasonable means, to escape. International law compels him to give the enemy no other information about himself than his name, rank and [serial] number; but when he has done this the war, for him, does not end.[20]

He saw life in prison compounds as 'a special sort of hell', a hell experienced by Paul Brickhill and many others in Stalag Luft III and elsewhere in Germany. Bates characterised such prisoners as from behind the barbed wire looking out and planning:

> with such meticulous care and risk the business of getting back to the very point from which they had started. How meticulously and ingeniously did they plan it all readers of Mr. Brickhill's *The Great Escape*, with its account of masterly systems of pass forging [conducted by Brickhill with others], corruption and blackmailing of guards by sheer daylight cheek, and of Mr. Eric Williams' *The Wooden Horse*, with its astounding piece of schoolboy amateurism turned

19 'Bates, H(erbert) E(rnest) (1905-1974)', Margaret Drabble (ed.), *The Oxford Companion to English Literature*, Oxford University Press, 2000, 72; Dominic Head (ed.), *The Cambridge Guide to Literature in English*, Cambridge University Press, 2006, 77-8.
20 Brickhill, *Escape – or Die*, 11.

> professional, will already know [both from within the barbed wire of Stalag Luft III].[21]

Such adventures Bates saw in the eight stories written or re-written by Brickhill in his book: stories of desert escape, escape through Poland and Russia, escape through the charms of a woman, escape by canal and boat and escape from Malaya to Australia. For the fourth time in almost the same number of years Brickhill had written another *tour-de-force*, another great bestseller, another winner in the publishing world – this time for the RAF Escaping Society and for the charitable cause it represented, but it was to leave him exhausted and on the edge of a nervous breakdown. His own thoughts at this time revolved about a single word: escape. That is, to escape the heavy pressures of celebrity in London that both he and his wife had created through the nature of their work as a best-selling author and a top model.

Again – Margot and Paul

The married couple decided to escape the 'wave of distraction' arising from success and they had the money to do it. They suddenly headed for France to get away from it all and for Paul to find some idyllic peace to settle his troubled mind that was constantly haunted by the twenty-six months of incarceration in Stalag Luft III with all its depreciation and human suffering and misery. Paul was genuine in his desire to escape the blazing lights of celebrity of London's literary world despite making many friends in those circles. In one sense, it both drew and repelled him and made him feel claustrophobic, especially on crowded social occasions.

---

21 HE Bates, 'Escape', in Brickhill, *Escape – or Die*, 13-14.

Margot and Paul Brickhill looked for peace and quiet by renting a villa in the fashionable hilltop village of St-Paul de Vence (or Vence) in the south of France just fifteen minutes or so by car from the Mediterranean Sea and not far from the resorts of Nice and Cannes. They stayed there from January 1951 to February 1952 and then went back to Chelsea.

Artists and writers had begun to frequent the village from the beginning of the 1920s on a similar mission to that of the Brickhills. The trail blazers to St-Paul de Vence were Paul Signac, Raoul Dufy and Chaïm Soutine. They set up their easels in this peaceful village of Provence, as did Margot Brickhill later in 1951, attracted by the colours and the light of incomparable richness and intensity. The village was also the haunt in the 1920s of DH Lawrence, the famous novelist, short story writer, poet, critic, playwright and artist. He died there of tuberculosis in 1930 at the age of forty-four.

The tramway line between Cagne-sur-Mer and Vence via Saint-Paul began in 1911 and – still running in 1951 – opened up the place to the outside world. The 1950s were St-Paul de Vence's golden age hosting French and foreign movie stars drawn to the French Riviera by the film studios in nearby Nice as well as the famous Cannes Film Festival.[22] Paul and Margot found themselves in this milieu in 1951-1952.

A large photograph in *People* showed Margot, informally dressed in slacks and sandals, standing and contemplating her easel on the outdoor patio of their villa while Paul is sitting in an outdoor chair, informally dressed in a tee-shirt, shorts and sandals with a book on his knee and pointing out something to his wife in conversation. The accompanying caption reads: 'THE BRICKHILLS IN THEIR HOME – SINCE ABANDONED – IN THE SOUTH OF FRANCE. HE WENT

22 <www.saint-pauldevence.com/en>.

THERE FOR PEACE – BUT HAD TOO MANY CALLERS'. The last phrase thus sounded an ominous note:

> It would have been a wonderful place to work, but so many of the people who had been casually invited down for a week or two actually arrived that the Brickhills found they were getting less time to themselves there than they did in Chelsea. They stuck it out [for a year]... and went back to London for a rest [from entertaining friends].[23]

Such was the price demanded by fame.

Another large photograph depicted Margot as a London model with three others. Her formal attire was in striking difference to the casualness of her dress in the other main photograph which adorned the article in *People*. The caption for this one read: 'Margot Brickhill (right), an Australian girl Paul Brickhill met on the way to Europe [by ship], and other Hartnell models in gowns suitable for non-titled women to wear inside the Abbey [for the coronation of Queen Elizabeth II]'. This image and caption reveal that Margot was a celebrity in London in her own right, but in the French villa she was attempting to get back to the art she had been trained in at the National Art School in Sydney.

Margot's chance to work, in particular, for the famous Norman Hartnell came shortly after the Brickhills returned to London from France in 1952. Through her agent, she replaced one of Hartnell's regular models who was on holidays: 'I twirled out and walked around for the usual minute or so and then went back into the dressing-room to change ... Then the head *vendeuse* [saleswoman] came and said "Mr Hartnell wants to

23 'Mountain out of a Brickhill', 20-22.

see you in a suit'". She remembered that she became nervous and found it hard to get the suit on. But she did and Hartnell immediately offered her a full-time job, so impressed was he with her rather individual modelling style and poise. Margot was delighted and agreed. She soon became Hartnell's top model.

Life for a Hartnell model began each day at the Hartnell showrooms at 10am sharp. By 10.15 Margot was supposed to have her make-up on for the day's modelling and she then stood by for tedious fittings, which kept her busy until noon, in the dynamic workshops 'surrounded by excited French exclamations' from the large team of French seamstresses. Sometimes, this activity went on longer to 2.30pm with a few hurried coffee breaks.

Then at 3pm sharp, there was a major showing to an eager but critical audience in the 'long, grey-carpeted main showroom with its walls flanked by gilt chairs and its team of solicitous saleswomen hovering about customers'. Margot, leading five other swiftly working models, usually showed some 110 frocks that required eighteen changes for each model in little over an hour. Then from prospective customers came requests for certain frocks to be modelled again so that cautious purchasers could make up their minds to spend a lot of money. All of this was routine, but exhausting routine. On certain days Margot had long sessions at work beneath arc-lights while films were made for newsreels and television.

On 2 June 1953, Queen Elizabeth who had driven and mended military trucks in the Second World War arrived for her coronation in a golden coach pulled by eight grey horses. The ceremony in Westminster Abbey was packed with men and highly fashionable women, many in dresses designed by Norman Hartnell and, not a few, modelled by the Australian Margot Brickhill, the diva of London's fashion world.

The fashion frenzy, stimulated by the preparations for Queen Elizabeth's coronation and associated events, had swept London, the British Isles and even the rest of the English-speaking world. This was the first coronation to be seen by millions of people all over the world because of television. A feature film had also been prepared for cinemas so women had wanted to look their best wearing the highest of formal fashionable gowns and hats especially as the event would be relayed on the small and big screens.

In the coronation year, the prestigious house of Hartnell became 'a continuous whirl of excitement' and exacting work for Margot as one of its star models. It was exhausting and intensely interesting for her, but with certain stresses and tensions that began to affect her marriage. She had found her milieu which brought with it fame and a high degree of recognition in London's fashion world for high society. It was also a new world for Paul Brickhill to cope with as well as the highly competitive publishing hub of London he was involved in.

After the couple resettled in the Chelsea flat, Margot seemed to be floating 'in front of the cameras' and the eyes of England through the media and England's nobly bred and fashionable women. Paul at home was 'licking into shape' what he called 'the greatest story of all' – a personal biography of the famous legless aviator Douglas Bader. He was to call his book *Reach for the Sky* which would become a great success and a bestseller.[24]

Paul had spent many hours interviewing the exacting but famous Bader with a microphone in one hand, capturing everything he needed on a tape-recorder. When the tape was filled, Brickhill posted it off to a London typing agency and received the typescript back in twenty-four hours. Working hard daily on this basis, he had accumulated about 500,000 words in his typed files from the taped-recordings. It was

24 'Mountain of a Brickhill', 22.

indeed a mountain of data to sift through and refine into shape as a manuscript of patterned life experiential themes about one-fifth 'as bulky as the raw material'.

The captions of the other photographs in the article 'Mountain of a Brickhill' are instructive: 'Brickhill and manuscript [depicting Brickhill at his desk with typewriter]. Composition was an ordeal by red hot typewriter. Now he uses a tape-recorder to capture the basic information [and then conducts other forms of research]'. Another photograph shows Paul and Margot happily wandering hand-in-hand down a country track near their villa in southern France and the romantic caption reads: 'It's quite a feeling to make a success of life – and still be young. *The Brickhills are planning to return to Australia soon*'.

Another portrait of Margot in the same popular article heralds something of the same with touches of fame in it: 'Margot Brickhill in London – with bunches of flannel flowers. They are sent over [from Australia by air] for an Australian bottle (brush) party'.[25] The same photograph appeared in the *Newcastle Herald* and gives us more information about the nature of the party and other details in its caption: 'Australians All. Margot Brickhill, Norman Hartnell's only Australian model, takes delivery at London Airport of bunches of Australian flannel flowers and bottlebrush, flown to London by Qantas for the inaugural party of the Society of Australian Authors in Australia House. Margot is the wife of Paul Brickhill Australian author of three bestsellers including the "Dam Busters"'.[26] Maybe Brickhill's friend Peter Finch was in attendance for what seems to have been a farewell party for the famous couple.

A striking full-page portrait of Margot appeared on the cover

25 Mountain of a Brickhill', 22, 23.
26 *Newcastle Herald*, 25 November 1952.

page of the same issue of the fortnightly news magazine *People* (20 May 1953). She is obviously dressed in one of Hartnell's formal fashionable coronation outfits. The powerful, striking portrait of the top-billed model with penetratingly direct eyes is captioned: 'MARGOT BRICKHILL. Australian best-seller's wife'. *People* then heralded the arrival back to Australia of the famed couple in the media directed at an eager mass audience.

Part of the reason for their return was that Margot was pregnant with their first child. As she had grown up in Richmond, naturally the local paper ran a story on the birth. The Brickhills were congratulated by the paper on the birth of their son Timothy Paul at Wakefield Private Hospital in Auckland, New Zealand.[27] (As already related, Margot was born in New Zealand and had come to live in countryside New South Wales as an infant.) The Brickhills had obviously stopped over in New Zealand for the birth of their first child.

Paul, Timothy, Margot Brickhill

By November 1959, the Brickhills had been married for ten years, mostly spent away from Australia. They had lived in England, France, America, Florence in Italy and New Zealand. In an interview, Margot admitted that she had become tired of moving around so much. She was by then thirty-one years of age. The last time she had done any professional modelling was in Florence four years earlier. By mid-November, the couple had recently arrived in Australia on the migrant liner *Fairsky* with their two children, Timothy

27 *Richmond and Windsor Gazette*, 5 May 1954.

aged five and Tempe aged two. They intended to spend eighteen months in Australia while Paul completed the research and writing of a commissioned work on the history of the large-scale post-war immigration to Australia.[28] It was to be his sixth non-fiction book in a decade, but it never saw the light of day as a publication. In the following year, the Brickhill's marriage began to unravel. By 1964, they were divorced.

* * *

Back in 1954 a newspaper article 'Sales of Fiction Slump' explored the new reader preferences, pointing out that the real world was so exciting readers did not need in their reading 'fantasy' – in other words, fiction. More and more non-fiction books were selling well as fiction seemed to be fading. More books were thus sold: 'about diving beneath the sea' (for example Ley Kenyon's books) and 'adventures above the clouds' (works by Paul Brickhill and others). Particular reference was made to *Reach for the Sky* and Sir John Hunt's *Ascent of Everest*. By 1954 both these books had 'broken all records by selling more than 300,000 copies each in a few months'. Readers were asked also to consider the popularity of the *Kon Tiki* story by Thor Heyerdahl, *The Wooden Horse* and *The Dam Busters* as being 'still wildly popular'. High praise was then given to Brickhill's three main books as leading the trend away from fiction. The trend was marked enough to advise young would-be writers to turn to non-fiction if they wanted to make a real living with their pen.[29]

Back in 1953 the same year that Paul Brickhill was struggling to produce an authentic biography of Douglas Bader – *Reach*

28 'Author's wife is a "model mum"'.
29 'Sales of Fiction Slump', *Mail*, (Adelaide), 11 December 1954.

for the Sky – which was to rule the roost in the world of non-fiction, former member of Naval Intelligence Ian Fleming had published *Casino Royale* that began to pull book popularity away from non-fiction towards the exciting international thriller in fiction, but strongly imbedded in a loose interpretation of authentic political international affairs in the contemporary Cold War period of the 1950s.

In *Casino Royale* Fleming created the superhuman British agent James Bond (007), that is with a license to kill. In a series of books about Bond which followed, the author created such demonic scoundrels that had to be destroyed by Bond, such as Dr No, Goldfinger and numerous unpleasant and murderous Russians. Fleming had discovered a winning blend of fanciful sex with deadly connotations (especially for women), extreme violence and gourmet-style living that he never varied. Thrill followed thrill in the tradition of John Buchan's *The Thirty-Nine Steps* and Baroness Orczy's *The Scarlet Pimpernel* with the hero escaping unbelievably perilous situations.

The bell then began to toll for the popularity of well-written, exciting and authentic non-fiction dealing with events of the Second World War.

Before starting on the proposed book on immigration, Brickhill was intent on completing his first work of fiction centred in Paris, a terrorist thriller that was to be published in 1962 by Collins in Sydney entitled *The Deadline*. It was to be be his sixth and final book publication, apart from revisions of his real-life books, especially *The Dam Busters*. Between 1962 and his death in 1991, there was a shadowy silence where he was intent on becoming a non-celebrity even in the book world. Nevertheless, *The Deadline* is a competent thriller in the mould of Ian Fleming and John Buchan and has startling touches of our contemporary world of international terrorist threats and realistic possibilities.

In 1963 it was published in America under the title *War of*

Nerves by Morrow in New York. Fontana Books released it in 1964 in paperback. It failed in comparative terms to capture the public's attention as his bestselling non-fictions had done.

The Deadline, Paul Brickhill's final major book, is set in Paris of 1962 (that is contemporary time of its publication the same year). The main protagonist Robert Mackay is a young, virile and carefree Australian visiting Paris. Immediately the impact of the Second World War is skilfully evoked. Mackay is shown by a portly short town clerk outside the *Mairie* (town hall) and around the corner to where his Aunt Claire was executed by the Gestapo during the German occupation:

Neatly chiselled on the tablet were the words:

ICI EST TOMBÉE
CLAIRE BEAUDRON
HÉROINE DE LA RÉSISTANCE
FUSILLÉE PAR L'ENNEMI
LE 18 JUILLET, 1944
MORTE POUR LA FRANCE

> My own school French had no trouble with that, and I stood there silently in the spring sunshine by the yellowed wall, trying to detach myself from the present and visualise the handsome woman in her thirties standing on this cracked pavement just where I was standing myself and facing the firing squad of six German soldiers lined up on the cobble-stones of this little side road.

By using the first person narrative of his youthful hero, Brickhill is able effortlessly to create the accurate world of the recent past – a memorial of female heroism glanced at – in powerful visual written terms and evoke the authenticity of history, but in a fictionalised form:

> ... Then the shots, the falling body and blood running down to the gutter at my feet. It happened here in Marterre, this humdrum spot on the fringe of Paris, part dormitory suburb, part village, lacking either the pulse of the city or the charm of the open country.[30]

Brickhill soon snaps us back to the present and Mackay narrates in the rest of the tense and exciting novel his current adventures as almost a *film noir* hero thrown into a dangerous situation that he is only vaguely aware of. He does not fully comprehend its significance, like Richard Hannay in *The Thirty-Nine Steps*, until things are unravelled in the exciting climax.

Mackay is depicted by the author as a young, carefree visitor to France, on the main looking for a good time which he never has until the end of the story. He enters a Left Bank café, saunters up to the bar, orders a drink, casts a knowing, but naive eye around the room and spots a pretty girl. Suddenly, a shot is fired, followed by more. A man slumps over a table, another victim of the Algerian conflict, but a daily occurrence in Paris at that time impacting negatively on the lives of Parisians.

For Robert Mackay, who is unwilling to be drawn into a web of political intrigue and violence, it is difficult to understand. The victim of the shooting is Sidi Chebourt, a significant peaceful Algerian figure. His assassin is the feared terrorist radical Ben Chakry. The plot rumps up – Chakry must be caught and stopped, dead or alive before he can carry out his dark and frightening plot against the entire French nation, by poisoning the water supply of a provincial French city. The Paris police force is mobilised and a hunt of massive scale and urgency is on. Mackay is the only person able to identify the

30 Paul Brickhill, *The Deadline*, Collins, Sydney, 1962, 7-8.

assassin Ben Chakry as he is the only one present when the killing took place. The police are keenly aware of this and so is Chakry. The search for the killer intensifies at the same time as the heightening death threat to Mackay. The thrilling story maintains its immediacy to the end and the social realism of the authentic background to the adventure is particularly well-realised. There is also a mysterious *femme-fatale* heroine, Simone, added to the mix of exciting incident.

Sadly, however, it was to be Paul Brickhill's last hurrah – his swansong – before he faded into obscurity, living alone in a top-story apartment fronting onto the beach at Balmoral and the beauty of Middle Harbour. With this view from his window, he could contemplate and console himself about the loss of fame.

Peter Finch's home,
Greenwich Point, Sydney

The Brickhill family home,
Greenwich Point, Sydney

Greenwich
Public School

Greenwich Point Tidal Swimming Pool

North Sydney Boys High School, Miller & Falcon Sts, North Sydney

Skylight of the Sun *newspaper Building*

Sir High Denison as a young man

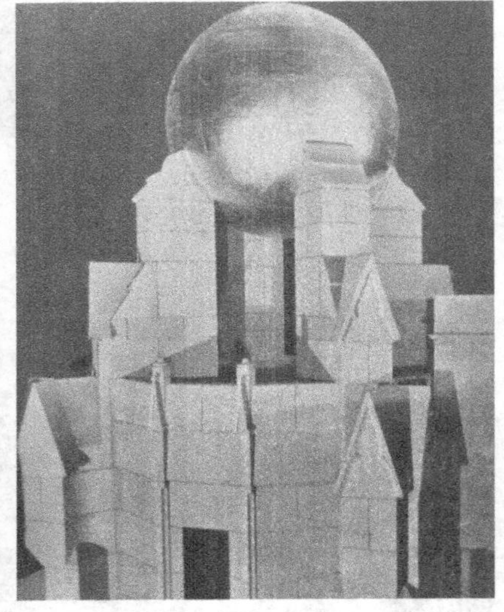

Sun symbol on top of Sun *newspaper Building, Elizabeth St, Sydney*

Interiors , Sun *newspaper building (now demolished)*

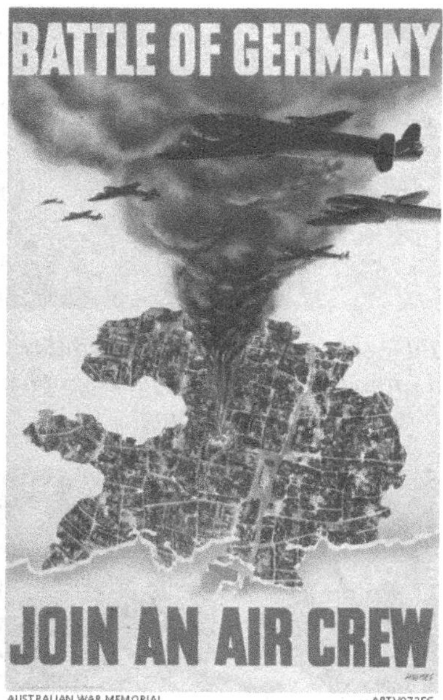

Posters from AWM (l-r): ARTV04316; ARTV07256; ARTV04273

Table set to celebrate 22nd birthday of Leading Aircraftsman/ photographer Ron Fleming

Early leading role for Peter Finch in Red Sky at Morning, *Australian film based on Dymphna Cusack's play*

Paul Brickhiil, successful toast of the London publishing world

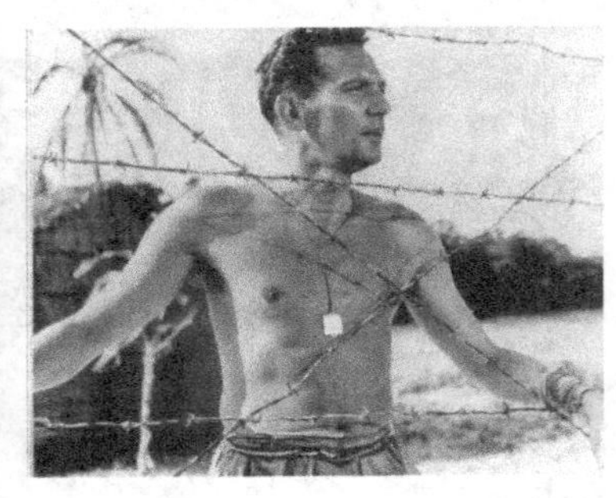

Peter Finch in his leading award-winning role in A Town like Alice *as a POW of the Japanese*

Paul (36) & Margot (24) Brickhill in St-Paul de Vence, village in southern France

Margot Brickhill with Timothy and Tempe

Margot (3rd from right, seated)
The principal Hartnell model for the coronation of Queen Elizabeth II, Westminster Abbey

Paul Brickhill's villa at St-Paul de Vence

Peter Finch, Man of a Thousand Faces, (l-r): as Jim Macauley in The Shiralee *(1957); as Flambeau in* Father Brown *(1954) and as Captain Langdoff of the Graf Spee in the Royal Command Performance film* The Battle of the River Plate *(1956)*

Margot Brickhill, cover girl for People

Paul Brickhill, early 1960s

Entrance to "Stancliff", the block of flats (below from the beach) where Brickhill lived between about 1964 and his death in 1991

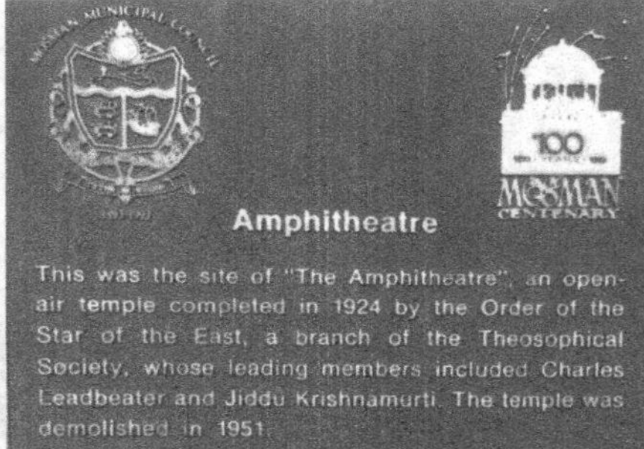

Plaque on "Stancliff"

Book covers courtesy of Bear Alley

King George VI, Royal Visit (16 May 1943) to Scampton after the raids on the Ruhr Dams

Micky Martin on BBC radio

Wing Commander Guy P Gibson VC, DFC & Bar, DSO & Bar

*Some of the Australian contingent after receiving medals for the Dam Raid, June 194
(left to right) Les Knight, Lance Howard, Mick Martin, Jack Leggo, Tammy Simpson, Spam Spafford, Dave Shannon, Bob Hay*

Squadron Leader John Williams shot down in North Africa, 1942. A POW in Stalag Luft III, one of the 76 who escaped, when recaptured, he was executed under Hitler's orders

John Williams DFC, Western Desert North Africa beside his Kittyhawk Mandrake *(both images courtesy of Louise Williams)*

The Norwegians: Per (Peter) Bergsland, Halldor Espelid & Jens Müller. Bergsland & Müller were successful in reaching England via Sweden. Espelid was recaptured and executed

'At the foot of the tunnel "Dick", the carpenter's shop'

'The tunnel at Stalag Luft III: the foot of the shaft'

Drawings by Albert Comber (1945, AWM)

Five Brickhill boys with father George & mother Dot (c.1921)
(courtesy of Bea Brickhill)

Paul with father, Clive, Geoff & Lloyd (courtesy of Bea Brickhill)

Left to right: Lloyd, Clive, Russell, Paul Geoff (c.1925) (courtesy of Bea Brickhill)

Brickhill reunion 1951, taken in the garden of the family home, Greenwich Point
Paul is 2nd from right (courtesy of Margaret Brickhill)

CHAPTER 8

THE CRACK-UP AND AFTER

> Paul Brickhill's pen flowed less freely as he grew older and he had become somewhat reclusive by the time of his death.
>
> – Geoff Simpson, *Guy Gibson Dambuster*, 57

Such retrospective judgement may convey an element of truth, but is a simplification of a complex personality and troubled life story. Certain aspects of a person's life can be shrouded in mystery that may never be fully solved.

The Dam Busters, *Reach for the Sky* and *The Great Escape* quite suddenly placed Paul Brickhill as an Australian author right at the top of the international bestseller lists. It had directly followed a long period of anonymous incarceration in a dreary prison camp where bored inactivity went on day after day outside the realm of economic employment and purposeful activity. It was an experience that was completely alien from civic life and individual aspiration. But by the 1950s in contrast, there was a price to pay for such enervating and exciting celebrity and notoriety in the media. London, in Brickhill's post-war experience, was the epicentre of the publishing world. Then in the early 1960s, the bestsellers stopped appearing and gradually the world seemed to forget Paul Brickhill. His world closed in around him as celebrity began to dissipate. He then slipped into a personal crisis of mental breakdown, sometimes fuelled by alcohol, that he believed was to last some twenty-five years and from which he emerged with great difficulty.[1]

In 1982 the journalist David Langsam interviewed Brickhill in his flat at Balmoral Beach in Sydney Harbour in a sensitive way and was able to unfold many of the author's personal experiences and anxieties since the beginning of the 1960s. Langsam met with Brickhill in "Stancliff", flat 53/ 6 Wyargine Street, Balmoral Beach.

"Stancliff" by the Harbour

"Stancliff" could be described appropriately as a five storey 'red brick citadel' of some thirty units or flats built on the site of the demolished Star Amphitheatre. The amphitheatre was built by the Order of the Star in the East, an offshoot of the international Theosophical Society which had been formed in 1913 locally by Mrs Annie Besant and Charles Webster Leadbeater. They had purchased three adjacent blocks of land sloping down from Wyargine Street to the beach in Balmoral. The dramatic Order of the Star of the East Amphitheatre was build in 1923 and demolished in 1950. "Stancliff" replaced it.

While not a distinguished piece of architecture, its imposing size, nevertheless, represents the origin of an important

1 David Langsam, 'After the Crackup', *Age, Saturday Extra*, May 1982.

building type and movement – the modern home unit. It played a major role in what was seen by many, including governments, as a model for the solution to the Sydney post-war housing shortage crisis and it suited Paul Brickhill to live there quietly and privately from his late forties to his death in 1991 at the age of seventy-four.

Another earlier "Stancliff" resident claimed: 'When we bought here it was the only place we could afford. Because of its location near the Heads [of Sydney Harbour], fears of invasion lowered the price'.[2]

The Hetherington View

By that time, Brickhill had also been extensively profiled by John Hetherington, a popular literary critic and journalist.[3] This 1960 interview, like the later one in 1982, took place in Brickhill's top-storey flat overlooking scenic Balmoral Beach and Sydney Harbour. David Langsam was an important interviewer who later revealed certain aspects of Brickhill's experiences and dilemmas with some sensitivity. Both he and Hetherington published different versions of their study of the author for slightly different purposes in various newspapers. They do not seem, in general, to be contradictory in their findings. The iconography related to these articles, however, is significant. One photograph used by Langsam shows a stressed contemporary image of Brickhill with his shirt undone down the front; others show him as a much younger man – some are press release file type of photographs displaying a smiling

2 Claire Mitchell, *Through the Heads To Balmoral, Sydney*, Claire Mitchell, Sydney, 2015, 62-63; 'The Star Amphitheatre Balmoral', pamphlet, Local Studies Service, Mosman Library, Mosman, undated.

3 John Hetherington, 'War launched an author', *Daily Telegraph*, 6 August 1960 (and in several other newspapers).

author, always smartly dressed, usually with a cravat and sports coat. The contemporary photograph of 1982 suggests that the subject was struggling through a stressful and troubled period in his life with the glory of fame well behind him. For Brickhill was open and candid about his mental life and the struggle he had had to maintain his sanity while living alone.

In 1962 John Hetherington was to give Paul Brickhill a prominent place in his book *Forty-Two Faces*, published in Melbourne, which consolidated Hetherington's many newspaper articles and profiles about prominent Australian authors. His chapter on Brickhill was prophetically entitled 'An End to Looking Back' that summarised the author's situation:

> Many a man spends a few months searching his soul ... when the thirties fall behind him and the fifties loom ahead. Paul Brickhill did this, but for him, the process lasted seven or eight years. This was in character, for Brickhill has a passion for thoroughness in whatever he does. He has never been able to work in any other way, whether the immediate task is to write a book, fly an aeroplane, or do anything else.
>
> ...
>
> But Brickhill's failure to publish a new book as year after year passed did not mean he was idling; on the contrary, for most of those years he was working perhaps harder than he had ever worked before, in the effort to find himself.[4]

Hetherington admits that for two years or so after *Reach for the Sky* was published, Brickhill turned his back on professional

4 John Hetherington, *Forty-Two Faces,* FW Cheshire, Melbourne, 1962, 165-6.

writing because of the 'tax-gatherer' and because he was busily preoccupied with being involved in the promotion of the sales of the book due to its 'immense success'. Brickhill was viewed by Hetherington as essentially a writer of 'dramatic narrative'. The author viewed himself this way as well, but writing 'out of fact' created for him, or any writer, a huge problem.

By 1962 Brickhill was no longer interested in writing for money, success or fame. 'He saw as one of the main articles of his creed: If I have something to say I want it to be in such a form that people will want to read it… I aim to avoid being dull or pompous and try to be readable and interesting'.[5] The books Brickhill produced by this date, including *The Deadline*, his first fiction and final book, provide a tangible illustration and proof that he achieved his aim. He was, indeed, a man of his word.

The Langsam View

In a shorter article for the *Courier Mail* with the by-line 'An author returns from his Great Escape', David Langsam relates Brickhill's personal struggles with the struggles of his protagonist Douglas Bader in *Reach for the Sky*, opening with a quotation:

> The good humoured barracking that had greeted his first efforts died away as people became aware that

5 Hetherington, *Forty-Two Faces,* 169-70.

> they were watching a man battling to do something that never had been done successfully before with only his guts to help him and a crippled life ahead if he failed. Refusing to accept that it was impossible kept him going.
>
> – Douglas Bader described by Brickhill in *Reach for the Sky*

Leading into this quotation was the context for the benefit of the reader, saying that just after the war Australian Paul Brickhill was one of the 'world's most successful authors', that he wrote 'blockbusting best-sellers of true war stories' and some were made into major films. Then he had 'a nervous breakdown', Langsam tells his readers, which lasted twenty-five years. The implication is obvious. Brickhill struggled with mental problems, but his protagonist Bader also had a most difficult struggle with a massive physical disability of the loss of both legs. And yet he succeeded. The unwritten question was, while Bader triumphed over his handicap, will Brickhill be able to do the same? The question remained hanging in the air until 1991 with many ebbs and flows of recovery.

Robert Willson writing a review of a recently published book about Roger Bushell, Brickhill's hero and leader of the "X" escape organisation in the mass escape at Sagan, mentioned that he came across Paul Brickhill many years before as a convalescent patient in an unnamed hospital in Sydney, possibly Concord Repatriation Hospital. Willson was able to have a long conversation with Brickhill as he 'had no other visitors that morning'. He must have met him in about 1962.

In the course of the discussion, Brickhill proudly showed him a proof copy of his latest book *The Deadline* (1962) which he had just received from the publisher Collins. As Brickhill had known Bushell in the POW camp at Sagan, Willson asked him to tell him more about his memories of the man and of the Great Escape. Brickhill generously obliged in his usual courteous and precise clipped manner.

When Brickhill had written *The Great Escape* in 1951, he did not have the opportunity to read through Roger Bushell's personal papers. The Bushell family released these only in 2013 or so – many years after Willson had met Brickhill in the Sydney convalescent hospital where he had been undergoing intensive treatment for his mental disorders. Brickhill had had no chance to explore these personal papers, diaries and letters that were deposited by the family in the Imperial War Museum, London, well after Brickhill's death.

Thus author Simon Pearson, by building on Brickhill's concise pioneering work so soon after the Second World War, had produced *The Great Escaper: The Life and Death of Roger Bushell* which was published by Hodder and Stoughton, and reviewed by Robert Willson who, by chance, had met Brickhill.

While this new book produced more colour and detail about Bushell's early life, Brickhill's view of his personality and character remained absolutely intact. Bushell 'burned within him a deep hatred of the Nazis and a determination to regain his freedom and to make life difficult for the Germans in the process'. And Simon Pearson agreed entirely with the long-deceased writer of bestselling wartime books, Paul Brickhill, that Roger Bushell was the 'organising genius behind all the escape exploits at Stalag Luft Three'.[6] The Brickhill influence remained strong in the early years of the twenty-first century. Much is still modelled on his work.

---

6 Robert Willson, 'Roger Bushell burned with hatred for the Nazis', Review of Simon Pearson, *The Great Escaper: The Life and Death of Roger Bushell*, in *Panorama, Canberra Times*, 26 April 2014, 26.

Paul Brickhill was depicted by Langsam in 1982 as sitting in his armchair by a window in the flat at Balmoral Beach, Mosman – that is, Edwards Beach – perpetually and thoughtfully gazing out to a view he knew so well. According to the journalist, his subject proclaimed: 'If I had a unit, say, in some side street in Gladesville, or wherever, I'd have gone around the twist years ago'. A room with a view is perceived then as a restorative device for mental problems. The view itself is lovingly described by Langsam:

> The view of the Pacific Ocean is framed on the left by North Head and on the right by Middle Head. The sea swells and rolls while top-less mothers lie on the beach in the Sydney sunshine.
>
> Across the water of Hunter's Bay are the naval depot the commando training school and the old quarantine station.[7]

Thus, mixed in with the majestic scenery is some military activity. Brickhill could watch this changing scene for hours. In the evening there were the lights of the Manly ferries crossing the harbour. So a soothing meditative experience for a man struggling with a mental disorder he honestly and courageously reveals to the public via such articles by intensive interviews of several inquisitive and invasive journalists who wanted to know.

In the longer article on Brickhill by David Langsam, 'After the Crackup' published later in the same year by the *Age*, the journalist begins by describing exactly the same view from Brickhill's window. When Langsam settled into the interview in Brickhill's lounge room, his subject – clearly nervous –

7 *Courier Mail,* 3 March 1982.

crosses to the kitchen and opens a carton of Summit Light cigarettes, thus implying he is a chain-smoker. He then pours himself a glass of Tab – implying he has gone on the wagon and is a recovering alcoholic. He then settles back in his armchair ready to answer any reasonable question asked.

By the late 1960s, Paul Brickhill had been completely written off by several journalists in the newspaper media around the nation. Some gloated on his seeming demise, enjoying tearing down what they saw as a tall poppy. The *West Australian* used the headline: 'Author: Golden Days Over' and they drew Brickhill himself into the discussion. 'Australian author Paul Brickhill said yesterday that the golden days for authors were almost finished'. He was of course discussing the publishing world in general. He claimed that he himself had finished writing books and he had actually been working for the taxation department for several years.

In December 1969 the famous author of six bestselling books of the 1950s arrived from overseas on the *Galileo*. In a stopover in Fremantle, he pointed out to an interviewing journalist that the high price of hard-covered books was ridiculous and was much of the cause in the drop in book sales across the board. Hard-covered books, he claimed, were now only bought by libraries and for birthday presents – otherwise, the general public were not buying.

As an example, he pointed out that *Reach for the Sky* in 1954 initially sold 500,000 copies in hard-cover. Such a book now – in 1969 – would probably not sell more than 30,000 copies. Currently, there were this number of new titles each year in Britain alone and bookstores could not keep up with them. New book publications kept flooding in.

He also said that he had decided to concentrate in the future on writing for film instead of writing books, but now the film industry was 'sick'. Most of the Hollywood film studios were going out of business and Hollywood was no longer the centre of the universe for film-making. And yet he intended to return to Sydney to do more writing.[8] He was obviously troubled and even confused by it all even though he perceived the current situation quite accurately.

Later, Langsam describes the sixty-six-year-old Paul Brickhill as a short portly 'former RAAF fighter pilot with a chocks-away-chaps moustache and long scars on his legs' – a permanent reminder of his war service as a Spitfire pilot who was shot down in the Tunisian desert in 1943. Langsam noted at this stage in the record of the interview that he was wounded in the back and scalp before he struggled free of the aeroplane and then was dragged by his parachute through an Italian minefield to the Italian wire after landing on the ground. Langsam recounts how his subject was kept incarcerated as a prisoner-of-war for the duration of the war in Stalag Luft III, thus the setting of his post-war eye-witness book *The Great Escape*.

French version

The Bookshelves in Flat 53

He noticed that his books still adorned his bookshelf: his two other 'million-copy selling books', mainly first edition copies of *The Dam Busters* and *Reach for the Sky* which had been translated into more than twenty languages. On display was a specially bound copy of *The Dam Busters*, a presentation from the Royal Air Force. He then

8 'Author: Golden Days Over', *West Australian*, 2 December 1969.

noticed the hardback editions of the same book in Swedish, French and Italian; the paperback form of the same book in Spanish, Czechoslovakian and German – all in apple-pie order. In pride of place was a statuette of Pan presented in gratitude by Pan books. And so newspaper readers are provided with a clear picture of Brickhill's writing achievements and his domestic pride in his accomplishments. His world of publishing was all around him in his living room where he lived quietly and modestly. All this, Langsam saw very much as past glories and symbols or trophies of his past fame and ecstatic celebrity in the 1950s. What the journalist did not realise was the value of the provenance of this collection.

After *Reach for the Sky*, the interviewing journalist claims, erroneously, that Brickhill stopped writing altogether. This seemed to have occurred after *The Deadline*, a novel as thriller which was published by Collins in Sydney in 1962 and marketed in the US under the title *War of Nerves*. It had not been the success that Brickhill had hoped for. Nevertheless, there is more evidence that exists that Brickhill continued to write at times when he was well enough. He was also involved from time to time working on revisions of his great bestsellers when they were republished. No matter what, he never gave up on writing in his flat overlooking Middle Harbour. After the 1960s, Langsam more correctly claims, readers of Brickhill saw only condensations of already published work.[9]

One of Brickhill's earliest stories as told to Allan A Michie, 'Tunnel to Freedom', was published in December 1945 in *Reader's Digest* just on his arrival in Brighton for rehabilitation after prison camp the same year. The story was the embryo of

---

9 For example, Brickhill 'Tunnel to Freedom', 167-92; Paul Brickhill, 'Escape or Die', in Charles S Verral (ed.), *Reader's Digest. True Stories of Great Escapes*, vol.2, Reader's Digest, Sydney, 1980, 310-50.

Escape to Danger (with Conrad Norton, 1946) and then *The Great Escape* (1951). It is clear that Paul Brickhill was still in uniform in 1945 and had not been demobilised when extracting the story word-for-word from the fighter pilot concerned.

This was the real beginning of Brickhill's new career as an author. 'Tunnel to Freedom' was re-published in 1980 in exactly the same format in *Reader's Digest. True Stories of Great Escapes.* Reader's Digest even appropriated Brickhill's coined title of his book (*The Great Escape*) as it had become very much part of the English language by then. In their second volume that year, Reader's Digest re-published another Brickhill short story in a new guise as 'Escape or Die'. This had originally appeared in the author's book with a similar title, *Escape – or Die* (1952) with its original title, 'It Feels Like This' – the last story in Brickhill's volume.

The investigative journalist Langsam, in his descriptions of Brickhill's fifth-storey flat, reasons that the author stopped writing and withdrew from the British world of celebrity and fame, why 'fame was no longer the spur' (Milton). 'Fame is the spur … (The last infirmity of the noble mind)'. What kind of personal crisis had the once famous author slipped into?

Langsam began by providing a little more background about not many people knowing that Brickhill was an Australian born in Melbourne in 1916 and had spent most of his life living in Sydney. (This is still the case today.) He was 'invariably thought of' as British. The Australian *Who's Who* failed to list him while the International edition carried 'a respectable 14-line entry'.

In his long interview, Langsam, however, noticed that when his subject talked about his past war record and experiences, he nervously clutched his glass of Tab – thus indicating he suffered from what we now know as post-war traumatic stress syndrome. Brickhill claimed he kept no alcohol in the apartment and only had an odd drink 'with an old flying chum' when they were able to meet. He had remained the typical RAF veteran who does not like what he termed 'line-shooting'. Instead, he quickly and quietly related short amusing anecdotes about the past. Being well read, he offered the journalist carefully-considered opinions ranging from the Sinai peacekeeping force of the early 1980s that he felt could rapidly turn into some more serious conflict – he was right – to taxes and Government writing grants and the bias given to fiction writers. Clearly, he was well informed and kept up-to-date with the worlds of politics and literature, taking a deep interest in them. In his gentlemanly style, he was expansive to his guest about his own knowledge of affairs in the literary and political world spheres of life. For a while, he avoided more personal matters. He tended to set up a protective wall around himself – as we all may do in an interview intended for media outreach.

This also reflected his considerable international background in investigative journalism before and immediately after the Second World War. He said, however, at a more personal level that he felt too restless to listen much to radio or watch much television. He preferred the newspapers, a fondness for a form he had gained in his early experiences and had considerable achievements in.

He spent most of his time reading a wide range of books, both fiction and non-fiction, magazines and newspapers. He proudly displayed his daughter Tempe, the beautiful model of the month on the front cover of *Vogue* that was placed on top of a neat pile of magazines in his sitting room. This was a most impressive full-colour portrait of a beautifully attired model who had the direct and intelligent look of her mother. It was clear she was following in her mother's footsteps who had made an impressive appearance on the front cover of *People* in May 1953. The likeness of mother and daughter was remarkable. The *Vogue* cover carried the headline 'CELEBRATING the AUSTRALIAN WOMAN who you are now [—] your new priorities'. Under the portrait was 'Tempe Brickhill Model music student'.[10] No mention is made on the cover that she was the famous daughter of the great Australian writer Paul Brickhill, or indeed the daughter of the great London model Margot. She was there in her own right and her father was bursting with pride about his daughter and rightly so.

The sum total of Paul's concentrated research in the early 1960s was to produce an extra 12,000 words each for *The Great Escape* and *The Dam Busters* weaving in what had been left out due to the United Kingdom's Department of Defence secret classification when the two books were originally published in the early 1950s. This activity required significant research and editing.

Despite Brickhill taking on several projects since, nothing much was completed or finalised in any shape or form, despite the world-wide success of the three feature films based on his 1950s books. Nevertheless, he still had a vast collection of Second World War escape stories to tell that he had failed to capitalise on fully.

Reflecting on Past Fame

With an emotional effort, Brickhill recounted for the interviewer his celebrity experiences of the 1950s which he had now left behind: 'The Brickhills became part of the

10 *Vogue*, April 1981; Langsam, 'After the Crackup'.

London social set. Publishers and agents and all sorts of people wanted to meet them and they were expected to be generous and receive people, what Brickhill calls "wear the faces". He exposed his acute discomfort with being, along with his wife, a London celebrity.

Brickhill then claimed fervently:

> I never had any illusions about it. I used to have a quiet giggle to myself, of having to appear to be eminent, but I hadn't and still haven't basically changed. One is forced into a certain amount of it. When you've got so many irons in the fire you have to be 10 different people in two days and yet still retain one's own inner integrity or rather, sense of humor and to be able to laugh at the whole charade.

Clearly, a sense of integrity and humour were significant to Brickhill still at the age of sixty-five, despite having had his life travelling awkwardly and with difficult emotional strain since about 1955 or 1956.

One can only imagine how Paul Brickhill must have felt after receiving Electric Shock Therapy (EST) as a treatment used on occasions to alleviate his current mental condition during the troubled 1960s and 1970s. Ken Kesey, the American author, in his outstanding book *One Flew Over the Cuckoo's Nest* in 1962 graphically described the process:

> You are strapped to a table, shaped, ironically, like a cross, with a crown of electric sparks in place of thorns. You are touched on each side of the head with wires. Zap! Five cents' worth of electricity through the brain and you are jointly administered therapy and a punishment for your hostile go-to-hell behaviour, on

> top of being put out of everyone's way for six hours to three days, depending on the individual. Even when you do regain consciousness you are in a state of disorientation for days. You are unable to think coherently. You can't recall things. Enough of these treatments and a man could turn out [... a] drooling, pants-wetting idiot at thirty-five.[11]

With EST Paul Brickhill, on a number of occasions, felt he had wandered around, after the treatment, in a daze for at least two weeks. It was like the ragged edge of sleep – a grey zone between light and dark, or between sleeping and waking, or living and dying. The individual does not even know what day it is for a time. The person has to fight out of it intact, or risk losing the wholeness of a personality forever. The cure seemed worse than the problem, but EST was popular in Australia up

until the 1990s.

It would now be impossible to estimate the effect on Brickhill of EST, even taking into account that it was taken voluntarily on medical advice during the 1960s and 1970s – a prolonged troubled time for the famous author living alone at Balmoral Beach.

While EST was a popular treatment for many forms of mental illnesses in Paul Brickhill's day, psychiatry is nowadays leaning more towards cognitive and drug-intensive therapies. Whether that is a good thing, who can say.

11 Ken Kesey, *One Flew Over the Cuckoo's Nest,* The Folio Society, London, 2015, 67-8.

Brickhill himself claimed that his breakdown lasted twenty-five years during which time he volunteered to undertake different treatments including psychotherapy and EST. After this time and showing great courage, he decided in the early 1980s to talk about his condition publicly in an attempt to help others.[12] Brickhill's "coming out" was therapeutic in nature and, most probably, suggested by his psychiatrist or local medico. This, in turn, led to a trail of journalists to his upstairs flat, wanting to interview the once bestselling author.

One journalist wrote melodramatically that by the end of the sixties war books were passé and Brickhill, like the ruins of his Spitfire in the Tunisian Desert, was forgotten.[13] This cruel judgement was not completely true. All his books at the end of the sixties were still in print and selling well. Paperbacks of his six 1950s books were still popular – especially translations of *The Dam Busters* in French, Italian, Spanish, Greek and Czech. He had recently received a statue of Pan that some interviewing journalists were later to comment on when they gained an opportunity to interview him. The statuette was to commemorate his achievement as being the first author to sell over a million paperback copies of *The Dam Busters* for the publisher Pan-Macmillan. He also possessed a specially bound tribute copy of the book presented to him by the Royal Air Force.

Apart from *War of Nerves*, Paul Brickhill had stopped publishing after *Reach for the Sky* due to a variety of mental breakdowns that caused writer's block at the time. His readers, however, continued to see condensations of his 1950s books appearing in anthologies, omnibuses and so on, including the *Reader's Digest*.

---

12 'An author returns from his Great Escape', *Courier Mail*, 3 May 1982.
13 'An author returns from'.

He was never forgotten by the older military buffs of the Second World War as well as film enthusiasts of famous wartime movies like *The Dam Busters*, *Reach for the Sky* and *The Great Escape*. Many subsequent war films also heavily reflected influences from his books.

To visiting interviewing journalists who he trusted, he was genial, hospitable and generous with his time. These investigative journalists included Graham Cavanagh for the *Australian*; David Langsam with an intensive and extensive interview for the *Age*; John Hetherington on several occasions; Liz Porter and others.[14] To some, he opened his soul about his mental health problems.

Apart from the occasional series of investigative journalistic articles by writers who explored aspects of Brickhill's mental health problems in later years via interviews with the once famous author himself after his divorce, military historian Craig Wilcox, in more recent years, has uncovered evidence of Brickhill trying to resolve his personal psychological struggles. He had returned to Sydney permanently with his wife and two children in the late 1950s after a restless period moving from place to place in Europe, America and elsewhere. This was after completing *Reach for the Sky* and the extensive research it had entailed which seemed to have exhausted him mentally.

When he settled with his family in a magnificent home at Clareville near Avalon on the Northern Beaches at Pittwater, he was struggling to achieve a mental balance. At the same time, he was attempting to write his first novel. Unfortunately, his marriage was also falling apart due largely to post-traumatic stress from his wartime experience. He drank heavily and even sought

14 Others include: Graham Cavanagh, 'Paul Brickhill reaches for his pen again', *Australian*, 6 December 1969; Liz Porter, 'Dam Buster plans another war thriller', *Sunday Telegraph*, 15 July 1981.

spiritual help from the evangelistic Church Army, an Anglican mobile organisation who were visiting St Mark's Church. Brickhill attended their publicised 'Community Hymn Singing and Answers to Questions' session and later wrote that he had gained some spiritual benefit and insight from his contact from members of the Church Army and their outreach about depression and mental illness. And yet it was just not enough during a troubled time.

After the completion of his novel *The Deadline* – so aptly and ironically titled *War of Nerves* in America – Brickhill spent the rest of his life 'largely forgotten by his readers'. The Church Army publicity leaflet of the late 1950s revealed his early spiritual search,[15] which was later culminated in his sixties by regular Bible readings and the comfort of Sydney Carter's spiritual poem, "Anonymous".

Visits and Friends

In the late 1980s, Tony Humphrey was conducting a survey in the large block of flats on Balmoral Beach where Paul Brickhill lived by himself. Not realising that the great "larger-than-life" famous author lived in the fifth floor corner flat, he knocked on the door. With his usual courtesy and friendliness, Paul opened the door and participated in the survey. Tony then suddenly

15 Craig Wilcox, 'A leaflet signaled hope for the troubled author who had risen to fame with The Great Escape', *SL Magazine*, Winter 2012, State Library of New South Wales, 31.

realised who the man with the clipped moustache was. He had no expectation that he was living there so modestly. Tony stood in awe of him as he had read all of his books as a youth and admired them very much. He remembers, now in 2016 aged eighty-three, how Paul invited him into his flat and they had a most pleasant chat for an hour or so that Tony found most interesting. The discussion was relaxed and Paul told Tony some fascinating stories about World War II in a most rational way. Tony left thinking he had had a brush with fame – he had met a great man who had the spirit of generosity and had a keen sense of being an Australian. To Tony, Brickhill was every inch the dashing Australian Spitfire pilot of fable who had become a famed author and had lived a fascinating life.

Several others who knew Paul Brickhill responded to letters to the editor and articles placed in the *Manly Daily*, *North Shore Times* and the *Mosman Daily*. They regarded him as a gentle person who led a sometimes isolated and troubled life from the beginning of the sixties. He kept to himself much of the time.

"Meg", a respondent, recounted that she had met Paul Brickhill in the early sixties in the country town of Wagga Wagga where he was conducting a weekly radio program on the local wireless presenting wartime stories of daring and adventure. They became good friends for about three years, after which they parted company.

At the time they met, Paul was offered to stay on a sheep station outside of Wagga Wagga with some friends of "Meg"'s family. He happily bedded down on the homestead's vast verandah with views of the wide countryside landscape. This was much better than the claustrophobic atmosphere of a small hotel room in town.[16]

Back in Sydney, "Meg" visited the Brickhill family home at

16 Author's interview with "Meg", 22 February 2016.

Greenwich Point where Paul was staying temporarily in a one room apartment. She was able to find him a more appropriate accommodation at Balmoral Beach, Mosman, where he moved into the fifth floor flat and where he was to live for the rest of his life. He could go up to his door by the staircase that had large windows looking out to views of Middle Harbour which made him comfortable with his claustrophobia that plagued him on a daily basis. The flat had extensive views of Middle Harbour, the Sydney Heads and the sea beyond. It was light and airy with plenty of sunlight. It allowed him to look out at the landscape and seascape.

"Meg" and Paul frequently discussed his famous books. He gave her a collection of first editions. She had methods to calm him down when he became agitated, strategies to assist his depression and levels of high anxiety. Paul's younger brother and his wife told her privately that, since Paul had met her, he was a lot brighter and much less depressed – she had been able to achieve a better outlook for him, at least for a few years.

Unfortunately, other problems began to beset him and his mental health deteriorated. In the end, "Meg" felt she was not strong enough to cope and she had her own family responsibilities. She was about thirty-one when they met; he was about forty-eight. After three years of close friendship, they had to part company. She could not find the strength to endure such 'a troubled soul'. She was compelled to leave him, as kindly as possible, 'to his fate'.[17]

A recurring theme in Paul Brickhill's imagination, especially during the troubled 1960s to 1980s, was reflected in something Paul once wrote: 'It was an indefinite purgatory. Life marked time, but despair and emotions didn't'. And then there was

---

17 Correspondence from "Meg", 4 January 2016.

always a persistent undertone of fear.[18] He suffered from a wartime stress syndrome that never quite left him throughout the rest of his life.

On reflection as an older wiser man in 1982, Brickhill felt his greatest contribution to the world and to literature was his book *Reach for the Sky* – a detailed objective biography of the legless British RAF fighter pilot and POW – like Brickhill himself without the handicap – who was still very much alive. Brickhill told Langsam with great sincerity that he was 'most grateful and privileged' to be given 'the opportunity to be the medium for Bader's tale of determination and courage'. Brickhill was Bader's personal choice of author.

And Brickhill was acutely accurate about his subject's remarkable achievement. Many beautifully written passages in the book illustrate this:

> Getting into the cockpit was not the trouble he [the legless Douglas Bader] thought it might be. He put his foot into the slot at the side of the rear cockpit and Ross [his friend and sometimes co-pilot] gave him a heave up. Then, clutching the leather-padded rim of the cockpit with his left hand it was simple to grab his right calf and swing it over into the seat. He eased himself down delighting instantly in the old, familiar smell of an Avro [aircraft] cockpit, the blend of castor oil, dope, leather and metal that rolled the months back more subtly and potently than any other sense. Sitting in the familiar seat, eyeing instruments and crash-pad and taking the stick in his hand, sent a flush of enchantment through him. He set each foot on the rudder-bar and pushed each end in turn – it

18 Brickhill and Norton, *Escape to Danger*, 5.

> was easy; nerveless in the foot but sensitive in the shin and right thigh. He'd literally be flying by the seat of his pants.[19]

Much of Brickhill's writing in his publications presents the same conciseness, immediacy, sense of reality and verve. He was the master of dramatic narrative like Ernest Hemingway and John Buchan. There is nothing that can quite match Brickhill's exciting personal narratives of wartime adventure. He was always drawn to human drama within the broader themes of modern technological warfare making him one of the masters of popular historiography that remains memorable and, therefore, classic in the Homeric sense.

Troubles Soared and Fluctuated

For Brickhill, after *Reach for the Sky* was written, his troubles soared: he returned to Australia and did not like what he saw. He soon moved restlessly to New Zealand, Canada and Italy. By this time, he admitted he had been under immense strain for many years, some aspects of it dating back to the long stagnant, but threatening period he had spent in Stalag Luft III in eastern Germany during the war that left many, sometimes hidden, psychological scars. His marriage to Margot had turned problematic for both partners with no one to blame, especially as they were both public figures and, therefore, under more strain because of it.

Brickhill courageously opened up about his personal problem of mental illness on occasions. He kept on emphasising the immense strain he had been under. Early in his life, even before the war, he described the 'obsession' he had in his journalistic

19 Brickhill, *Reach for the Sky*, 102.

work with the Sydney *Sun*. No doubt this was also a desire to succeed in a profession owned by his family – both his father and grandfather were pioneering and eminent journalists. Nevertheless, in the 1982 interview by Langsam, Brickhill was in the mood for self-analysis well aware that he would be revealing much of his mystery to the general public if Langsam was prepared to publish an entirely frank account of their conversation.

He recounted his study of aviation during his training at Narrandera and Ottawa. He had been bored with the theory of meteorology classes, he told the interviewer, and spent the time daydreaming of flying (like the heroes of his books, Douglas Bader, Guy Gibson, Micky Martin and others). Despite this, he had great success with an examination essay he wrote for the theory course at Ottawa. His instructor told him, because of his writing skill, his paper was forwarded to air force headquarters with the recommendation that it become a standard training manual. In other words, he had succeeded brilliantly in the theory of elements of the Empire Air Training Scheme.

The interview by Langsam, as recorded in the media in its jump-start narrative of events, then jumped to the end of the war. It was pointed out that Brickhill, while still in uniform, was given leave from the RAF to report on the European situation for the Sydney *Sun*. This seemed to be part of his personal repatriation to civilian life. He opened up 'that he had difficulty mustering up the courage to climb on board a bus'. He was clearly suffering from post traumatic stress from his war experiences, especially as a prisoner-of-war at Sagan. 'As were many others, the war had taken its toll'.

Nevertheless, Brickhill stated that he enjoyed his posting to New York after being demobilised from the RAAF (via the RAF in London). On returning to Australia to take up a sub-editor position with the daily paper in Sydney, he found it 'a bloody misery' in which his nervous problems exploded as the routine work bored him.

Consequently, he returned to London in 1949 and on the way he met and later married Margot Slater. She was 'an Australian who became a model for the prestigious showroom of Norman Hartnell' and, therefore, became a celebrity like himself in the London social scene. He pointed out that he rapidly wrote four books one immediately after the other, and then returned to Australia. Their son Timothy Paul was born in 1954 and Tempe in 1957. By 1956, the Brickhills had travelled to Florence, Italy. Paul by this time was suffering badly from high blood pressure, depression and extreme tension. A fashionable Italian doctor who he consulted prescribed Reserpine. This later became well known in the medical world as a potentially dangerous drug for patients suffering from depression, but it was one of the few available at that time for some treatments.[20] Paul Brickhill was forty years old at the time.

Much concern later would arise about Reserpine actually causing further deep depression that could lead to suicide. This was reported mainly in uncontrolled studies using heavy dosages. Reserpine could cause nasal congestion, nausea, vomiting, weight gain, gastric intolerance, gastric ulceration, stomach cramps and diarrhoea. The drug was reported as actually causing hypotension, rather than preventing it, and also bradycardia. It could even worsen asthma. It created drowsiness, dizziness and nightmares. Brickhill already suffered from these because of his war experiences. Such were the side effects of the drug, some of which Brickhill was to suffer from after taking the intensive treatment in Florence.

Reserpine was isolated in 1952 from the dried root of *Rauwolfea serpentina* (Indian snakeroot), but it had been used

---

20 Langsam, 'After the Crackup'.

for centuries in India for the treatment of insanity and snake bites. Reserpine was later discontinued in the United Kingdom due to its perceived side effects. In some countries it is still available as part of a combination of drugs for the treatment of hypertension.

At sixty-five, Brickhill still believed that the Italian treatment of Reserpine triggered what he defined as his quarter-century breakdown. This would be difficult to verify now, but for eight weeks in Italy Brickhill received the Reserpine treatment and suffered what he called 'the horrors'. The interviewer noted that Brickhill 'got up from the armchair' at this point in the conversation. His face was red, his knuckles white:

> 'Right, right, okay …' he said, steadying himself. 'I'd have to go to the doctor, in Florence, for an intravenous injection of the stuff every second day just to hang on.
>
> 'For the next two years, I couldn't get myself organised and then when I began to come out of it, I discovered that I had entirely lost my easy conscience as a writer'.

In other words (or lack of them), Brickhill found that his troubles included the mysterious, but very real disablement of what has been widely described as 'writer's block'.

He found this a 'ghastly' condition as all his adult life, before and after the war, had been spent writing to a deadline. His earlier book had come to him easily: 'I started at the beginning and went on blithely through'. But now he found he did not know what he was doing, he was so disoriented in his mind. This would have been difficult for the man to admit as it cut through to the core of his being. He courageously admitted that the condition lasted about twenty-five years with various ups and downs. At times he found he could not even write letters. But some days were clear days and then he was able to write a letter or two.

The complete structuring of a book, however, seemed on most days to be beyond him despite the fact that many times he thought of ambitiously writing down his ideas – his mind was still a fertile, imaginative place – but he found it impossible to get any of them out fully. Book writing progressively became an impossibility. He claimed optimistically that he suddenly found his way out of it all when he was about sixty-three. The darkened clouds that had hovered in his mind began to lift and disappear and he was ready and eager for the work of writing again for the first time in many, many years.

From that moment, he began to address a vast backlog of correspondence that had come in his mailbox at the bottom of his five-story block of flats. It was piled neatly in one of his rooms. He did not throw anything away. He had obligations he wanted to fulfil, including resuming neglected friendships which had previously come his way as a famous author. Unfortunately, many had already passed away.

Awareness of Self

Brickhill's awareness of himself was clearly articulated to his interviewer Langsam. He said: 'I am aware now if I allow myself to become overstressed in any way, I will not be able to get anything done. And this is a terrifyingly difficult thing to explain to anyone'.

The advice people had given him, he soon found was worthless: 'Just sit down to the typewriter and write. It'll come. But it's not that easy…', he exclaimed. Several weeks before, he saw on television an interview with Don Dunstan, the former Premier of South Australia. Likening Dunstan's illness to his own, he noted that Dunstan had collapsed two years before and his doctors had told him that 'if ever he got himself into any stress again, it was going to knock him flat'. Brickhill found this analysis 'quite, quite true' in his own case:

> People may not understand, but I find that if I get one little bit extra of stress, like a straw on a camel's back, I find that I can get nothing done. I cannot even read. And that's exactly what happens to me. As soon as I'm in overload, when I'm obliged or when people want me to do so-and-so I've got to withdraw and keep a low profile.

The discussion then shifted to his last publication of 1962, his first novel *The Deadline* which he appeared very disappointed with. It was a book, according to the interviewer, he did not really want to talk about. The book started well enough – as Brickhill put it – but as the pressure mounted from the publishers and others to have it completed, he found it impossible to cope 'with the increased strain'. At the same time, his marriage was falling apart. Margot had decided to pursue her own career separately. She was a highly intelligent and accomplished woman. The couple separated and later divorced.

It was about at this time that he moved from his family home on the Northern Beaches of Sydney. Later, he purchased a new apartment for himself at Balmoral Beach where he was to live alone for the rest of his life. He remained tight-lipped about his marriage or blamed it on his mental problems.

The days he spent since his divorce in 1964 involved taking an occasional swim and walking a mile or two every day – a matter of getting out in the fresh air away from the confines of his comfortable flat by the beachside. By 1982 and suffering increasingly from health problems, he found the later forms of exercise too difficult and tended to stay indoors except for visits to the doctor and hospital treatment. But, as an aging man, he felt there was no need to get too excited about anything. The royalties of the reprints of his books kept coming in making him financially comfortable. He now spent his days just coping with the world around him since he felt he could no longer write, or need to anyway.

His spiritual life seemed to have altered for the better. He was much influenced by Sydney Carter's religious poem "Anonymous". Its concepts were life-changing for him. He reflected on the poem, neatly dividing his spiritual life into three phases: in the air force on the battle front, he was an atheist; at Stalag Luft III as a prisoner-of-war, he became an agnostic, and later, during a very difficult time, he came to believe in a supreme being or force. This did not mean that he found conventional Christianity acceptable. He was turned away from the church in terms of regular attendance as it filled his new-found belief with unnecessary guilt.

The words of the songwriter and poet Sydney Carter in his work "Anonymous" were constantly evocative for him and opened up a new form of spirituality which he related to with ease:

> Forget my name is Jesus
> From now on I
> I am anonymous
> Do not trust people who
> hang me like a millstone
> round your neck.
> Do not look at me but
> what I am pointing to.
> The Jesus who
> keeps saying 'I am Jesus,
> look at me
> there is no substitute'
> is an imposter. Do not trust
> the Christ cult of
> personality, I came
> to turn you on and not
> to turn you off,
> to make you free and not
> to tie you up.
> My yoke was easy and
> my burden light
> until they make
> salvation copyright, and
> all in the name of Jesus.
> So forget

my name was Jesus,
From now on
I am anonymous.[21]

By accident, Brickhill discovered the Carter poem in a book he received in the mail from his publisher – a quasi-religious English song book *Blueprint*. It contained exercises in comprehension and creative writing. The poem seemed to have a profound, calming effect on Brickhill's life, in his later years now a man in his sixties and ailing physically and mentally. For him, "Anonymous" was a lesson about a depersonalised, non-judgemental god. It made more sense to him than conventional church life and encouraged him in feeling not alone in his belief.

Brickhill took to reading the Bible with newly-discovered vigour, he revealed to Langsam, and realised that his ability to dig and research was, somehow, still intact. He had started in a most private way to make a comeback to what he really was: 'I have always been determined I would not give up. Only once in 1978 [he revealed] did I think: "Don't kid yourself, you're not going to make it". Then things began to open up'.

Langsam started to realise, as the interview in the cosy Balmoral Beach apartment at 'Stancliff" continued, that his

21 Songwriter Sydney Carter (1915-2005) was a member of the Society of Friends (Quakers) and lived in England where he died aged 88. He achieved the remarkable feat of composing two of the most popular songs sung by British school assemblies all over the United Kingdom, one being "Lord of the Dance" (1963) – an adaptation of a Quaker hymn. Carter was a folk poet of the people, a holy sceptic and an iconoclastic theologian which were characteristics that seemed to appeal to Brickhill in his final years. Carter satirised self-righteous faith to be without doubt, he argued, was godless pride. He wrote two books, *The Rock of Doubt* (1978) and *Dance in the Dark* (1980) which may have appealed to Brickhill: 'Follow where the bird has gone/ If you want to find him, keep travelling on'.

subject's 'devastating emotional problems' now seemed to be a thing of the past. And yet emotionally he swung like a pendulum during the exhausting interrogation. The man was courageously catching up on the twenty-five-year backlog of unanswered mail. And fan letters were still pouring into his mailbox from a wide range of countries. At his age, he was looking forward to completing a new book.

Towards the end of the long interview, he told Langsam that his new book was completely researched and eighty percent was written (and had been for some years). But now he was determined to finish it and have it published. He may have been inspired by the interview itself. Since his death, the manuscript remains undiscovered and undisturbed.

He would not talk to Langsam about its contents: 'I don't want to call my shots'. He was confident, nevertheless, that it would have a market when completed. He had no doubts that publishers would be keenly competing for it. It would be Brickhill's first major work in nearly thirty years. Sadly, it never was.

Shown to the door of the flat with 'a twitch of his moustache and a shake of his left index finger', Langsam was farewelled by Brickhill in the best RAAF tradition: 'Now mind, no line shooting [in your article, stick to the truth], all right?'[22] As Langsam left the towering block of flats, his mind was still full of the stunning outlook, the panoramic view and light of Brickhill's apartment and the generous living/dining room together with its three bedrooms, all neatly organised.

Long after Brickhill's death in 1991, the flat was to be extensively renovated and sold, perhaps again in 2015. The remains of the author's life had totally disappeared, but he was still known affectionately to other residents living in the

22 Langsam, 'After the Crackup'.

complex. He had been the distinguished author for many years with his gentlemanly friendliness and impressive style. His fame rubbed off on his neighbours and they were immensely proud of him.

The Amphitheatre and Peter Finch

Langsam may have recognised the irony expressed on the historical plaque on the beachside below the massive building:

> Amphitheatre
> This was the site of "The Amphitheatre" an open air temple completed in 1924 by the Order of the Star of the East, a branch of the Theosophical Society, whose leading members were Charles Leadbeater and Jiddu Krishnamurti. The temple was demolished in 1951.
> – Mosman Municipality No 11

The information on the plaque raises interesting connections as it was the Reverend Charles W Leadbeater who brought the infant Peter Finch, Brickhill's closest childhood friend, to Sydney by ship at the bequest of his grandmother and placed him in the Theosophical infants boarding school, The Manor, at Mosman.

> The Manor in Mosman is a huge Victorian building overlooking Sydney Harbour [as Brickhill's flat later was] … It was here that CW Leadbeater, an old Oxonian and formerly an English vicar and now a self-styled bishop, had embraced the trappings and rituals of the Catholic Church without the hellfire and brimstone and founded the Liberal Catholic Church … In February 1926 when Peter [Finch aged 9] arrived, the mixed community of children and adults

> staying at The Manor were given courses in Esperanto (world language), Astrology, Art, the reading of the Bhagavad Gita and Meditation. In other words, ideas, ideas, ideas were buzzing around The Manor like flies. But first, Peter had to learn to read and write English.[23]

It is an intriguing question to ask how much the slightly older Brickhill was influenced in childhood by his young friend's worldview. We will never know. Something, somehow, must have attracted Brickhill, from about the age of forty, to choose to live the rest of his life on the same site as the Open Temple since demolished.

When Brickhill and Finch, as young sixteen-year-olds, were fellow cub reporters at the *Sun*, Finch took Wednesday afternoons off to attend acting classes at Mosman. They were likely conducted at the Star Temple in its meeting rooms beneath the building by some forgotten acting company. When he considered buying the flat at "Stancliff" did Brickhill consider these connections?

Be that as it may, the year before Langsam conducted his revealing and extensive interview with the once famous author, journalist Liz Porter in her newspaper article with the rather misleading banner heading 'Dam Buster plans another war thriller' revealed more about the author's proposed new book: 'Best-Selling Australian war novelist [*sic*] Paul Brickhill is about to make a literary comeback – with a story even more thrilling than The Great Escape'. The article was accompanied by a smiling portrait of the moustached Brickhill holding in his right hand a large model of a four-engined Lancaster bomber of Second World War vintage (see p.257). The caption helpfully reads: 'Paul Brickhill with a model of a Lancaster bomber, the

23 Dundy, *Finch, Bloody Finch*, 41.

plane that featured in "The Dam Busters"'. The photograph tended to dominate the written article along with the banner headline. Above it is a sympathetic comment: 'After 20 years forced break, Paul Brickhill is back at his typewriter'.

A New Book?

After claiming Brickhill had hardly touched his typewriter of twenty years and been able to live comfortably on the proceeds of bestsellers like *The Dam Busters*, *Reach for the Sky* and *Escape – or Die*, Porter reports eagerly that he is writing another biography like the Douglas Bader saga. Nearly every journalist including Porter implied that Brickhill was royalties rich.

In the interview with Langsam a year later, Brickhill was cagey about the subject of this new book. Not so when he was subjected to probing but charming questions by the intrepid Liz Porter who had taken her photographer along with her to the flat at "Stancliff" Balmoral Beach. 'The new book will be a biography of an old friend called John Dodge', he had openly stated to her. She revealed to her newspaper audience that: 'Mr Brickhill, a former World War II fighter pilot who still sports a natty RAF style moustache met the talented soldier spy when they were inmates in the German Stalag Luft Three prisoner-of-war camp'.

She informs the public that Dodge was an American cousin by marriage of Winston Churchill and quotes that Brickhill described him as a tall, handsome twenty-year-old in 1914. At the start of the First World War, he got on the first ship to England from New York and four weeks later he was in action in the Dardanelles, Brickhill narrates freely to Porter. Dodge fought on Gallipoli, was three times wounded and decorated twice. He was naturalised as English through his mother and stepfather, but he never lost his connections with the United States. He completed the war as a Lieutenant-Colonel and became the youngest battalion commander in the British Army. Brickhill continued with a summary of his subsequent story: 'Two or three years later he was captured by the Bolshevik secret police in Russia and was imprisoned, [and yet] escaping by an extraordinary means'.

As soon as the Second World War was declared, 'he camped on the steps of the War Office'. In his forties he was offered a staff job with a brigadier rank, but he dropped back to major so he could be in combat. In France, he was rounded up by the Gestapo after the country had fallen to the Nazi invasion. He ended up in a death cell at Sachsenhausen concentration camp in Germany near Berlin. Sachenhausen K2 was one of the newly expanded concentration camps by the Gestapo as ordered by Reichs-führer Heinrich Himmler. Many died in this camp after having been systematically tortured and few escaped.[24] Dodge expected to be taken out at any moment and shot.

'He was taken out all right!' claimed Brickhill to Porter, 'but was finally released and given a secret message [close to the end of the war] to his cousin Winston Churchill in London'. He was, in fact, carrying a secret peace proposal from sections of the Nazi government wishing to give in. They knew that they were about to be defeated. According to Brickhill, as Dodge travelled east through Nazi occupied territory, he 'got into all sorts of adventures and was in and out of Gestapo hands all the way'. There are touches of John Buchan and Ian Fleming about Brickhill's oral account to Porter. He quickly pointed out that John Dodge finally reached London safely and was subsequently awarded the Military Cross for bravery.

In response, Porter noted that all Paul Brickhill's books drew heavily on his war experiences and then she gave her readers a

24 Peter Longerich, *Heinrich Himmler,* trans. by Jeremy Noakes & Lesley Sharpe, Oxford University Press, 2012, 242, 246-7, 482.

quick summary of their contents: about how he was shot down over Tunisia and ended up in Stalag Luft III which gave him the insider's view to enable him to write *The Great Escape*, 'a gripping and true story of a brilliantly-conceived mass escape'.

Brickhill told Porter something of his experience in the German prison camp more than forty years earlier: 'I was in charge of security of the forgers who needed to work by a window in good light'. And then he added: 'But I missed out on the draw for the escape tunnel' – in retrospect not such bad luck; of the seventy-odd who escaped only three 'made their way to freedom'. The rest were recaptured and fifty were executed under Hitler's direct orders. Then Brickhill talked about how he was shot down in North Africa in the first place after he was shot in the back by an enemy plane. He then pointed out fiercely that his new book was 'well on the way', but admitted: 'Largely because of ill-health I haven't written anything of substance for years'. Porter recognised that 'churning out four highly-researched best-sellers in as many years took a heavy toll on Brickhill'. He opened up about this issue: 'By the time Reach for the Sky came out in 1954 I was coming apart at the seams'.

But at the time of her interview, a 'peaceful atmosphere' prevailed in Brickhill's Balmoral Beach flat, 'with its magnificent beach and harbour views' where the ex-RAAF man was 'throwing himself back into writing again'. Porter noted that his 1950s books were still in print and readily available overseas – but, ironically, hard to find in Australia even though he was an Australian author.[25] In his home country he was very much a forgotten man.

It seems that the biography of John Dodge was never completed or the whole manuscript was lost somehow after

25 Liz Porter, 'Dam Buster plans another war thriller', *Sunday Telegraph*, March 15, 1981.

Brickhill's death in 1991 when his possessions were removed from his flat. Either way, it never saw the light of day. It is, however, clear that after a long hiatal gestation Brickhill had decided to combine a biography à la *Reach for the Sky* with a wartime and espionage thriller. Already in *The Great Escape*, he had touched on the American-born and educated John Doyle, especially in the final chapters and had subsequently become fascinated with his full life story, but it was ultimately not to be.

* * *

It is clear that, from the time Paul Brickhill settled into his Balmoral Beach flat in the early 1960s, he was at times to live a troubled existence and endure a prolonged struggle to maintain his mental balance. Between 1960 and his death in 1991, he received intermittent press coverage and consideration. Sometimes, there were excited reports about a new book on the way and film rights.

At other times, there was hostile press with harsh headlines such as: 'Author: Golden Days over',[26] and even an obituary: 'Writer's ambitions unfulfilled'.[27] Sometimes, he was subjected to interviewers who sensationalised or exaggerated vital matters. In a strange sense, the once famed Australian author, somehow, remained newsworthy.

It was clear he was a troubled, uncertain man full of contradictions and vague ambitions whose literary success in the public eye was long behind him. In poor health, his marriage gone, depression often beset him. The last years of his life were often obscured by the legend of his early glamour as a writer which had dramatically emerged in the early 1950s. After all, he

26 *West Australian*, 2 December 1969.
27 Newspaper Obituary unidentified, Archives, Paul Brickhill file, Australian War Memorial, Canberra.

had coined terms like "the great escape" and "the dambusters". And yet his claimed work on the adventures of John Dodge "The Dodger" was an exciting and captivating new beginning just like Fleming's discovery of James Bond, his fictitious super hero.

His reported interviews with the press provided, nevertheless, an almost unbearably bitter-sweet portrait of an aging, but once great author whose repartee still gleamed with wit. And yet he was still very much of the 1950s era with its emphasis on social-realistic, true-to-life, but comfortingly idealistic war stories from the perspective of the triumph of the Allies over the evils of the Nazis. Brickhill continued to inhabit this world passionately from his point of view with great authenticity.

Every now and then, the press claimed loudly that the author had reached for his pen again. In early 1967, the *Canberra Times* announced that Australian author, the famed author of *The Great Escape*, was preparing a script for a new film on RAF POWs in Germany during the Second World War. This proposal followed on the tail of the popularity of the feature film by director John Sturges *The Great Escape* (1963) starring Richard Attenborough, Steve McQueen, James Garner, Charles Bronson and James Coburn with a screenplay by bestselling author James Clavell of *Shogun* fame (also an ex-POW), but based on Paul Brickhill's book in all its nuances.

The new but totally different screenplay, announced in January 1967, was to be based on a real-life hero Wing-Commander Harry Melville Day DSO, OBE, who had been in Stalag Luft III (the location of *The Great Escape*) with Paul Brickhill. Like the author, Day had survived the war within the prison camp. By this time, he had a holiday villa in Monaco while normally a resident of England. Day travelled to Australia to discuss the script of the proposed new movie with Brickhill himself.

Brickhill told the journalists that the story of the proposed film would be about 'an RAF officer prisoner in Germany during the war'. He said the script would be ready in two or three months and the film would be produced in America by an American company. He also pointed out that after completing the screenplay, he would follow up with a book of the film (not the other way as before). The media noted that the author's three earlier books had been made into highly successful films.[28] Like many other Hollywood projects, it was never accomplished despite its potential.

Reaching for the Pen Again

In 1969 again, Graham Cavanagh, in the *Australian*, wrote the headliner: 'Paul Brickhill reaches for his pen again'. Cavanagh solemnly and dramatically announced that in early December Paul Brickhill had come 'out of his non-writing exile yesterday'. The author had announced he had returned to serious writing sixteen years after his last major work. Brickhill confessed that he had pulled out of the 'rat race' and had 'been sitting around' ever since: 'But it's no kind of life, so I go back to work', he said in an interview by the *Australian* journalist in Melbourne Port on the Italian liner *Galileo* that had just arrived. He said he was on his way to his 'little pad' in Sydney (on Balmoral Beach). He argued that he had been away from writing as there was no point working for the 'tax collector all the time'. He claimed that, because 'you have' written books that had been made into motion films you were 'rolling in money'. He went on in this vein referring to the cost of lawyers, accountants, agents, friends, relatives and tax collectors. Such situations made a 'pretty big dent [financially]in the whole thing'.

He argued strongly that a writer needed 'isolation and freedom' to work, to be fully productive and it was a dilemma

28 'Brickhill's new film', *Canberra Times*, 27 January 1967.

he felt keenly. There were troubles that came with earning large amounts of cash – he noted that in one year he had earned a quarter of a million dollars, but this situation was problematic. He felt at times that he was taken for a 'sucker' because of his fame in editions of *Who's Who*: 'I just got sick ... of all the bums and bludgers that gathered around...'.

He described *The Deadline* (1962) as a lesser work after great international success of his earlier works. He had great plans for his comeback with three books – two novels with a war base, one that would be made into a film by a Hollywood independent film company and the third non-fictional.

With his interviewer, Brickhill investigated the problems of writing. He pointed out that many people tried to write books, but rarely succeeded because they had daytime jobs that drained away mental energy as well as family responsibilities and activities. Then he pointed out that too many books were being published anyway and only few sold well. In England, he noted, there were 30,000 new titles a year – booksellers at the other end of the production line were faced with 500 new titles a week.

In this context, Brickhill had great success behind him. He was the second writer in the world, he claimed, to sell a million copies in paperback – *The Dam Busters*. The first was a new translation of Homer's *Iliad* written 2,000 years ago. Brickhill had calculated roughly that some five million full copies of his books in seventeen languages had been sold.[29]

A Legend in his Lifetime

At the time of his death, it seemed overly-easy for some fashionable critics to ignore or dismiss Paul Brickhill's

29 Graham Cavanagh, 'Paul Brickhill reaches for his pen again', *Australian*, 12 December 1969.

achievements as a writer. Between 1982 and 1991, his life had swung like an 'uneasy pendulum' between two extremes – to steal his own metaphor about Douglas Bader in *Reach for the Sky*.[30] But he was no recluse as the media often portrayed him. When he thought too much, he had giant moods and depression brought on largely by post-traumatic stress of war having been shot down and injured, having experienced life in a German prisoner-of-war camp and the treacherous long march to freedom. The repairing medical treatment he received in Brighton had proven quite inadequate, especially in the psychic sense for his rehabilitation and return to civic life. Fears remained with the wartime hero.

While Brickhill tried to resume his journalistic career after the war and achieving much as a foreign correspondent, he remained intensely troubled. Fame as a writer of best-selling non-fiction books in the first half of the 1950s took its toll – fame had a price to pay. But if his books seem to some as old-fashioned and in a genre of writing that became less fashionable (at least in its non-fiction form), his books have several virtues: they remain concisely written in the style of Ernest Hemingway; they are intensely gripping, well-researched narratives and form an impressive body of work that defined major sub-genres – escape stories. Brickhill excels in using the theme of courage against adversity in modern total warfare and played a major part in creating the popular historiography of the Second World War. He is a key reference in several modern war histories about Bomber Command.

Some revisionists have only chipped away at the edges of this solid 'if popular myth that Paul Brickhill helped to pour into the concrete' of memorials.[31] The author's golden days were never

30 Brickhill, *Reach for the Sky*, 69.

31 John Ellis, Obituary 'Paul Brickhill "Fears of a wartime hero"', *Guardian*, 5 May 1991.

over and are embedded in the time-slip of three enormously classical, but very British movies, *The Dam Busters*, *Reach for the Sky* and *The Great Escape*, and continue to be replicated and reinforced in many others, both British and American.

During the last decades of his life, Brickhill continued to reach for his pen and work on several projects. There were developed ideas about new books and films during the span between 1962 and 1991. But who could judge this man? He struggled courageously on, alone and lonely, in his Balmoral Beach flat.

It should not be forgotten that his boyhood dreams with his school friend Peter Finch were fully and magnificently realised. Paul Brickhill's great days never really left him. His great books took on a life of their own in many different languages and serve to be fine explorations of the nature of warfare and of courage in warfare.

It is no wonder that, like Homer's *Iliad*, they sold millions of copies and have a place of honour in public libraries and second hand bookshops. (Somewhere in the world, they still remain in print.)

Paul Brickhill lived a lonely life between the 1960s and his death in 1991 in his upstairs three-bedroom flat above the beach and yet the sky-blue days at Balmoral Beach were ample recompense and had the fortunate sense to him of living in a private Eden. The once renowned author died quietly one evening alone with the view of the Sydney Heads before him.

* * *

The funeral service for Paul Chester Jerome Brickhill was held at St Clement's Anglican Church Mosman on 29 April 1991 at 2.30pm. Elegies were presented by Lloyd Brickhill, Paul's brother, and Alan Jones, the well-known radio commentator.

Psalm 23 was read by Paul's son Timothy Brickhill. The service was conducted by Reverend John G Mason. June Imrie played the organ accompaniment to the hymns "Praise My Soul, The King of Heaven" and "As pants the hart for cooling streams".[32]

The assembled congregation gave thanks for the life of Paul Brickhill.

A few weeks after the funeral, Paul's youngest brother Clive was able to summarise subtly and with sensitivity the trials and tribulations of his brother's life that strikes an authentic note:

> From the excitement but stress of combat, to the trauma of being shot down with injuries, the horror of being trapped on the plane, the three [*sic*] years of imprisonment not knowing when he would be released, the restricted diet, the uncertainty, the shooting of 50 of his friends, the awful march under armed guard through a couple of hundred miles of snow freezing, the collapse of friends to be put in carts, these insults piled on top of each other left him a mental mess by the time he got to England where I believe he became very difficult when challenged with the slightest frustration as he interpreted the service procedure and discipline.
>
> Paul recovered enough to write his books, to marry Margo and have two beautiful children. But the scars were embedded and further stresses eventually caught up with him. As a psychiatrist who treated him in Sydney told me: 'Paul's capacity to withstand stress is marginal. Paul's early treatment from doctors I suspect did not help, with loads of

32 Copy of funeral service provided by June Imrie of Mosman.

> pills switching from one to the other [...] There is no doubt in my mind that Paul's war experiences were the basic cause of his post-war problems.[33]

In his last months his older brother Lloyd noted, after seeing him, that he was recovering sufficiently to put 'his business affairs in order', but more than that to re-establish with Tempe and Timothy 'the warm, loving and rewarding relationship' which had been 'too often strained' especially when he experienced mental and physical health problems. This brought him 'a peace and contentment he had not known for many years'. He told Lloyd that he had 'achieved all he wanted out of life'. He died alone in his flat less than two weeks later.[34]

---

33 Clive Brickhill to Tempe and Tim, Toowoomba Qld, 11 May 1991.
34 Lloyd Brickhill, eulogy to Paul Brickhill, 24 April 1991.

BOOKS TO FILMS

CHAPTER 9

THE DAM BUSTERS: BOOK TO FILM

The Return

When Paul and Margot arrived in Melbourne as Australian celebrities from London in August 1953, he had just finished writing the draft biography of the famous war hero Douglas Bader, who had lost both legs before the Second World War. Despite this, he had become an iconic legendary RAF fighter pilot of the Battle of Britain and other exploits. Paul Brickhill told the eager journalists who came aboard their ship to interview him that the provisional title of his fifth book was '*Reach for the Sky*'. He had a great ability to select the right title as a selling point on the cover of a book.

Already, he had published the bestsellers *Escape to Danger* (with Conrad Norton), *The Great Escape*, *The Dam Busters* and *Escape – or Die*. He was then the biggest best-selling and best-known author worldwide of war books that told of realistic but exciting air raids behind the lines into the enemy territory and equally gripping escape stories from prisoner-of-war camps during the war. In the titles of three of these books was the expressive word ESCAPE and it was what the people were wanting to read about as non fiction after the war.

In the public eye, Brickhill was a superb war book man and so Australian newspaper men swarmed into his cabin, full of excitement about a home-grown celebrity as soon as he arrived in the Melbourne dock on the *Orontes*.

Being a dapper moustached shrewd journalist of eminence in the newspaper world, Brickhill knew he needed a surprising opening story to tell that would sell copy and excite readers. Knowing how to build excitement and arresting news stories with the press, he gravely announced he had ambitious plans to change direction completely and write three books about Australia and therefore 'give away' writing war thrillers. One proposed book was to be about living in the city and two were to be about country life since he had experienced both in Sydney and Narrandera before going to England in the RAAF. Whether they would be fiction or non-fiction he did not disclose and now we will never know as they were not completed, or perhaps not even started.

Brickhill's public comments suggest some uncertainty about his writing future and an anxiety about being prolific, of keeping up the pace in writing and publishing he had already established in the previous four years or so. Maybe he also wanted to blot war entirely out of his mind.

His second disclosure to the excited press followed swiftly. He said the plans to make a feature film version of 'The Dam Busters' had begun, but they seemed to have been curtailed or delayed somewhat when the new Three Dimensional (3-D) film industry had been introduced by Hollywood (and the possible flight sequences of *The Dam Busters* story would have been particularly appropriate, perfect for a 3-D adaptation, but this was never to be).

In his final statement, he revealed that film options had also been sold for *The Great Escape*.[1] It was, however, to take another ten years for this to be accomplished and released as a film.

A few days earlier, the Brickhills aboard the *Orontes* had passed through Fremantle on their way to Melbourne. There Paul was lauded by the local press as Australia's most successful author: 'He has had four best sellers in "The Dam Busters", "The Great Escape", "Escape – or Die" and [originally] "Escape to Danger"'. Another book that the press described as just finished 'tells the story of the famous legless Battle of Britain fighter pilot, Group Capt. Douglas Bader – "Tin Legs Bader" who is still flying in his civilian job'.

Clearly, the press felt that he had picked another big winner and they were right. They also commented: 'Mr Brickhill now intends to concentrate on a book with an Australian setting'. No mention in the Western Australian press at this time was made about film rights for the author's books. He decided not to mention them. At the Fremantle stopover, however, he did mention that he was bound for Sydney after 'four years of almost non-stop writing in England',[2] producing four books and

---

1 'No New Thrillers', *Argus* (Melbourne), 20 August 1953.

2 'Popular Writer Plans Book on Australia', *West Australian* (Perth), 14 August 1953.

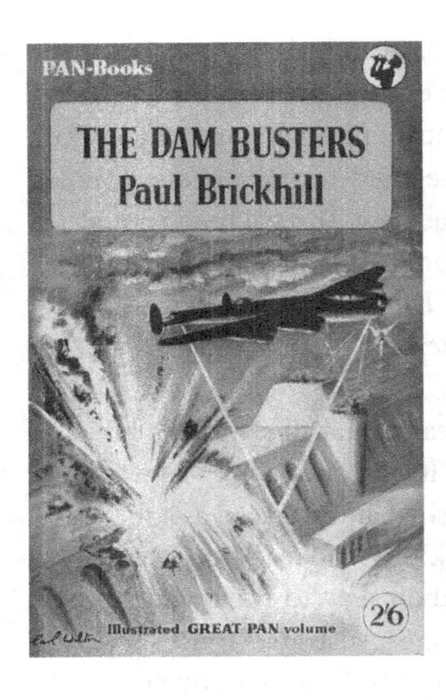

one completed and accepted manuscript – *Reach for the Sky* – which was to be released early the following year in March 1954.

Hitting the Jackpot?

The well-dressed, cravat-wearing Brickhill (as shown in his newspaper photograph) was frequently depicted in the mid-1950s by the press as the Australian writer who had 'hit the jackpot', a gambling term meaning great success. Described as 'dapper', he was characterised as 'the most successful author in Britain'. Like other authors, he was required by publishers to promote the sale of his books, making him a public figure. The news media soon picked up that Brickhill had gained £15,000 for the film rights of *The Dam Busters*.[3] He earned the same amount for the film rights of *Reach for the Sky* gained in October 1954 only about eight months after its first release as a book.[4] One correspondent for the *Sydney Morning Herald* claimed by late November that year that Brickhill had earned nearly £70,000 for the book sales and serial and film rights.[5]

The Dam Busters, *The Great Escape* and then *Reach for the Sky* became dramatised radio serials in Australia as precursors

3 'Australian Writer "Hits Jackpot"', *Advertiser* (Adelaide), 19 October 1954.
4 'Australian Author's Big Success', *Chronicle* (Adelaide), 21 October 1954.
5 'Big Sales for Air Ace Book', *SMH*, 22 November 1954.

to the feature films, thus building a strong audience response and following that culminated in crowded picture theatres when the feature films were shown to mass audiences. The public could not get enough of the portrayal in drama of the 'magnificent courage and gallantry' of war airmen, either in the air or underground in escape tunnels.

The serials of the three books were broadcast at the height of the popularity of radio drama in Australia before the introduction of television. In early September 1954 'Radio Round-up' acclaimed:

> Mr Paul Brickhill must have completely pixilated [Station] 5AD. On Wednesday evening the station gave the first episode of yet another radio adaptation of one of that gentleman's novels ... "The Dam Busters" and "The Great Escape" gave us some excellent radio [drama] and this third offering "Reach for the Sky" looks like doing the same.

The critic felt that it was unfortunate that the serial was limited to being broadcast a half-hour per week on commercial radio. The first episode ended 'on that tragic day when, for a 10/- bet the airman attempted the reckless low-level stunt that crashed his plane and cost him his legs'.[6]

The audience around Australia were anxious to hear more. Brickhill's inspiring recreation of Douglas Bader's life was on everybody's lips and he soon gained an iconic legendary status in the eyes of the public that has sustained itself ever since, even though the author was largely forgotten and had disappeared from sight.

---

6 John Quinn, 'Radio Round-up', 'Still reaching for air', *Mail* (Adelaide), 4 September 1954.

Radio Dramatisations of the Books

In the radio adaptation of *Reach for the Sky*, produced by Morris West, prominent Australian Thespian, the virile young Sydney actor Rod Taylor was given the plumb role of the legless Bader. He was a great success. His performance was to dominate the drama as he captured Paul Brickhill's sense of precise authenticity. In one sequence the script called on him to climb out of his bed with great difficulty, get on to his crutches for the first time and go down a hospital corridor to the bathroom without any assistance. When it came to recording, Taylor refused to have the sound effects man tap a crutch on a piece of wood on one microphone while he made sounds of effort on another. Instead, he did this whole scene himself manipulating the crutches:

> For several minutes he made the others in the studio believe that he was Bader, a man on crutches that he couldn't manipulate very well making his slow and painful way down a corridor. On air the only sound listeners heard was clunk… tap… tap… gasp, as he almost fell and steadied himself tap … as he went on.

As a powerful actor, Taylor created the whole scene despite the limitation of radio and made listeners feel Bader's determination and 'angry effort' simply by using those few authentic sounds effects.[7] He instinctively knew the audience of the age were looking for authenticity.

Like Brickhill, Taylor achieved fame in the 1950s, but as a film star of major Hollywood and British feature films: *Giant* (1956), *Raintree County* (1957), *The Birds* (1963), *Young*

7 Kent, *Out of the Bakelite Box*.

Cassidy (1966) and *The High Commissioner* (1970). With rugged strong appearance and a good voice trained in radio, he presented powerful physical characterisations of an authentic nature. His acting career roughly paralleled that of Peter Finch, Paul Brickhill's schoolboy companion. Taylor pursued his film career mainly in Hollywood whereas Finch did the same in Britain where he met up again with Brickhill in the 1950s.

Earlier in April 1954, *The Dam Busters* as a radio serial drama had been broadcast nationally in Australia on commercial radio also produced by Morris West who later became, like Brickhill, an international best-selling author. He produced many radio serials in the mid-1950s for his independent company with maximum dramatic effect. West adapted the serial from Brickhill's book and cast it with leading radio actors, with Rod Taylor playing the lead as Squadron leader Guy Gibson. As with Bader later, Taylor captured the physicality and determination of the character. Paul Brickhill acted as narrator throughout the series. The series of *The Dam Busters* replaced Morris West's popular crime serial "Alias the Baron" in the same prime time slot on commercial radio at 8.30pm every Thursday and 9pm every Sunday.[8]

Morris West was a prolific writer and highly popular producer and writer of radio drama. He produced a long string of highly popular exciting radio serials including *Dick Barton*, a detective series, *The Bartons of Banner Street* (first serial to reach one thousand episodes), *The Story of Alan Carlyle, Prince of Peace* (the life of Christ), *The Affairs of Harlequin* and *Paradise of Cheats*. Listeners were thrilled and enthralled by his serialised classics of writers such as Conan Doyle, Sabatini, Thackeray, Jules Verne and others that brought him

8 'Dambusters' From 5AD Tomorrow', *Advertiser* (South Australia), 10 April 1954.

closer to the adventure elements of Brickhill's work. And he had commercial sponsors lining up for his work. He did both highly romanticised fiction and real-life adventures. He never wasted a minute – it was thrill after thrill.[9]

As an independent radio producer, West was highly successful in the early 1950s. As well as national broadcasts, his company readily sold to South Africa, Canada and New Zealand including the Brickhill serials that stimulated wide interest in the books from which they were adapted as well as the three major films.

Later West became internationally famous with his best-selling books: his non-fiction *Children of the Sun* (1958); his religious thriller novels – *The Devil's Advocate* (1959) and *The Shoes of the Fisherman* (1963), both made into blockbusting feature films. West left radio drama at the right time when the industry began to collapse. Nevertheless, his radio serial ventures with Brickhill's three books were the highlights of a successful career in radio production. He was central to the last five years of radio's golden age of drama.

The 1954 radio serials of *The Dam Busters*, *Reach for the Sky* and *The Great Escape* were superior productions by Morris West as the independent producer of national radio shows of significance. West's company, Australasian Radio Productions, was well known to Australian and New Zealand listeners. It achieved large audiences nationally and distributed some of its productions elsewhere to the United States, Canada, Great Britain and South Africa.

Paul Brickhill wrote the radio script of twenty-six episodes of *The Dam Busters* assisted and edited by Morris West and Gordon Grimsdale. The series was centred round the 617 Squadron and

9 'Monk returns to the World. Morris West renounced his vows and is now a wealthy radio man', *People*, 14 January 1953, 15-17.

was replete with air force activities and suspenseful adventures of true-life war experiences. The all-star leading cast were Rod Taylor, as already recounted, Allan Trevor and Coralie Neville. The production was billed as a documentary drama. Supporting cast included theatre and radio luminaries Charles "Bud" Tingwell (also an ex-RAF pilot in real life), David Eadie and Alexander Archdale. A number of the supporting actors were ex-air force men which added to the drama's sense of authenticity along with Brickhill's narration. Each episode was thirty minutes long with a cliff-hanger ending in each to take the audience to the next episode. The serial's influence in Australia was significant in that it made the wartime exploits of the 617 Squadron famous, especially those of flying aces Guy Gibson, Micky Martin and Leonard Cheshire.

The serial *Reach for the Sky* had a similar impact on the Australian public, helping to make Wing Commander Douglas Bader the most famous hero of World War II. It was an even bigger production than that of Brickhill's earlier bestselling book, running for fifty-two episodes. Rod Taylor played Bader in episodes 1 to 36 and another leading actor Bruce Stewart took over and played him in episodes 37 to 52. Again the supporting cast was made up of a stellar group of leading Australian actors well known to Australian radio audiences: Dinah Shearing, Neva Carr Glyn, John Meillon, Ray Barratt and Lyndall Barbour. The first broadcast was on 28 July 1954. The show was a bigger hit with the listening public than *The Dam Busters*. It was broadcast when radio was a great influence on public taste and values. The mythology of air force heroes was at its height and they are still held as fond memories for most senior Australians.

The Great Escape – the third of the radio serials – was also scripted by Paul Brickhill, Morris West and Gordon Grimsdale. Again, Rod Taylor was the lead in a distinguished male cast that included Guy Doleman, Kevin Brennan and Bruce Stewart. For this serial the cast was particularly ensemble in nature. There were twenty-six episodes like *The Dam Busters*. In this case, it was an all-male cast, unlike the other two, and began to be broadcasted on 8 October 1954. Basically it was the story of the mass escape of RAF officers from the German prison camp at Sagan.

For Paul Brickhill and Morris West, all three 1954 serials were outstanding successes and drew in a huge collective audience of listeners. The episodes were high on adventure and suspense and fulfilled the community's need for exciting near-present real-life experiences that mitigated against the dull routine of Australian suburban life.

The Dam Busters – beginnings in Reality

At 7.30am on 17 May 1943, Jerry Fray, a Flying Officer with No 542 Squadron, took off in his photo-reconnaissance Spitfire for a sortie over Germany to assess damage of a recent secret bombing raid. At 30,000 feet and one hundred miles east of the Ruhr River, he sighted what looked like a bank of cloud further to the east. As he flew closer, he realised it was the sun glinting on a mass of water that strangely filled the valley below the Moehne Dam. It was a stunning bizarre sight – the floodwater was about a mile wide in the valley and was still gushing through a huge breach in the dam wall. Fray was overcome by its immensity and the destruction it had done.

He took a series of photographs of the damage below the Moehne Dam and then flew on to the Eder valley where the damage and flooding appeared even more extensive. More photographs were taken, but an approaching enemy aircraft forced him to turn for home at full speed. His Spitfire was unarmed.

Fray's aerial photographs were pin-sharp and, on the

following morning they were released and appeared on the front page of every British newspaper to stimulate public morale. The Air Ministry had also issued a short communiqué outlining the target as three Ruhr dams and stated: 'The attacks were pressed home at a very low level with great determination and coolness in the face of fierce resistance' – something of an understatement in the English manner.

With the belief that the three dams were central to the supply of water for factories, hydro-electric power, the coke ovens of the steel mills at the heart of Germany's war economy, the British newspapers went absolutely wild over the achievements of the 617 Bomber Squadron's successful raid. The *Telegraph* in London proudly proclaimed: 'With one single blow the RAF has precipitated what may prove to be the greatest industrial disaster yet inflicted on Germany in this war'. Thus the legend of the Dam Busters was born in media propaganda[10] and the 617 Squadron was to achieve a lasting celebrated status which was reinforced after the war by Brickhill's book and its adaptation into a stirring feature film that became Britain's biggest box office success in 1955.

Today, the film remains a much loved British classic.

In his book Paul Brickhill made excellent use of Jerry Fray's graphic reconnaissance photographs the morning after the attack, but he backed them up with equally graphic descriptions that caught the reader's attention.[11] He ably captured one of the defining moments in the air of the Second World War. But he was able to see it more subtly from the German side of things:

---

10 Taylor Downing, 'War on Film. The Dam Busters', *Military History Monthly*, Issue 32, May 2013, 40.

11 Paul Brickhill, *The Dam Busters*, Herald-Sun Reader's Book Club, Adelaide, 1953, images between 96 & 97.

> Three kilometres down the valley from the Moehne lay the sleeping village of Himmelpforten, which means Gates of Heaven [in German]. The explosions had wakened the village priest, Father Berkenkopf, and he guessed instantly what was happening; he had been afraid of it for three years He ran to his small stone church, Porta Coeli (which also means Gates of Heaven – in Italian) – and began tugging grimly on the bell-rope, the signal he had arranged with his villagers. It is not certain how many were warned in time. In the darkness the clanging of the bell rolled ominously round the valley and then it was muffled in the thunder moving nearer. Berkenkopf must have heard it and known what it meant, but it seems that he was still pulling at the bell when the flood crushed the church and the village of the Gates of Heaven and rolled them down the valley.[12]

Thus Brickhill, through the human factor of a specific incident, created an appropriate metaphor for the larger disaster.

It is interesting to note that the director Michael Anderson in his film does not seek to exploit this tragic scene despite its effective qualities of irony and, thus, deal with the impact of the raid on the civilian population of the valley. As part of the wave of British film of the mid-1950s, Anderson strikes instead a triumphal note that avoids any anti-war sentiment or theme. In one of the few shots devoted to the German response in the valley after the raid, he depicts a group of five or six men clambering up an industrial rigging in a desperate attempt to avoid the mounting flood. They are all in military uniform – there is not a stranded civilian in sight. Nevertheless, the Gates

12 Brickhill, *The Dam Busters,* 105-6.

of Heaven incident was an important opportunity badly missed by Anderson, the director of the film.

His film in no way exposes the dark underbelly of heroism – the effect that war had on civilian society. Like Jose Ferrer's *Cockleshell Heroes* made in the same year which deals with blockade-running German ships, the strategy for knocking out vital industrial water supplies in *The Dam Busters* film celebrates heroic achievement and sacrifice in the field of conflict solely on the British side. The dangers to non-combatants is not explored. Brickhill's book did this too, but he did at least glance at the other side of things with the eye of compassion.

The flood in reality went many miles and took more villages: 'a tumbling maelstrom of water and splintered houses', as Brickhill ably put it. With vivid writing in the book, he captures the moment of disaster and brings it all to life: '... beds and frying-pans, the chalice from Porta Coeli and the bell, the bodies of cattle and horses, pigs and dogs, and the bodies of Father Berkenkopf and other human beings'.[13]

Given the somewhat restricted availability of official documents after the Second World War in the 1950s, Paul Brickhill made a good fist of describing the degree of devastation in the Ruhr after the attack on the dams. He described how the Moehne and Eder Dams were emptied and how 330 million tons of water spread 'like cancer' through the western Ruhr valleys: 'the bones of towns and villages lifeless in the wilderness' that had been created by the sudden and violent floods. It was truly an 'ordeal ... by water'. Here is at least a touch of TS Eliot's *The Waste Land* in Brickhill's thinking.

13 Brickhill, *The Dam Busters,* 106.

A New Waste Land

For fifty miles both from the Moehne and the Eder coal mines were flooded and factories were in a state of collapse. Fritzlar, one of Hitler's largest military aerodromes went under water: 'the landing ground, hangars, barracks, and bomb dump'. Roads, bridges and railways simply disappeared under the initial force of the water. Canal banks were washed away, power stations had disappeared and the Ruhr foundries were without water for making steel. Communication systems had broken down.

More importantly, as the fair-minded Brickhill saw it, official German contemporary reports described the situation as 'a dark picture of destruction'. 400,000 men (at least) including 1,250 soldiers were diverted quickly to repair the damage in the valleys and the dams. There had been the loss of war production of 100,000 men for several months. The final situation was that 125 factories were either destroyed or badly damaged, about 3,000 hectares of arable land were ruined, 25 bridges had vanished and 21 more badly damaged. The livestock losses were 6,500 cattle and pigs that once fed the nation. The German population had to tighten their belts yet again – and yet German morale had not been significantly dented which immensely disappointed the British government.

The human and moral price was that 1,294 people were drowned in the floods and most were civilian workers. As Brickhill carefully pointed out, most were not Germans – there were 749 slaves and prisoners-of-war among the dead. There had been a Russian POW camp in the valley almost immediately below the Eder Dam.[14]

But this was at the close of the story of the raids on the dams, not the beginning.

---

14 Brickhill, *The Dam Busters*, 114-5.

In both the book and the film, the story of how a brilliant inventor Dr Barnes Wallis comes up with the idea of a bouncing bomb and how a new bomber squadron made up of the more renowned pilots in the RAF, 617 Squadron, are gathered together under Wing Commander Guy Gibson to carry out the daring, high-life risk mission to bomb the dams.

Such a story of a bombing mission was well-known to the post-war British population, but they were most eager to have the story retold in fine detail for them on film. And so one of the best British Second World War films ever was made.

The Dam Busters premiered to a packed admiring audience on the twelfth anniversary of the Raid in May 1955. Brickhill's book had been first published in 1951 and reprinted on several occasions to keep up with the great demand. The release of the film gave it another prolonged boost. The film version relates the first half of the book only – up to page 124. Brickhill's history of the 617 Squadron goes through to page 284 and the end of the war, detailing many other events involving the continued courage of the squadron.

The rest of the book could have been developed quite handsomely into a sequel – a second feature film on its own merit.

The 617 Squadron and its Fame

The film does not touch on the events concerning the 617 Squadron after the attacks on the dams. As Sir Arthur Harris put it (and Paul Brickhill dutifully reports): 'We'll make 'em a special duties squadron'.[15] So the 617 were sent on a series of specially conceived and secret raids on a variety of significant targets. Brickhill colourfully labelled it "Sniper Squadron"

15 Brickhill, *The Dam Busters*, 142.

with the Australian Ace Micky Martin playing a major role in effective low level bombing.

Leonard Cheshire replaced Guy Gibson as squadron leader and worked closely with intelligent agencies and officers. Like Gibson, Cheshire was to be awarded the Victoria Cross for bravery. Targets included U-boat submarine bases (nests) in France, Belgium and Norway, the location of important German secret weapons and canals and other war supply routes and locations. They smashed a number of German secret weapon bases with powerful effect and had great success in sinking the great German battleship *Tirpitz* in the northern Norwegian fiord of Tromso where it was being refitted. They also sank Germany's last pocket battleship *Lutzow* sheltering in Swinemunde deep in enemy territory in the Baltic Sea. None of this exciting action was to feature in Anderson's film version.

The filmic treatment of Brickhill's book is thus different to that of *Reach for the Sky* and *The Great Escape* where the book and the film begin and end at roughly the same point.

Paul Brickhill's career was strongly enhanced by *The Dam Busters* as a writing project. The Air History Board had searched for someone to research and write the detailed history of the 617 Squadron, mainly because of the fame it had achieved in the eyes of the British public during the war from the time of the announcement at the war's height of the successful raid on the dams onwards, together with the iconic symbolism of the award of the Victoria Cross to two of its members, Wing Commander Guy Gibson (VC, DSO and Bar, DFC and Bar) and Group Captain Leonard Cheshire (VC, DSO and 2 Bars, DFC) who took over from Gibson after the dam-busters raid.

An English author attempted the work on the squadron's history before Brickhill, but found it beyond him and 'threw in the towel'. The Air History Board had then found 'the very man' for the job, 'an Australian who had just arrived back in this country' – Paul Brickhill. The Board recognised Brickhill's earlier achievement with *The Great Escape*.

They persuaded him and then steered him into a mass of released primary source documents so that he could write the history which made him into a crowning doyen as an author of best-selling war stories.[16] The moment had been right for him and enhanced with strong official support. They were desperate for him to complete it at any cost. He was to receive rave reviews.

The British press were ecstatic! 'In all the history of arms there is no finer epic', wrote Hugh Dundas extravagantly in the *Daily Express*; Guy Ramsay in the *Daily Telegraph* claimed: 'I found myself reading at a pace equalled only by the speed of the narrative. The author has quickened his pages with breath-stopping excitement of the air'; it was claimed in the *Nottingham Guardian* that the book 'makes the nerves tingle'; and the *Truth* was emphatic: 'One of the greatest war books ever written'.[17]

With such reviews and many others like them that capture the excitement of Brickhill's style, it is no wonder that film producers became intensely excited and interested in adapting the book for the screen. The *Sunday Mercury* considered it to be 'A whole book of thrills', while the *Belfast Newsletter* recognised its visual elements – 'A vivid story from beginning to end'. It satisfied the book reader's hunger for realism, for true life stories:

16 Wilcox, 'Fall from the Sky', 131.

17 Dustcover commentary, Brickhill, *The Dam Busters*.

> Here is a story, related with breath-taking realism, stranger and more exciting than fiction, which, whilst portraying all the grimness of war in the air, does not forget the laughter in off-duty moments, and the disappointments when theories and plans were upset.

The book was just made for the movies. As an Australian, Brickhill, by circumstance, had beaten English writers of non-fiction to the punch and was the envy of the literati in sophisticated London circles – the Australian who was invading their territory with a typhoon of words. He was turned into a literary celebrity of the first water and was fêted everywhere he went.

In essence, the film adaptation of *The Dam Busters*, closely based on the first half of Brickhill's book, was a carefully crafted British war epic in which the Ruhr dams are destroyed in 1943 by Dr Barnes Wallis' bouncing bombs. The director was Michael Anderson (his first film as an independent director). Its two outstanding stars were Michael Redgrave as Barnes Wallis and Richard Todd as Guy Gibson. It also had a cast of experienced actors, notably Basil Sydney as Air Chief Marshal Sir Arthur Harris. The film, in documentary-style black and white, was 125 minutes in length with never a dull moment. It contained a stirring march by Eric Coates and a well-paced and edited story. Most of the many scenes are short and sharp and to the point. Tension builds as in Brickhill's book to the climatic scene.

Shaping the Film Version

The film's producers wanted to make it as realistic as possible, but entirely from a British angle. They decided to shoot it in black-and-white which was considered to be more authentic and less theatrical, giving it a grainy realistic quality. As well, sequences could be more easily blended in black-and-white with documentary footage taken during the war, including Jerry Fray's graphic reconnaissance photographs taken from the air the morning following the raid. Black-and-white was also easier on special effects.

The celebrated playwright and screenwriter Robert Cedric Sherriff (1896-1975) was employed to write and develop the script based on Brickhill's book. Sherriff's World War I play *Journey's End*, starring in its first performance in 1929 a not well-known young Laurence Olivier, was a smash hit on the West End stage of London and played for several years to packed audiences. Sherriff in his play had captured to great effect men's intimate relationships in the claustrophobic atmosphere of an officer's dugout in warfare in the trenches of the Somme. He then easily applies the same feeling and emotions within the interior of bomber planes in *The Dam Busters* to express the same threat to the human factor in subtle gesture and reaction in such a confined and dangerous space. With great care, Sherriff draws most of his dialogue from Brickhill's book.

Sherriff's highly experienced approach to scriptwriting was realistic and low-key and a useful corrective to the romantic conception of war, both in his famous play *Journey's End* and in the film script for *The Dam Busters*. Such an approach considerably enhanced the film, while still capturing the verve and immediacy of the author's prose style.

By the time he had begun the script for the film, Sherriff had already gained much valuable experience in the film world by adapting novels, including *Goodbye Mr Chips* (1939) and *Odd Man Out* (1947), and had published several successful novels and other plays in his own right. His script for *The Dam Busters* was nicely understated and naturalistic in tone. Moreover, his war service with the 9th Battalion East Surrey Regiment in the Great War provided him with a deep and indelible understanding of the nature of war and of the human condition as well as a sensitive background to the behaviour of men. Sherriff saw action at Vimy and Loos and was badly wounded at Ypres in 1917. He was awarded a Military Cross for bravery in the face of the enemy.

The turning point in Sherriff's writing career came in December 1928 when his play *Journey's End* was staged at the Apollo, later moving to the Savoy for a long run. The story of the play about a doomed soldier in the trenches at St Quentin as the German Spring Offensive of 1918 approaches was inspired by Sherriff's own letters home from the Western Front in the Great War.

The play shot its author to fame, so he continued to produce with ups and downs. His original play continues to reappear.[18] He was almost the perfect choice to write the screenplay for the film adaptation of *The Dam Busters* book because of his real-life experience of war and the connection of his writing style with that of Brickhill – understated and economically precise.

RC Sherriff – The Screenplay

In his autobiography, significantly titled *No Leading Lady* because of the phenomenal success of his 1929 play *Journey's End* which had no female characters, RC Sherriff recognised he was back in the same territory with his screenplay of *The Dam Busters*, beit not in the frontline trenches but in the battle of the air in enemy territory in the Second World War. This was to have 'no leading lady', but it worked perfectly for the box office. It was a late success for him: 'I wrote the screenplay of *The Dam Busters*', he reminisced, 'which hit the bull's-eye and took me on top of the world with the film studios'. From then on were golden years for the playwright as he recalled.

18 Geoff Simpson, *Guy Gibson Dambuster*, Pen & Sword Aviation, Barnsley, 2013, 159.

It was an Indian summer for him as a writer and, for twenty years after the release of *The Dam Busters*, he produced more plays (including radio plays), novels and television screenplays before his death in 1975.[19]

The preparation for the film saw great attention to authentic detail. Many of the survivors of the 617 Squadron were consulted as well as some of the next-of-kin of those who had died in the bombing raid on the dams, or subsequently on other missions that involved the 'Suicide Squadron', as it was more commonly known. Many of the outdoor scenes were filmed at RAF Scampton in remote Lincolnshire, eastern England on the North Sea – the squadron had actually flown from here in 1943 – and at the headquarters of 5 Bomber Group at Grantham, the Lincolnshire market town on the River Witham – from where the mission had been directed.[20] Grantham and Scampton had hardly altered since the war's end in appearance. The wartime atmosphere of such places was carefully recreated.

Roughly two years had been spent preparing and researching the film. The leading actor Richard Todd who played to role of Guy Gibson, the famous leader of the mission to knock out the dams, spent much time talking to people who had known Gibson, including Barnes Wallis, the inventor of the bouncing bomb used in the raid, Gibson's wife Eve and his father Alexander, the Australian flying ace Micky Martin and even one of Gibson's former schoolmasters.

Group Captain Charles Whitworth DSO, DFC was appointed as technical advisor for the movie. Whitworth was Station Commander at RAF Scampton throughout the squadron's stay there and present at most of the briefings of pilots and crews

---

19 RC Sherriff, *No Leading Lady. An Autobiography*, Victor Gollancz, London, 1968, 349.

20 Downing, 'War on Film. The Dam Busters', 40-1.

by Gibson. He also broke the news of the death of Gibson's dog Nigger after one of the final briefings.[21] Thus he was closely associated with the story of 617 Squadron. As well, Barnes Wallis, Dave Shannon, Micky Martin and Ralph Cochrane lent their assistance and expertise to the film project by providing advice and comment.

Richard Todd as Guy Gibson (right) in secret planning for the attack on the Ruhr dams in The Dam Busters

The attention and care to authentic detail paid off in the production of the film (as it had done in Brickhill's book). Most of the actors playing the flight crews and the higher command looked absolutely authentic for their parts.

Todd was appropriately right visually and in personal style for Gibson: both were short, stocky but neat in build, youthful-looking and vigorous in appearance with similar round faces. Todd was actually thirty-five years old when he played the twenty-four-year-old, but this did not seem to matter in the black-and-white filming technique used. He was perfect for the part and he had his own heroic war experience as a World War II commando leader that he was able to draw upon. Todd had been in the 6th Airborne Division and had parachuted down at Pegasus on D-Day and had taken a leading part in explosive frontline action with great courage.[22]

21 Alan W Cooper, *The Men who breached the dams. 617 Squadron, 'The Dam Busters'*, Pen & Sword Aviation, Barnsley, 2013, 154.

22 Downing, 'War on Film', 41.

Richard Todd, who later wrote his autobiography *Caught in the Act* in 1986, said of the nature of courage in tackling life's hardships: 'It is rather like something that happens to men in war. You don't consciously set out to do something gallant. You just do it because that is what you are there for'. In his straightforward characterisation of Guy Gibson in the film, Todd had captured this keen sense of understatement in the nuances of his mannerisms that meshed neatly with Sherriff's screenplay and Brickhill's book. While some critics later disparaged it as stiff upperlipism, it was, nevertheless, authentic and captures the mood of the time in a definitive way.

Some of the strongest visual images of the film on the windswept coast of England showed two figures, striking in their contrasting appearance: the neat, short uniformed and caped Richard Todd standing close to the untidily civilian-clothed and more than six-foot Michael Redgrave in a flapping overcoat with his hair freely blowing in the wind. Both are symbols of modern war; both are the most significant individuals in the story; both have undaunted but unconscious courage – the bomber pilot and the intrepid inventor, both indelible images in their scenes together. They were just doing what they were there for.

The Performers

The performance of renowned thespian of stage and screen Michael Redgrave as Dr Barnes Wallis, the engineer and inventor of the bouncing bomb, was a superb commanding portrayal of a slightly eccentric and independent vigorous man. It was an important cornerstone of the film. Wallis and Redgrave were exactly the same height – tall and rangy with flowing grey hair. Redgrave adopted a pair of round spectacles exactly like those worn by Wallis and even tied his tie with exactly the same type of knot.

In the early episodes of the film, the audience is captured by the inventor's experiments using humble marbles and a tin bath in the side garden of his house and then interest is maintained as he persistently struggles with ongoing technical difficulties, red tape and official lack of interest in and even opposition to his work.

In March 2015, Dr Mary Stopes-Roe of Birmingham, the daughter of Barnes Wallis, described the same incident as the one used in the opening scene of the film. She called it 'our marbles game':

> A year after our marbles game, on 17th May 1943, the raid [on the Ruhr Dams] was reported [in newspapers] in graphic and detailed celebration. I was away from home at boarding school, but I knew at once what it had been about. The relevance of the marbles and the water-tub game became clear, and I wrote an exuberant, overjoyed letter – 'up the marbles, wonderful marbles' – to my father. I still have it.

In the copy of *The Dam Busters* presented to Barnes Wallis after the war, Mary Stopes-Roe found that her mother had written several comments in faint pencil. One was 'Helped by his children who never divulged a word to anyone'. Mary Stopes-Roe remembered, however, that it was not a matter of virtue. Wallis was never secretive and had not warned his children not to talk about it. At the time the children had no idea of what the real purpose of the garden game was.

The game was touchingly and authentically recreated in the first sequence of the film by Michael Redgrave as Barnes Wallis with four child actors playing the parts of Wallis' children in the side garden of a suburban villa. It was filmed on the real location of the Wallis residence in the open countryside.

It was a completely authentic recreation of real life as had appeared too in Brickhill's book. The four children had been recruited to help their father in a rather strange game. He borrowed some of one of his daughter's marbles, designed a catapult used to fire them and had his wife carry out a large old tin wash tub to a garden table on the side of the garden terrace. The tub was filled carefully with buckets of cold water from the kitchen. Mary's brother recorded the number of skips or bounces over the water made by each marble and each was related to the height of the catapult and the angle of discharge. The other children searched for the lost marbles in the back garden. Mary's mother took a photographic snap of the game and this was used to begin the famous film with the incident.[23]

There were tensions surrounding the threats to cancel the entire wartime project. Redgrave captures the psychological tension within the well-focussed and determined, brilliant inventor fighting against all odds.[24] And it is as Brickhill portrayed his personality in the book.

Redgrave spent time with Wallis during the making of the film, capturing nuances of his mannerisms and gestures. Memorable scenes involving Redgrave were in the operations room during the raid and where success becomes evident. These are beautifully restrained as is Redgrave's profound sorrow on learning of the cost of the raid on aircrew lives. In their scenes together, Todd and Redgrave work beautifully in unison while creating distinctly contrasting mannerisms in their understated characterisations.

Taylor Downing has convincingly argued that the grey-haired Redgrave presents Wallis in classical terms as the eccentric

---

23 Mary Stopes-Roe, Introduction, Paul Brickhill, *The Dam Busters,* Folio Books, London, 2015, xiii-xiv.

24 Colin Burgess, *Australia's Dambusters. The Men and Mission of 617 Squadron*, Australian Military History Publications, Loftus, 2013, 243-4.

inventor, the stereotype of British films of the time – a portrait of a 'bumbling boffin struggling against the grey, unimaginative "Men of the Ministry"' – the individual against the system. Nevertheless, this is how Brickhill originally conceived him.

> Wallis did not look like a man who was going to have much influence on the war; he looked more like a diffident and gentle cleric. At 53 his face was unlined and composed, the skin smooth and pink and the eyes behind the horn-rimmed glasses mild and grey; crisp white hair like a woolly cap enhanced the effect of benevolence. Many people who stood in his way in the next three years [of the war] were deceived by this, having failed to note the long upper lip which gave stubbornness to the mouth and was the only visible clue to his persistent refusal to be diverted from his purpose. Even his friends did not quite understand this because Wallis, in a vaguely indefinable way, was a little insulated from the rough and tumble of ordinary life by a mind virtually on another plane, immersed in figures and theories. They knew him as a gentle, if rather detached aircraft designer, and it was not till later that they began to use the word 'genius'.[25]

Brickhill typically paints a portrait of character in a single paragraph. Redgrave's performance deftly captures all of this as does Sherriff's screenplay.

Redgrave was too good an actor not to realise the stereotype imposed and lifted above it with a series of subtle nuances of self-awareness as he portrays the inner tensions and strains within the

25 Brickhill, *The Dam Busters*, Herald-Sun, 1953, 15.

character. His intimate relationship with his wife played skilfully by Ursula Jeans, an experienced stage actor of suitable age, is nicely handled in a few homely scenes. Despite the dramatic simplification that is usually necessary in a feature film, the historical record is rather different. The idea of disabling the Ruhr industrial zone of west Germany by bombing the dams had been discussed by an Air Ministry committee in 1938. Barnes Wallis in real life as a much admired aeronautical engineer was given a great deal of encouragement to try out his new idea. As was shown in the film (but after much dramatic reluctance in this form of drama), he was given permission to use water tanks, to borrow aircraft to drop mock bombs and, from the beginning of 1942, he had access to an actual disused dam in mid Wales to blow up. He had enthusiastic support in high places that was more than the film implies in some of its key scenes. But it was tense drama, for the sake of tense drama.

Sir Barnes Wallis

In reality, Air Chief Marshal Sir Arthur Harris of Bomber Command remained hostile to Wallis' plan: 'the maddest proposal as a weapon that we have yet come across'. He did not like the idea of risking his 'precious Lancasters and their human crew' on a precision raid for which the Lancaster as an aircraft was not designed. He saw the whole operation as a major distraction from his policy of destroying the German war economy and machine through area bombing. The actor playing Harris in the film, Basil Sydney, did at least touch on some of this in his commanding and totally convincing performance.

In the film Harris is correctly presented as a bluff no-nonsense commander – thus a very authentic performance. Nevertheless, the film fictionalises the story when Harris comes round to enthusiastically support the idea of the raid and to admire Wallis, the brilliant inventor behind it. In reality, Harris jealously guarded Bomber Command's right to select its own target. He thus resisted pressure from the Ministry of Economic Warfare that wanted to bomb the Ruhr dams. It was only the intervention of the Chief of Air Staff Sir Charles Portal that made the difference together with Churchill's keen approval in February 1943.

Portal ordered Harris to carry out the raid to be codenamed officially "Operation Chastise". In his turn, Harris reluctantly told the new commander of Group 5 Bomber Command, Air Vice-Marshal Ralph Cochrane, to form a new squadron to carry out the mission. As in the film, however, Harris chose Wing Commander Guy Gibson to lead the squadron.[26]

After cruising carefully at a leisurely pace through the research experiments and frustrations of Dr Barnes Wallis in which Michael Redgrave's subtly brilliant performance dominates the screen reinforced by his physical size and his bursts of dynamic energy juxtaposed against the sombre dress and dark overcoats of a collection of critical London bureaucrats, the story is increased in pace and drama by the director Michael Anderson.

A sense of urgency is effectively created about the actual mission. Gibson has barely eight weeks to train his crew for low-level flying before the German dams reach their high tide – the most effective time to bomb them, thus a dramatic deadline. At the same time Wallis, as the designer of the Lancasters, frantically works on the modification to the bomb so that they will be able to carry the bouncing bomb known by its codename "Upkeep".

Even when the film was made after the book was published, parts of the secrecy act were still in force. Thus in the film the

26 Downing, 'War on Film', 42.

giant bomb is obscurely depicted as spherical slung under the Lancaster. In actual fact, it was cylindrical more like a huge depth charge or mine, sixty inches in length and fifty inches in diameter containing 6,600 lbs of Torpex explosive. In addition, each Lancaster contained a giant rotation system which back-spun the bomb at 500rpm, so when it hit the water it rapidly skimmed along it.

The film imagines a scene where Richard Todd as the hard-working and snappy Guy Gibson takes a rare night off to visit a London variety show in a popular theatre where he gets the idea of using two spotlights to focus on the surface of the lakes of the dams to establish the exact height where the bomb needs to be dropped.

In real life, this idea came from Ben Lockspeiser, the director of Scientific Research at the Ministry of Aircraft Production where experiments had already taken place for using spotlights to establish optimum height to depth-charge German U-boats.[27]

The film's final climax – the raid itself – accords with historical reality and worked close to Paul Brickhill's text. Only a few weeks before Operation Chastise took place, Wallis believed that the bombs had to be dropped from sixty feet to achieve their objective not, as originally planned, at 150 feet. So changes to the design of the bouncing bomb continued to the last minute. The operation was scheduled for when the spring waters – 'the tide' – behind the dams would be at their greatest height and there was a clear moonlit night.

It was at a certain time in annual weather history when the rivers entering the lakes made by the damming were swollen by the Alpine melt of the spring. This would raise the water level of the dams to their maximum point that would ensure maximum damage to war industry if the dam walls were breached. The

27 Downing, 'War on Film', 42.

weather experts could accurately predict on what particular day this would occur. These two requirements were emphasised in the dialogue and the visual qualities of the film. Pressure was on all the real-life characters of the film which effectively heightened the over-all tension. It was indeed a stunning wartime achievement that everything fell into place at the correct time.

On the day that the night raid was to take place, in a highly effective group scene set in a conference room, the aircrews were told for the first time – by Todd as Gibson – what their targets were. Redgrave as Wallis was there to explain everything on maps and charts to reinforce Gibson's stern statement. For the film, the actual original scale models of the terrain were used to add to the authenticity. Richard Todd then sternly instructs his crews 'to get every detail in your heads until you know them with your eyes shut', in the same manner as Gibson would have instructed the real crews.

Michael Anderson – Film Director

The film as directed by Anderson was able to record the story of the raid on 16 May 1943 with great accuracy considering the difficulties of recreating the actual flight of the war planes in the whole operation with all its technical problems. The aircrew interiors in the Lancasters were built as sets at Elstree Studios. They moved on a platform as the various actors moved the joysticks and thus created a kind of flight simulator. Aerial prepared film of the route across the Holland canal and Germany on the Ruhr River and then flying around the dams was then back-projected on the walls of the outside of the cockpit interiors of the set.

The Derwent reservoir in Derbyshire was used for the broader dam shots. (The actual Dam Busters of 617 Squadron practised bouncing their bombs on the Derwent reservoir before their celebrated raid.) As director Anderson excelled himself in achieving the realistic effects he wanted in the dramatic climax (which took several weeks to get them right technically).

The end of the film in itself is low-key and not particularly triumphalist in tone. Eight of the nineteen aircraft did not return – only seventeen had been used in action on the dams. The camera lingers on the bedrooms of the aircrew who were never to return and their sacrifice was underlined in visual rather than verbal terms with close-ups of various personal objects and items in the empty rooms. After a gentle tender encounter with the worried Wallis on the tarmac, Gibson walks off, alone and a lonely figure, to write letters to the families of those who died on the mission. This is a quiet, yet emotion-charged final scene that closes the story so effectively. It is well remembered by viewers to this day. No words needed to be said.

Earlier, only Harris is elated telling the deeply troubled Wallis that 'now you can sell me a pink elephant'. Again, the reality was quite different with Harris. The mission had proved to him that Lancasters should not be used again in such precise bombing missions. As Brickhill also points out in the later part of his book (that was not used in the film), other aircraft, in particular Mosquitos, were used for precision raids which was the real lesson that Harris took from the dambusters raid.[28]

* * *

Like a number of other British films of the 1940s and particularly the 1950s, *The Dam Busters* as a war film was intended in general as a reasonably exact reconstruction of historical events and the emphasis was on the collective, a group of aircrew doing the right thing in the right manner as inspired by Paul

---

28 Downing, 'War on Film', 43.

Brickhill's compelling factual book of the exploits of the RAF in the Second World War.

Like other English filmmakers, Anderson was sensitive to the interplay of roles in wartime, particularly between Richard Todd as Wing Commander Guy Gibson and Michael Redgrave as the civilian inventor Barnes Wallis. Both characters are stand-out heroes in their various ways, but belong also to two groups of men with a common social understanding working together. This genre seems to have first been articulated during 1942 with Noel Coward's and David Lean's *In Which We Serve* whose evocative title suggests the same worldview. *In Which We Serve* was one of the prime inspirations of the war-time period, just as Michael Anderson's *The Dam Busters* achieved the very same goal after the war in 1954. Nothing much had changed for British cinema as it was a highly popular theme and drew enthusiastic audiences. Paul Brickhill achieved the same level of inspiration in his book of the same name. To give its age, *The Dam Busters*, both as book and film, spoke of a group of national understated heroes who carried triumph from the shadow of failure, defeat and frustration. They did, as the actor Richard Todd later pointed out, what they were there for. As an epic of war as film, it combined the glories of the past with an implicit call of the future.

With a seeming documentary exactness, the film ably encompasses the dangerous experiences of British bomber crews in a desperate raid over the German Ruhr dams. It was a film that paid homage to those who served in both arenas of war, in the home country (Barnes Willis and the Air Force Executive, Guy Gibson, etc) and over enemy territory. There was no dissension about the value of fighting the German aggressor who is never characterised. In the film, individual German characters do not exist. Unlike in some later films, the German military are unseen, not sighted.

The Dam Busters as a film was beautifully shot, superbly performed, edited with tremendous pace (just like Brickhill's book). It still stands up sixty or so years after as a fine tribute to the men of the 617 Squadron at the time of the raids on the dams. Theirs was a great and well-recognised achievement.

For its time, its special effects look impressive and deeply engaging. It is also a lasting tribute, as Brickhill's book is, to inventiveness, improvisation and understated courage. Brickhill and the film gave a very British telling culturally of a very British story. This is probably why even today many people regard Paul Brickhill as an Englishman rather than an Australian writer – an attitude that does not really include a close analysis of his literary work.

Eric Coates, a composer who tended to specialise in signature tunes and light music, wrote the famous musical march theme for the film ("The Dambusters March") that expresses the corporate understated courage of all those involved in the raid on the ground, like Barnes Wallis and Arthur Harris, and in the air like Guy Gibson and the aircrews. Coates used a theme he had written before even seeing the film. It was to become inextricably associated with *The Dam Busters* in the same way that the "Colonel Bogey March" was associated with David Lean's *The Bridge on the River Kwai* (1958). "The Dambusters March" took on a life of its own and is still a popular favourite today. It was also used in two Carling Black Label advertisements for lager: one in which a German goalkeeper in a football game is seen catching the bouncing bomb and another when a tourist swimmer throws his towel that bounces across a pool to reserve his deckchair on the other side.

As already demonstrated, the damage caused by the raid was severe as depicted in the film, graphically but without much detail. As well as flooding power stations and factories, railways had been washed away and mud and silt was deposited over a huge area. The final estimation of the death toll was about 1,300 civilians killed in the flooding including 500 Ukrainian slave-workers living in the valleys below the dams. Nevertheless, German engineers repaired the damage with remarkable speed, skill and efficiency. Within six weeks, water supplies to the factories of the Ruhr had been fully restored. In a massive effort the breaches in the Moehne and Eder dams were repaired. By September they were working almost normally again.

On the other hand, Germany had to divert huge resources in a massive relief operation. The Germans allocated much needed anti-aircraft weapons to guard the dams for the rest of the war, thus severely weakening other military placements. The irony of the entire British campaign against the dams was that, in the longer term, it had almost a negligible effect on the German war effort in general.[29]

To recognise the 25th Anniversary of the Dams Operation, a thanksgiving service was held at St Clement Danes Church on 19 May 1968. Paul Brickhill apparently did not attend. It was preceded the day before by a reception that started with a showing of the film at the Warner Theatre in Leicester Square. Nearly all the survivors were there including Barnes Wallis. After the film, there was a cocktail party attended by the actor Richard Todd who had enjoyed his best-known role of his acting career as Wing Commander Guy Gibson VC. It was also one of his most compelling performances. Sir Arthur Harris, Sir Ralph Cochrane and Charles Whitworth, the former station commander at Scampton where the 617 Squadron were based in the Dams campaign, were in attendance. Whitworth had worked closely with the film project as technical adviser.

The Thanksgiving service had been presided over by the Reverend JER Williams DFC, a former pilot with the 617.

29 Downing, 'War in Film', 42-3.

Richard Todd delivered a passage from the Funeral Oration of Pericles and the lessons were read by Micky Martin, the leading Australian ace of the dambuster operations, and Leonard Cheshire VC who Paul Brickhill admired so much (more so than Guy Gibson in his book).[30]

As Brickhill emphasised in his book, the story of No 617 Squadron went well beyond the raid on the Ruhr dams as shown in the squadron's regimental badge with its motto: '*Après moi le déluge*' (After me, the deluge). Between May 1943 and April 1945, they flew a total of ninety-five operations in which 189 aircrew were lost. But the legend of the Dam Busters was set immediately after the raid and consolidated after the war in film and book.

Despite the deathrate, the positive thing to come out of any war is comradeship which frequently turns into lasting friendships. For the 617 Squadron these two factors have been evident. Since the early 1960s, several members have been meeting regularly. The initial major trigger for reunions was the launch of Brickhill's book by the publishers Evans Brothers Limited in London in 1951. All of the survivors were invited and, therefore, got together for the first time since the war. The phenomenal success of the book had the tendency to cement their relationships, their joint celebrity and need to meet each other on a regular basis. They all became well-known national heroes. Brickhill had thus turned them into lasting legends in their own lifetime.

The Royal World Première

In 1955 the Royal World Première of the feature film in

---

30 Cooper, *The Men who breached the dams,* 155; Burgess, *Australia's Dambusters,* 246.

London was to bring the men who breached the dams together in a formal and very public sense that fêted their wartime achievements in an official and public manner. The Première was held over two days at the Empire Theatre in Leicester Square on 16 and 17 May. The timing marked the twelfth anniversary of the actual raid on the dams. Apart from the surviving crew in attendance on the first night there was Guy Gibson's wife Eve and his father, Alexander Gibson.

The Première was indeed a Royal one in nature: on the exciting first evening, Princess Margaret, at the height of her popularity, was the official guest arriving in a limousine to a red carpet reception surrounded by crowds of excited cheering onlookers and fans lining the streets around the Square overlooking the Empire – the crowd caring not for the rain showers. Umbrellas were up above enthusiastic spectators. On the second evening, the Duke and Duchess of Gloucester presided over the event in a less exciting way.

Princess Margaret met the star actor Richard Todd, resplendent in evening suit, and his wife. (They also attended the second evening.) Then she met survivors of the squadron in the theatre's vestibule as well as their wives and the widows and mothers of those who had not survived – a touching scene full of emotion and British pride of place. Margaret handled the situation with fitting aplomb looking every inch like a glamorous film star herself in a magnificent evening gown.

On the second occasion, the Duke and Duchess of Gloucester at first met with a duller group of film executives. The situation did not spark the emotions of the first night, but the two Royals handled the occasion with competence. The crowds were still there and uniformed young RAF men provided an impressive guard-of-honour on both nights. Needless to say, the appropriately named Empire Theatre was packed inside on both occasions and the applause for the film was long, loud and enthusiastic.

The film's reception in Australia in May 1956 was equally ecstatic and glamorous. A Hollywood style Australian Première of *The Dam Busters* at the Hoyts Windsor Theatre in Melbourne had His Excellency the Governor of Victoria Sir Dallas Brooks and Lady Brooks. They were the Queen's representatives. Sleet, gale winds and rain did not prevent the success of the occasion amongst the Melbourne elite. All the movers-and-shakers were there at their glamorous best. As the *Argus* would have it, Lady Brooks threw a gay challenge at the 'gloomy atmosphere' of the night in her 'leschenaultia blue gown with scroll braiding round the rounded neckline and with white fox furs on her shoulders'. The formal wear of other women in attendance was described in detail. Indeed, the movie played to a glamorous, overdressed audience of prominent Melbournians and received generous applause.

The Men of the 617

A leading guest at the Australian première was Wing Commander Micky Martin, the recognised leading light in the legendary dambuster raid. Before the show, he had dined at Government House with Sir Dallas and Lady Brooks. The thirty-eight-year-old Martin was one of the most decorated and celebrated Australian serviceman of World War II apart from Arthur Roden Cutler VC. He had a AFC, two DSOs and three DFCs. He had arrived in Melbourne in late April 1956 especially for the film première in which Australian actor Bill Kerr had played his part.

The media depicted Martin as a 'blithe, boisterous air ace', full of humour. He noted to the *Argus* when interviewed: 'The days of the Lancasters and [other] conventional planes are nearly over'. He quipped: 'It's P for Pushbutton – not Popsie now', referring to his famous Lancaster bomber nicknamed "P for Popsie". The journalist labelled Martin as 'one of the real live stars in May1943' – a major part of the Dam Busters legend. Describing him as small and wiry, the journalist provided his biography that sang his praises:

Wing Commander "Micky" Martin

> [He] had left Australia (home town Sydney) in 1938 on a world trip, joined the R.A.F. at the outbreak of war.
>
> Because of his audacious low-level bombing exploits, he was singled out to form 617 (Suicide) Squadron to bust the Ruhr dams.
>
> He made 90 missions in his famous Lancaster P for Popsie and became Australia's greatest bomber pilot.[31]

As confirmed by Paul Brickhill in his book, all of this was substantially true and is reinforced in the film by Bill Kerr's effective cameo performance although he didn't get much of the dialogue by Sherriff who saw the Empire pilots as faithful retainers in the background of the English stars of the movie.

Martin was directly under Wing Commander Guy Gibson, leader of the raids on the Moehne and Eder dams. When he arrived at Essendon airport from England to attend the Melbourne film première he was met by Squadron Leader Jack Leggo, the current President of Legacy and his old navigator. By this time, Martin was working as operational planning chief at Allied Air Force Headquarters outside Paris. He was still

31 'Glamour rose above it all', *Argus*, 3 May 1956; Michael Fitzgerald, 'Sit in chair – be an air ace', *Argus*, 30 April 1956.

carrying with him a fluffy grey koala mascot that was also featured in the film. At the Wednesday night première, he had a reunion with "Tommy" Simpson, another of his dambuster crew.

When Martin viewed the film first at the London première, as he was watching his beloved P for Popsie skim across the Moehne Dam at sixty feet with flack bursting all around after the plane before him was shot down, he rushed out of the cinema and had 'a stiff whiskey'.[32] This shows how some of the dambuster survivors viewed the film of their exploits.

Several Australians in the aircrews of the 617 Squadron had paid the ultimate price during the Second World War. They were:

- Flight Lieutenant Robert Norman George Barlow, DFC (killed in action on 16 May 1943)
- Flying Officer Charles Rowland Williams, DFC (killed in action on 16 May 1943)
- Flight Lieutenant Leslie Gordon Knight, DSO (killed in action on 16 May 1943)
- Pilot Officer Frederick Michael Spafford, DFM, DFC (killed in action on 16 September 1943)
- Flight Lieutenant Robert Claude Hay, DFC and Bar (killed in action on 12 February 1944)
- Flying Officer John Irvine Gordon, DFC (killed in action on 13 February 1944)
- Flying Officer Stanley George Hall (killed in action on 13 February 1944)
- Flying Officer Ian Stewart Ross (killed in action on 12 January 1945)

All of these names appear on the Roll of Honour. The inscription reads: 'May their example be an inspiration to us, now and in the

32 Fitzgerald, 'Sit in chair'.

future. Marshal of the RAF The Lord Tedder, GCB.'[33]

Only the full circumstances of the deaths of Flight Lieutenant Norman "Norm" Barlow and Flight Lieutenant Leslie Gordon Knight, including location, have since been discovered. Robert Norman George Barlow who, like Paul Brickhill, sported a pencil-thin moustache, had trained and graduated at the Empire Air Training Scheme in Ottawa, Canada. He was from the Melbourne suburb of Carlton. He learnt to fly in 1928 and gained a pilot's licence. He had the honour to begin the proceedings for Operation Chastise by being the first to take off on a clear, bright evening in his modified Lancaster. The section of six aircraft was bound for the Sorpe Dam under Norman Barlow's captaincy.

They made their way across the North Sea flying extremely low at fifty feet, not in strict formation but mainly in visual sight of one another. Two of the planes were lost over the water. Barlow's passage was along a south-easterly route across Holland, but crossing into Germany at a low level to avoid radar, he crashed into fairly invisible high-tension cables supported by tall pylons, 'hung like a spider's web across the Lancaster's path.' The aircraft ploughed into a field near a pond a few hundred yards further on where it burnt furiously. There were no survivors. The bomb they carried did not detonate and was recovered by German military who were able to uncover its secrets. The time was 23.50.

High tension wires difficult to see at night were responsible for the death of Norm Barlow of Melbourne and his crew at Haldern-Herken, north of Rees in Germany before reaching the Sorpe Dam. At the time, the local mayor, photographed with the huge bomb, believed it to be a fuel tank because of its cylindrical shape.

---

33 Burgess, *Australia's Dambusters,* 230.

Barlow's Upkeep bomb had rolled about fifty metres from where his Lancaster had crashed and had instantly burst into flames. And so was recovered intact and defused by the Luftwaffe who then shipped what was still a mysterious device off to a weapon examination depot at Kalkum near Dusseldorf for more intensive examination. A group of Luftwaffe officers and uniformed Gestapo (as with the photo of the local mayor) were photographed on site before the bomb was removed.

Norman Barlow had an intense interest in flying as demonstrated in his letters home. In one he wrote about 'thrilling experiences dodging flack, searchlights and night fighters', while at the same time wanting the war to end quickly. Just before the Dam Busters operation, he wrote to his mother: 'Today I discovered I have been awarded the DFC… boy am I happy… I tried to send you a cable today but the post office is closed until Monday'. Sadly, Monday never came for Flight Lieutenant Barlow.

A quiet dedicated man, Flight Lieutenant Leslie Gordon Knight of Camberwell, Victoria, successfully returned from Operation Chastise a legendary hero. His attack in "N-Nuts" modified Lancaster on the Eder Dam with the first wave's last available Upkeep bomb was 'absolutely copybook' despite the most testing requirements. As he flew away, elated by his success, he had the satisfaction of seeing the valley in full flood. Bob Kellow, Knight's wireless operator, provided the excitement of the event in his report:

> Les positioned our aircraft for our second run, got down to the required 60 feet, negotiated the dog-leg, adjusted the speed to 240 mph and headed straight and level for the dam wall… I heard the bomb aimer say 'Bomb gone!' and the engines roared as the nose of the aircraft lifted as we climbed to pass over the

> dam and then a large hill directly ahead of us. Les had to pull the nose up quite steeply … to clear the hill … I looked back at the dam falling behind us … Suddenly a large, black hole appeared in the centre of the dam face, about 30 feet from the top, and the water was gushing out.

Michael Anderson faithfully recreated this incident in the film.[34]

The Dortmund-Ems Canal Raid was to prove even more demanding. Knight's outstanding skill at night flying at a low level did not save him and his crew. Over the target, Knight and his crew failed to spot tree tops poking out above a heavy fog. They ploughed through the branches losing the use of both port engines and damaging control surfaces. Knight was left with no option but to request that he jettison the dead weight of the bomb and try to get back to base in England. By the time they approached the small Dutch town of Denham, it was becoming impossible to keep the Lancaster flying straight and level. Knight realised they would never be able to negotiate the sea crossing.

Thereupon, he dragged the Lancaster as high as he possibly could and his seven crew mates parachuted clear. Alone in the bomber, Knight tried to pull off a controlled forced landing in a field, but hit trees and nosed into the ground where the wreckage burned furiously killing Knight. Nevertheless, five of his crew managed to evade capture and got back to England in about six weeks.

---

34 Chris Ward & Andreas Wachtel, *Dambuster Crash Sites, 617 Dambuster Squadron Crash Sites in Holland and Germany,* Pen & Sword Aviation, Barnsley, 2013, 32-4, 76-80; Burgess, *Australia's Dambusters,* 18-21, 35-7, 45, 52, 199.

Bob Kellow was profoundly upset when he finally heard the news of his skipper who, by his actions, saved the lives of his crew:

> It was not until I arrived back in England that I learned that Les had died that evening we baled out … Les apparently made a near-perfect wheels-up landing, but unfortunately the enemy had dug a deep ditch across the field and piled earth from the ditch to form a wall about six feet high. The aircraft slammed into the wall and the impact broke Les' neck. He was killed instantly.[35]

The Australians

The six Australian crewmen of No 617 portrayed in Michael Anderson's film included, in a prominent place in the actual raid on the dams, Les Knight as played by Denys Graham, whereas the prominent Australian stage and screen actor Bill Kerr played the flying ace Micky Martin (as already related): 'Two more beers, please waiter'; Ronald Wilson played Dave Shannon; Nigel Stock (who was also in the film *The Great Escape*) played "Spam" Stafford; Basil Appleby played Bob Hay and Tim Turner played Jack Leggo. In real life, however, there were thirteen Australians in the three formations of the dambusters raid and they were heavily decorated on the achievement of the raid, except for – funnily enough – Les Knight, "Tammy" Simpson, "Lance" Howard and "Charlie" Williams.

They were:

35 Burgess, *Australia's Dambusters,* 97.

- Flight Lieutenant HBM "Mick" Martin, DFC
- Flight Lieutenant DJ "Dave" Shannon, DFC
- * Pilot Officer LG "Les" Knight
- * Flight Lieutenant RNG "Norm" Barlow, DFC
- Flight Lieutenant JF "Jack" Leggo, DFC
- * Flight Lieutenant RC "Bob" Hay, DFC
- Pilot Officer RGT "Bob" Kellow, DFM
- Flight Sergeant TD "Tammy" Simpson
- Pilot Officer BT "Toby" Foxlee, DFM
- Pilot Officer CL "Lance" Howard
- Pilot Officer A "Tony" Burcher, DFM
- * Pilot Officer FM "Span" Spafford, DFM
- * Flying Officer CR "Charlie" Williams[36]

It is obvious that giving all these men a speaking part with actors playing their roles would have turned Anderson's film into a reconstructed documentary rather than a film drama as it was meant to be. Anderson did show in the film how important Australian pilots were to the success of the No 617 Squadron when Richard Todd as Guy Gibson is taken to choose the members of the squadron: 'I'd go for these two Australians if I were you', suggests Group Captain Whitworth, pointing to photos of P/O Knight (played by Australian expatriate actor Vincent Ball) and then to Micky Martin (Bill Kerr). 'Like to have David Shannon'. And so the scene continues with Canadians and two New Zealanders chosen as well.

Anderson's film captures the severity of the death toll of the aircrew in the famous raid by concentrating on Michael Redgrave's anguish as Barnes Wallis in the last scenes when he learns something of the deaths and thus questions whether the whole enterprise was really worthwhile – a touch of anti-

36 * Killed in action in the war; list in Burgess, *Australia's Dambusters,* 3.

war sentiment. Ten out of the nineteen Lancasters used, Paul Brickhill tells, were coming home after their dangerous encounter with the Ruhr dams 'hugging the ground, 8 tons lighter now in bomb and petrol load and travelling at a maximum cruising, about 245 [mph], not worrying about petrol; only about getting home'. By the time they reached base 'fifty-six beardless men out of 133 were missing and only three got out by parachute at a perilously low height to spend the rest of the war miserably in prison camp [an experience Brickhill was to share with them and then write about extensively before writing *The Dam Busters*]'.[37]

The Australian Flying Officer Charles R Williams DFC was killed when his Lancaster bomber crashed in northern Germany in the dambusters 1943 raid; the incident was alluded to in the film by one of Richard Todd's tense reactions while leading the attack as Guy Gibson.

Charles Williams spent the first thirty years of his life in north-western Queensland. At the war's outbreak, he volunteered for the air force to see the world and to fly. He took part in the Empire Training Scheme that Prime Minister Robert Menzies had committed Australians to in 1939. Williams had been commissioned as a wireless operator/ air gunner before he arrived in England in late 1941. He joined 61 Squadron flying Lancasters and made many English friends while on leave. He volunteered for the 617 Squadron. To his family, Charles could only write: 'How I do wish I could tell you everything I would like to … but until the war is over I cannot tell anyone'. In the attack on the dams, sadly, Charles' plane hit a high voltage cable near the River Rhine. The entire crew died instantly.[38] The feature

37 Brickhill, *The Dam Busters*, 110-3.

38 EC Fry 'Death of an Airman', Ann Curthoys, AW Martin & Tim Rowse, *Australians from 1939*, Fairfax, Symes & Weldon Associates, Broadway, 1987, 24-5.

film drama recorded the event and captured the suddenness of the loss of contact with the plane and the deadly explosion.

* * *

The great renowned New Zealand filmmaker Peter Jackson has wanted to remake *The Dam Busters* as a feature film for a long time and was even about to start filming a few years ago, but he has since been busy involved in making *The Hobbit*. For *The Dam Busters* a new script has been written by Stephen Fry to replace the RC Sherriff original. The wealthy ex-television presenter David Frost has purchased the rights to the Paul Brickhill book, but the new version will use the untouched half of Brickhill's book as well as feature many aspects of the story that were not known or revealed because of the secrecy act at the time Brickhill wrote the story in the first half of the 1950s. Ten Lancaster models by Jackson have already been make. After much debate and controversy, in the new film Gibson's dog is to be called "Digger" rather than "Nigger" – thus history can be changed for political correctness alone. At the time of writing, there is not a timetable for its release and filming has yet to begin, but the legend is as healthy as ever and continues to be reset and reset again.

The last survivor of the dambusters raid died in August 2015. Squadron leader, Flight Lieutenant John Leslie ("Les") Munro was born in Gisborne, New Zealand. After the war, he went back to farming. He joined the Royal New Zealand Air Force (RNZAF) in 1941 enlisting on 5 July. He arrived in the United Kingdom on 20 October 1941. He flew in the 97 Squadron in 1942/43 before becoming part of the 617 Squadron on March 1943. He was awarded the DFC gazetted on 11 June 1943 by which time he had flown in twenty-one operations; the DSO was gazetted on 28 April 1944. By this time, he had flown in forty-one operations. He was promoted to Squadron Leader and released from service on 5 February 1946.[39]

Les Munro took off for the dams in the first formation. He was hit by flak over Vlieland and the plane's radio and intercom went dead, as was depicted in the film. The other aircraft of the formation crossed the coast and turned sharply south-east and made their way across the Zuyder Zee. 'The rising full moon lent them an even more sinister look as they thundered over the low sand dunes and swung inland towards Germany'. But Les Munro, being hit on the approach to Vlieland, was eventually forced to turn his Lancaster 'W-Willie' back to Scampton. Munro later wrote in his book *Bomber Boys*:

> I would have been at 70 or 60 feet when we were hit over [the island of] Vlieland on the post side of the aircraft. The intercom immediately went dead. I felt the thump of the shell. The damage from that shell exploding blew a hole in the side of the aircraft where the squadron code letters were, but didn't cause much damage on the other side, and no damage to the rear gunner and his turret...

But as it was impossible to make repairs, Munro made the wise decision to return to base. As he wrote: 'It was just one of those things'. When Munro reflected on it, he felt relief. The damaged plane and the return to base probably saved his life: 'Even to this day I think if I had gone on there was a strong possibility I wouldn't have come back'. Munro was in the minority in the 617 Squadron, there were only three pilots left from the original: the Australian Dave Shannon, New Zealander Les Munro and the American Joe McCarthy who

39 Cooper, *The Men who breached the dams,* 194.

now flew under Group Captain Leonard Cheshire in the 617. The rest that survived moved on to other squadrons. Cheshire had made them heads, that is flight commanders, of three flights under his organisation. The raid on Mimoyecques proved to be the end of an era for Leonard Cheshire VC and then David Shannon, Joe McCarthy and Les Munro – they were all posted as "tour expired". The big secret German guns of Mimoyecques had been buried and blocked by them in a raid and were never fired on London.

Shannon, McCarthy and Munro from three separate nations were all veterans of the original mission to the Ruhr Valley and they had defied the odds by flying on. They had done more than enough. They had put in two years of flying the most hazardous of operations. The Australian David Shannon had won two DSOs and two DFCs before he left 617 Squadron as a wing commander, like McCarthy and Munro. Shannon completed sixty-nine operations without a meaningful break.[40]

Les Munro came into prominence recently with the proposed sale of his war medals. Not only was he the last surviving pilot by 2015 of the famous 'Dambuster' raids, he was one of only two New Zealanders in the team selected by Gibson. He died at the age of 96 on 4 August 2015 at the same time as this book was being prepared. Munro was played in the movie by distinguished New Zealand actor Ewen Solon. Munro decided to sell his impressive New Zealand Order of Merit, DSO and DFC group and put the money towards the RAF Benevolent Fund's Upkeep of the Bomber Command Memorial in London – a magnanimous gesture. He wanted to ensure that 'the men of Bomber Command who had lost their lives during the Second World War will be remembered with pride for generations to come'.

40 Burgess, *Australia's Dambusters,* 42, 43, 44, 61, 103, 116, 140, 238.

The Squadron Leader's decision to sell his medals sparked something of a public controversy in New Zealand. Suddenly, seemingly out of nowhere, came a raft of people horrified that Munro's medals might leave New Zealand. He was urged to reconsider and keep them in the country. Some suggested that New Zealanders should club together and buy the medals – they were worth a large amount on the medal market internationally, thus allowing the donation to proceed. A few even hinted that Munro should be forcibly restricted by the government by blocking the sale under the country's *Protection of Objects Act.*

Fortunately, any such action proved unnecessary as Lord Ashcroft stepped in with an offer of £75,000 to be donated to the RAF Benevolent Fund on the proviso that the medals were to be donated to New Zealand's Museum of Transport and Technology (MOTAT) in Auckland. This offer diffused the political situation and took the heat out of the debate.

Before this time, some of the more violent reaction to the original sale was an eye-opener. The fact that Squadron Leader Les Munro was awarded these medals for his bravery during one of the most dangerous RAF missions in Europe during the Second World War did not seem to be taken into account (as well as the subsequent missions he was engaged in, including the D-Day invasion of France). To claim that he should not be allowed to do whatever he wanted with the medals was in itself ludicrous.

There was a consortium of museums in New Zealand that tried to persuade Munro to change his mind and keep the medals in the country. They did not want the medals of one of the two New Zealand Dam Busters to go overseas at any cost. But the museums, however, did not have the necessary resources to bid for them. Lord Ashcroft's generosity solved the problem and brought the controversy to a successful conclusion.[41] The death of Les Munro occurred on 4 August 2015. There is no one left now with a living memory of the night of the actual raid on the Ruhr Dams.

* * *

The Dam Busters as a film turned Brickhill's more complex book into the straightforward war mission genre, albeit of a carefully wrought and factual nature. Its phases are well established: a military strategy underlying the purpose of a military mission is delineated; men are thoroughly trained and disciplined in preparation; they are sent on the dangerous mission, but succeed in its accomplishment in the course of which heroic deeds are performed; some of the men return safely to base, others do not; some regrets are expressed, but a sense of triumph pervades the atmosphere; life returns to normal. To achieve this direction in the film's genre-driven story, the director Michael Anderson eliminates themes and issues raised by Brickhill that may complicate the thrust of the action. Such matters as the impact of the raid on the civilian population of the Ruhr Valley is totally ignored. In doing so, Anderson barely films half of Brickhill's book so that the total concentration is on the military mission and its achievement. Thus the film is prevented from rambling and maintains its high-octane tension.

Nevertheless, the film is a fine example of this type of war genre and provides subtle light and shade touches, particularly in the well-realised characterisation as played in a masterly

41 'From the Editorial Desk. Whose medal is it anyway?' and 'Munro's medals to stay in NZ', *Medal News*, May 2015, 5, 6.

manner by Michael Redgrave and Richard Todd with neatly understated nuances.

It is a film of its time in that it respectively celebrates male camaraderie and admires effective leadership and responsible decisions. It is quite simply a classic war movie that expresses comfortable sentiments, unlike Stanley Kubrick's brilliant *Paths of Glory* and David Lean's fine film, *The Bridge on the River Kwai* filmed a few years later in 1957 where there is a questioning of moral absolutes and anti-war arguments are generated in the comments of various characters in tense situations.

The Dam Busters, however, is fundamentally a tribute to successful and highly innovative military action. The focus is the unfolding chronological narrative of the squadron, its mission and achievement albeit painful with little reference to the broader issues of war. And yet the brilliant screenplay by RC Sherriff with his exact interpretation of Brickhill's work ensures *The Dam Busters* remains an outstanding example of its genre, remaining a favourite of film buffs of all types.

For Michael Anderson, *The Dam Busters*, a patriotic and intensely British World War II story, was his first major breakthrough success as a director in his own right having worked with and been strongly influenced by powerful English directors like Anthony Asquith, Noel Coward and David Lean. His use of black-and-white film to display authenticity and the historical truth of war is achieved in a masterly manner.

Anderson got his first start as an independent director in 1947 and then continued to direct one or two fairly minor feature films each year, including the gripping, well-made second feature in 1953 *The House of the Hour* – also based on a book like *The Dam Busters*. This helped to have him chosen for the filming of Brickhill's bestselling non-fiction book. All of Michael Anderson's films between 1953 and 1959 were well received by cinema audiences and highly popular with them,

Guy Gibson (Richard Todd) & Barnes Wallis (Michael Redgrave) in The Dam Busters

including the highly regarded identity-crisis thriller *Chase a Crooked Shadow* (1957) in which Richard Todd was again the leading man in a nerve-wracked performance that extended his range. Before that, Todd – again in uniform – in the *Yangtse Incident* played the trapped naval commander in a fact-based gripping story rather similar to his commanding Guy Gibson portrayal and familiar ground for the actor who was a Second World War hero himself. Anderson directed it with great skill ramping up the tension towards its dramatic climax. Like *The Dam Busters*, it was a collective tribute to the bravery of the men in uniform and in harm's way during the whole incident. In three successive years, Anderson used Todd's considerable talents as a leading man.

Anderson's film of *The Dam Busters* does recognise through Richard Todd's performance and Brickhill's treatment in his book that Guy Gibson was one of the outstanding flyers and leaders in the RAF. He had been in command of 106 Squadron and had flown two bomber tours of duty and one night-flying tour (mentioned in the film but not depicted) before being selected to command 617 Squadron. In the film, he arrived spectacularly at Scampton in a Lancaster making a grand entrance for Richard Todd since Michael Redgrave had dominated the film up to this moment. As well as the VC, Gibson had won the DSO and DFC twice and was the most decorated pilot in Britain. He was thought of by many to be cocky and arrogant (unlike Leonard Cheshire who succeeded him).

Gibson was awarded a VC for leading the dambusters raid and thirty-three other decorations were handed out, making No 617 Squadron the most decorated in the air force. After the raid, Gibson was sent on a lecture tour of the United States and wrote up his wartime career in *Enemy Coast Ahead*, but he was killed before it was published. His wife Eve insisted it be recognised as a source for the film *The Dam Busters* along with the work of Paul Brickhill. This was agreed to. Brickhill flew to America where she lived to appease her.

Guy Gibson was killed on 19 September 1944. The Mosquito he was flying crashed in Holland while returning from a raid. By this time, he had flown 175 sorties over occupied Europe.[42] Anderson's triumphant film does not record his death. At the end of the film, we see him walking away alone in the dark, up the road to his quarters in Scampton where he intends to painfully write letters to the beloved relatives of the fifty-three men killed. And so, immediately, the film ends on a sombre note.

Much later in 1995, Richard Todd gave his shrewd assessment of Guy Gibson from the point of view of the actor who played him and had to 'get under his skin'. This was contained in a letter to a thirteen-year-old schoolboy who had contacted him for an

42 Downing, 'War on Film', 41.

assessment in studying a famous person. The aging 'handsome, blue eyed' actor who always appeared 'with an erect military bearing' (perhaps because of his short stature like Gibson) wrote with precision:

> He was a young man of great physical and mental courage, allied to determination and stubbornness. He was a brilliant pilot but reckoned to be overshadowed in this respect by (his dams raid colleague) 'Mickey' [*sic*] Martin. He was a born leader of men but not entirely popular with those who served with him, since he was quite cold and calculating and inclined to be very 'cocky'.
> He was extremely ambitious both professionally and personally and yet very protective towards his subordinates. Had he survived the war he would have had a highly successful career in the RAF.[43]

Squadron Leader George "Johnny" Johnson also gave his thoughts about Gibson that were echoed in the vital raid scene in the film:

> I think the true demonstration of leadership came on the actual attack on the Moehne Dam. He made the first attack and assessed the strength of the defences. As he called in each subsequent crew to attack he flew alongside them to attract some of the defences. To me that says, 'You are doing this, I am doing it, we are doing it together'. That to me is the essence of good leadership, always from the front.[44]

43 Cited in Simpson, *Guy Gibson Dambuster*, 151.
44 Also cited in Simpson, *Guy Gibson Dambuster*, 150.

The assessment of the actor who played the part and the eye witness account to the actual events collide in their opinion with perfect precision.

Guy Gibson (on ladder) and crew

CHAPTER 10

REACHING FOR THE SKY
Film, Reality and Book

In any feature film worth its salt as a biography (a Bio-pic, as they are called) of a famous or celebrated person, the choice of actor to play the role of the main protagonist is crucial to its success or failure as a feature film in the box-office. Such was the case for *Reach for the Sky*.

Released after World War II in March 1954, Brickhill's book strongly confirmed thereafter the iconic and legendary status of Douglas Robert Stewart Bader[1] as an air force war hero. In framing the filmic character, the experienced director Lewis Gilbert had to take into account the fact that Bader was older than most of the fighter pilots who had fought in the Battle of Britain. He was born in 1909 on 21 February. The pre-war professional RAF pilot had lost both legs in a devastating aircraft accident on 14

1 Pronounced 'Bahder'.

December 1931 when flying a Bulldog trainer and performing a low-flying stunt. Showing determination, physical courage and confidence in winning against all odds, Bader had learned to walk with two prosthetic metal legs without the use of a walking stick, hence his nickname "Tin-Legs" Bader. From the beginning, he refused to use a stick even to steady himself. With the aid of carefully placed film shots, the actor was required to be convincing in his movements in rehabilitation as the film would depict his gradual stumbling advancement in mastering the art of relearning how to walk. Using the latest techniques of the time, Bader was taught how to walk at Roehampton rehabilitation hospital with his artificial limbs being constantly adjusted to enable his continued progress. This situation was faithfully recorded in the film sequences in documentary style.

The actor also had to give a good hint that, before the accident, Bader was a competitive athlete who was a brilliant aggressive all-rounder at cricket and a fine rugby player who had been close to selection in the national team as a fly half or inside centre to play against the visiting South African Springboks national team just prior to his accident. He played for the famous Harlequins Rugby Union Club as a star first-grade centre three-quarter. He was a champion competitive boxer in the RAF team. As well, he was absolutely dedicated to the squadron's masculine social life in all its facets.

When Lewis Gilbert chose popular film actor Kenneth More in 1956 as Bader the die was cast. More had had enormous recent success in the light comedy *Genevieve* about a veteran car rally from London to Brighton, as well as a more melancholic film adaptation of Terence Rattigan's play *The Deep Blue Sea* co-starred with Vivien Leigh that showed him to be a dramatic actor of subtle depth and compelling strength. In it, he played 'a shiftless, schoolboyish ex-RAF man' that implied, by chance, some of Bader's youthful characteristics.

Soon after, he had the main role in Gilbert's reverential film biography of Bader, the legless fighting ace based very closely on the book by Paul Brickhill. More played the part to the hilt and it made him a matinee idol in the British cinema. Later, he played in Gilbert's *Sink the Bismark!* another successful war film. He was also good as a naval officer in the lead part in 1957 in *A Night to Remember* about the sinking of the *Titanic* in 1911. In 1958 he played Richard Hannay in a remake of *The 39 Steps* based on John Buchan's spy novel. Further on with an all-star cast, he played in Guy Hamilton's *The Battle of Britain* (1968) in which in real life Douglas Bader had played a major part. More did not repeat his performance of Bader, but instead played a senior executive RAF officer behind the scenes.

The box-office success of *Reach for the Sky* turned Kenneth More, who was born in 1916, the same age as Paul Brickhill and Peter Finch, and thus a little younger than Douglas Bader, into a top-ranking film star. It was a major turning point in his career.

More started his stage career as a stage hand at the famous Windmill Theatre which presented vaudeville. He then had a spell in repertory followed by service in the Second World War in the Royal Navy. He found a niche as an actor in early television drama productions. The fifties saw him make a big name for himself in British comedy feature films like *Doctor in the House* (1952) with Dirk Bogarde, another popular British star. He appeared in the comedy *The Sheriff of Fractured Jaw* in 1958.

As the great war hero in *Reach for the Sky*, More was particularly convincing as Bader. His jovial, energetic very English style was most appropriate and made him one of the most popular of all post-war British stars, apart from Dirk Bogarde. He died in 1982 after playing in major television series, like *Father Brown Detective* and *The Forsyte Saga*. More's last feature war film was *Oh! What a Lovely War* (1969), the satire based on World War I documents, in which he played Kaiser Wilhelm II.

Lewis Gilbert, the director of *Reach for the Sky*, was born in London in 1920. He was brought up in a music hall family. Originally a child actor who started on the stage at the age of five, he later became interested in film direction. His firmly based tradition was to keep the audience entertained as in the music hall. He was invalided out of the RAF in 1944 and joined the British Instructional to work for the RAF Film Unit as a director of documentaries and war propaganda. With his documentary experience and style of romantic and entertaining social realism, he made six good solid war movies that were 'winningly acted, thrilling and moving'.[2] They started with the underrated *Albert RN* (1953) that helped to provide material in tone and style for John Sturges' *The Great Escape* in 1963, *The Sea Shall Not Have Them* (1954) and *Reach for the Sky* (1956). These were all highly successful in the box office. Then he made *Carve Her Name with Pride* (1958) – most probably his best film – followed by *Sink the Bismark!* (1960) with Kenneth More again and *HMS Defiant* (1962). These six films were predominantly grey and realistic using black-and-white film and authentic locations. They were all tributes to the determined way of life of wartime British heroes, either civilian or military.

In 1961 Gilbert made the sensitive non-war drama *The Greengage Summer* about coming-of-age and a blighted romance, again with Kenneth More who appeared to be his favourite actor. *The Greengage Summer* expanded Kenneth More's range away from wartime heroes and into flawed

---

2 David Quinlan, *Quinlan's Film Directors*, BT Blatsford Ltd, London, 1999, 124.

sensitive characterisations that he was to continue with for the rest of his acting career. The war movies were amongst Gilbert's best, apart from the well-realised *The Greengage Summer*. Later, he made three James Bond movies: *You only live Twice* (1967), *The Spy Who Loved Me* (1977) and *Moonraker* (1979).[3]

Paul Brickhill was careful not to write a hagiography about Bader who, in some respects, was a controversial, difficult public figure who tended to be bullish and who always believed he was in the right. He took occasional pleasure in opposing authority. Some of this was carefully represented in Brickhill's book which sold nearly 200,000 copies in its first year of release. It was a huge success for the author that, apparently, became a source of some annoyance much later for Bader.

In 1955, film producer Daniel M Angel purchased the book rights for £15,000 (a little more than a third of a million British pounds in today's currency). Then Angel brought in Gilbert to write the screenplay based on Brickhill's book and inspired by it with some simplification to suit a visual rather than a written suspense drama. This was a matter of reworking the facts slightly. From his wartime experiences, like Brickhill, Gilbert knew how the RAF operated and understood well its mores and cherished traditions. He liked the masculine world of flyers and this made him reverential towards the life and hard-fought achievements of Bader.

When it came to adapting Brickhill's book, Gilbert believed he had to smooth out the rough edges of Bader's character for consumption by the cinema audience and make him even more simply heroic. Public image forged in wartime newspapers had to be preserved in the feature film. Gilbert was more intent on

---

3 George Perry, *The Great British Picture Show*, Pavilion Books, London, 1974, 164, 179, 181, 184, 200, 221, 272; Lloyd & Fuller (eds), *The Illustrated Who's Who*, 171, 311.

shaping a model, inspirational British hero, understated and yet still a little opinionated, charmingly confrontational, thus fitting neatly into Kenneth More's crisp jovial style and splendid timing of dialogue. He was presented in the film as unflappable, persistent, courageous and perpetually pipe-smoking and very British Public School middle class in speech and deportment (as was Bader in real life).

In the opening of *Reach for the Sky*, we are drawn to a small light, almost fragile plane taking off against an ominously darkened cloudy sky. Implied is a tense feeling of foreboding about the future. The titles appear: 'KENNETH MORE in REACH FOR THE SKY based on the book by Paul Brickhill. THE STORY OF DOUGLAS BADER'.[4] We soon realise that More as Bader will dominate the screen from the very beginning to the end with a huge number of close-ups capturing every nuance of expression in the actor's face as the character encounters both the highs and the lows of life, humour and tragedy. Brickhill's episodic narrative style in his biography of Bader was most suited to the development of a screenplay and Gilbert as screenwriter was able to capture its essence while reducing the written episodes to suit the pace and the visual narrative of a feature film so as to ensure elements of entertainment for the cinema audiences of various social backgrounds. Brickhill's precise and particular detail helped to capture authenticity in every scene and sequence.

Brickhill's own characterisations were sharp, precise and consistent in their serial form which provided an occasional punch-line to end each episode. His palpably visual character

4 *Reach for the Sky*, based on the book by Paul Brickhill, Director Lewis Gilbert, screenplay by Lewis Gilbert, Producer Daniel M Angel, starring Kenneth More, Muriel Pavlow, Lyndon Brook, Lee Patterson & Alexander Knox, 136 minutes, black & white, 1956 (The Rank Collection DVD Video).

sketches of minor characters assisted the several screen actors to play out their parts. As an example, Alexander Knox as the surgeon Dr Leonard Joyce who removed both of Bader's legs in major operations has his character to a tee:

> 'Excuse me, Mr Joyce [Alexander Knox], but we've just admitted a young Air Force officer after a bad crash. Could you have a look at him?'
>
> The rest was understood: she had assisted Joyce at many operations and he was a man of few words. He took his coat off and followed her back to the ward, and shortly was saying that he would wait and see if the patient came out of shock enough to try and operate. He was young and strong. They must at least try.
>
> … a man in a long white surgeon's coat and cap standing by his [Bader's] head who looked scholarly and said in a quiet voice: 'Hallo, old chap. I see you've had a bit of an accident. Don't worry. Just lie back and we'll soon have you fixed up'.[5]

Lewis Gilbert was astute enough to lift the piece of dialogue straight out of the book where suitable and use a similar scene structure in the film. Thus, in this sense, Brickhill collaborated with Gilbert in script writing. Knox, a fine character actor specialised in such dignified upper-middle class roles, dominated the tense scenes at the hospital with a quiet but alert manner. He was a Canadian actor who arrived in England in the 1930s where he was later to become a successful novelist and playwright. He made his first film in 1938. Going to the United States, he built up a sterling career as a character actor.

---

5 Brickhill, *Reach for the Sky*, 50-1.

Once again in England in the 1950s, he gave some remarkable performances in British films, especially in the important hospital scenes in *Reach for the Sky*. Later, he played another role as a military doctor in *Fräulein Doktor* (1969). He was particularly effective (as he was in *Reach for the Sky*) in director Joseph Losey's two remarkable films *The Damned* (1962) and *Accident* (1967).[6] In *Reach for the Sky*, Knox presented a presence of quiet but powerful authority, exactly as Gilbert wanted and exactly as Paul Brickhill had originally written it. Providing the most compelling cameo of the entire film, Knox matched Kenneth More, scene-for-scene. The two actors achieved a symbiotic relationship of documentary realism. Throughout the film Gilbert was able to draw upon a bevy of fine British character actors who played their parts with a high degree of skill. They were all cast appropriately.

Brickhill's separate successive scenes in his book, visually linked with interiors and cloudy landscapes, gradually but surely tightened the suspense and Lewis Gilbert's direction in the movie followed a similar pattern while maintaining the entertainment values through some hilariously funny episodes. He exploited More's comic touches well. This was also a major characteristic of Brickhill's writing which was punctuated with typically Australian punchlines, as in the famous *Bulletin* short stories.

Both Brickhill and Gilbert were married to a dramatic documentary social-realist style: a narrative where key details become symbolic of hidden understated, emotionally-charged feelings, as when More – depicting Bader – now in artificial legs, sights his old rugby boots, now useless, hanging in his bedroom locker and has them thrown away. The viewer is made to feel his loss of physical ability; his playing the game as he used to – full of energy and fierce sporting competitiveness. Brickhill's

6 Lloyd & Fuller (eds), *The Illustrated Who's Who*, 242.

written reportage thus is made into dramatic moments in the screenplay with complete respect for the author's intentions.

After the titles and subtitles flow through for the viewer with the biplane scene forming the background without the audience in the cinema seeing the pilot, a carefully-written statement defines the difference between the screenplay and the book:

> For dramatic purpose it has been necessary in this film to transpose in time certain events in Douglas Bader's life and also to reshape some of the characters involved in this story. The Producers apologise to those who may be affected by any change or omissions.

All is explained! The producer Daniel M Angel was very much aware that most of the protagonists in the film were still alive and active when the film was made, including Douglas Bader himself. The cinema audience could remember newspaper articles about the subject during World War II.

While Brickhill's book carefully deals in some detail with Bader's birth, ancestry, social class background, childhood, school days, including his prowess as a teenager sportsman, the film begins briskly in 1928, in a delightful comic scene with the young, neatly-suited, but carefree Bader making his way by motor bike to the Royal Air Force College, Cranwell (shown by a sign at the entrance gate). Kenneth More as Bader is seen merrily riding along a country road gazing enthusiastically at the sky and a plane flying overhead, symbolising his ambition and enthusiasm to be a pilot. While mesmerised by watching the aircraft above, he runs off the road falling off his bike on a mound of grass. His bowler hat is damaged and the headpiece flaps open, which soon after creates a comic scene to his great delight on his first parade.

In Brickhill's book, Bader dodges a stray cow on the road and lands off his bike, but the effect is the same although no cow appears in the film scene. More's subtle but gifted comic acting captures the character's youthful exuberant past, especially in the inspection scene of the new recruits at Cranwell where his bowler flaps open at precisely the wrong moment when the sergeant-at-arms inspects them. We picture Bader as a zestful fun-loving youth and are immediately attracted to his schoolboyish, lively cheeky persona.

In the inspection recruitment scene, Bader/More meets the featured actor Lyndon Brook who plays another cadet Johnny Sanderson, a composite character of several of Bader's youthful friends in real life making the dramatic narrative more straightforward and simple in entertainment terms. Brook also narrates parts of the story documentary-style in various scenes to ensure that continuity and the notion of real history taking place are maintained.

One scene quickly follows another while we find out Bader is a gifted natural flyer who learns extremely quickly, perhaps too quickly. But he is a cadet full of wild spirit and over confidence who gets into trouble with his mates late at night outside the college gates. As a prank he lets down the bicycle tyres of an overweight policeman. The next day he is reprimanded by the commanding officer: 'We don't want schoolboys in the RAF, Bader. We want men!'

The next brief scene shows Bader winning a cricket match single-handedly with a devastating display of big hitting with the bat. There is also a gay, happy dance scene with him and the other cadets in dress uniform. Bader/More dances merrily with a number of attractive young women who appear to find him immensely interesting and appealing. The story then quickly shifts to 1930.

By this time, Bader had been granted his "Wings" and is commissioned. He joins 23 Squadron at Kenley to fly Bulldog biplanes and is warned by a superior officer: 'Don't fly low aerobatics'. When a civilian flyer lays down a challenge, the impetuous, over-confident Bader/More cannot resist, sees red and does exactly what he was told not to do, thus establishing the theme of his occasional defiance of authority. The comedy has quickly turned to suspenseful and harrowing drama. By showing off demonstrating a low pass in the Bulldog, Bader crashes and his life is completely turned around. People at the aerodrome look on in horror for a long moment in disbelief and then race to the stricken pilot's aid. He is stuck unconscious in the cockpit of the smoking wreckage of the Bulldog.

Wreckage of Bader's Bulldog in real life. Bader's shoes front right

The crash scene was pivotal to Lewis Gilbert's film as the turning point between schoolboyish and peer group pranks that entertained as comic touches to the early harrowing scenes and the recovery sequence and serious culminating wartime heroics of the second half, both of the film and the book. A close-up of Bader's empty shoes at the crash site, with his bleeding body stretched out prone amongst anxious rescuers and friends at a distance from them, symbolise the change from act one to act two. In the final image of the crash scene, the camera zooms in for a close-up of the empty polished black dress shoes – a neat and foreboding symbol of what was next to take place.

It is interesting to note that Gilbert lifted the image of the empty shoes straight out of Brickhill's book to heighten both authenticity and individual tragedy. There is a page-length photograph in Brickhill's book of the crashed aeroplane a day or two after the incident.[7] It shows a startlingly dramatic wreckage that changed the hero's life and is captioned dramatically: 'The crash, 1931. Bader's [empty] shoes can be seen in the right foreground'. The uniting of the visual with the written was a vital part of Brickhill's graphic popular historiography that brought him much lasting acclaim with readers.

The hospital scenes, already recounted, are particularly well-done in the film as Bader/More hovers dangerously between life and death. In such moments Kenneth More provides a gut-wrenching, brilliant performance of depth. After Joyce (Alexander Knox) amputates Bader's right leg and, soon after, his left leg, he is at death's door and begins to drift away, almost peacefully. The narrator intones: 'he lay there fighting, fighting … slipping away'. But Bader then overhears, through the open door, a nurse in the corridor outside the room: 'There's a boy dying in there!' More, as the stricken Bader, mutters: 'We'll see'; his pecker is up again and he turns away decisively from death with its painlessness and begins with a rush of pain that carries with it consciousness and a mortal struggle, to recover slowly but surely. This struggle with death now has engendered a spirited and stubborn competitiveness.

Bader still does not know he has lost both legs. In the film, his pilot friend Sanderson (Lyndon Brook) is assigned to tell him. As soon as he wakes in bed, he is told, but still suffering from shock he does not take it in, saying very little. Later, Joyce says quietly: 'Very sorry, old chap. We had to take off the right leg [too]'.

Rarely does Bader/More nakedly reveal his innermost emotions. Impatient, he finds the task of recovery far too slow. In a moment of despair, he tells the nurse closest to him: 'I'd rather be dead'. In response the nurse (played beautifully by

7 Brickhill, *Reach for the Sky*, facing page 96. The photograph is most probably taken from Bader's personal collection.

Dorothy Alison) comes down on him hard, to teach him the lesson he will never forget: 'A lot of people have spent a great deal of time on you. They've worked for you, fought for you and prayed for you'. More shows by his expression that his character has turned the corner towards maturity and greater, almost overwhelming self-confidence and determination to succeed in life.

As recounted, the scenes at the Ministry of Pensions Hospital in Roehampton are powerfully achieved in the film. We experience as the audience how Bader is in genuine physical agony at first as he has to learn how to walk again and to turn left and right all over again with his new artificial legs. The doctor (sympathetically played by experienced grey-haired character actor Sydney Tafler) astutely supervises him. At every point in his development, through determination as a trained athlete, Bader achieves more quickly than what was expected by the training experts. More turns in another very fine, subtly articulated performance in this section of the movie. But the task ahead was by no means easy. In the dark of the cinema, the audience almost feels his pain just by watching. More gives a cathartic performance in these particular scenes while staying in character.

Even though the recovery is amazingly rapid, there is still a lot of struggle and falls to endure. Indeed, as the audience, we are taught a lesson of sorts. Every viewer is meant to applaud the determination and courage of the man. The effect on audiences is compelling. Even today, the film stands up to it in this particular respect.

Bader's next struggle in the film is against bureaucracy – a common theme in British war movies and also found in *The Dam Busters* with the inventor Barnes Wallis' struggles. There was nothing in the King's Regulations to support allowing a legless double amputee to be allowed to fly again in the RAF. Despite outstanding practical achievement back in flying school, Bader is eventually forced out of the RAF on a pension. He takes up a clerical position with the precursor to the famous Shell Oil Company. He impulsively marries his sweetheart (sensitively underplayed by Muriel Pavlow in counterpoint with Kenneth More) who he first met in a country roadside tearoom where she worked as a waitress. They meet on several romantic occasions providing the entertaining love theme of the film.

No male-female intense love affair interrupted the flow of the narrative of *The Dam Busters* as it has done in many other war movies. Neither Brickhill in his book nor Anderson in his film was particularly concerned about private lives – only about the mission at hand. By contrast, the moral support Douglas Bader's wife Thelma gave to her husband, especially through the war years, was extremely important and is underlined in the film by Pavlow's impressive performance. And this is why, after all, Brickhill dedicated his book to Thelma.

In 1939 after some negotiation at higher levels, Bader is again accepted into the RAF as a fully-fledged fighter pilot. He quickly rises through the ranks and becomes a famous ace. A famous photograph taken during the early period of the war depicts Douglas Bader standing heroically on the wing of his Hurricane fighter, leaning against the cockpit in his full flying gear. He is quietly smiling in a triumphant way – the message is obvious. Gilbert successfully recreates this scene with Kenneth More standing in a similar pose to that of the real Bader. Such settings heighten authenticity and the dramatic documentary style so evident throughout the movie, as in other British wartime feature films of the 1950s. Moreover, truth in fiction assists the creation of the post-war heroic legend of Bader as Brickhill had originally done so well in his famous and inspirational book of 1954.

More recent Second World War-in-the-Air histories, small and large, continue to reinforce the Bader legend in a similar way. Ira Peck's *The Battle of Britain* features a page-length photograph of Bader on the wing of the Hurricane – the same one that appeared in Brickhill's book – and another of Bader as an older man visiting the set for the 1969 war movie *The Battle of Britain*. Peck described the real-life Bader:

> Yet some of Britain's pilots *did* hate their enemy. One of them was Group Captain Douglas Bader, who flew a fighter despite having two artificial legs. This is how Bader describes his attitude towards the German invaders:
>
> 'We hated those airplanes with their iron crosses and their crooked swastikas flying into our English sky and dropping bombs indiscriminately on our British towns. Fighting alongside us were Czechs, Poles, Norwegians, Danes, Dutch, Belgians, and French, those gallant allies who managed to escape from their own countries and join with us in stopping the hated Hun from dominating the whole of Europe.[8]

Famous image of Douglas Bader

This portrayal reveals a harder aspect of the man, not found so much in Kenneth More's genial portrayal in the film, but is

8 Ira Peck, *The Battle of Britain*, Scholastic Book Services, New York, 1969, 63-5.

found subtly in Brickhill's book. Gilbert as director set out to soften the harder edge of the character, but in this portrayal by Peck, as an Empire man, he does not mention the Australian and Canadian pilots at all – to him, they are all Britishers and part of the British Empire that, by 1969, was crumbling badly, much to Bader's dismay.

John Vader's *Spitfire* also in 1969 provides a different page-length profile photograph of Bader looking like a young Marlon Brando – the caption reads 'Douglas Bader poses beside a Hurricane of the No 242 Squadron' – and even provides an extensive quotation about the Battle of Britain that uses the actual radio log from Paul Brickhill's *Reach for the Sky* where he quotes it.[9] Such an approach shows that Brickhill remained a recognised master of the subject.

In another published source about the Battle of Britain, a harsher portrait of Bader is provided while still retaining his heroic qualities.

> Wing-commander Douglas Bader, legless, opinionated and aggressive led the three squadrons of the 'Duxford Wing'. His pleas for the use of fighters *en masse* caused much controversy in R.A.F. Fighter Command. Bader's final tally was 23. He was shot down in 1941 and captured.[10]

But Brickhill had also dealt with this matter in precise detail.

Douglas Bader's public image and overpowering legendary status in the popular historiography of World War II remains

---

9 John Vader, *Spitfire*, Purnell's History of the Second World War weapons book, no 6, Macdonald & Co, London, 1969.

10 Lt-Col. Eddy Bauer, *World War II*, vol.1, pt 13, Battle of Britain, Orbis Publishing, London, 1978, 253.

dominant as exemplified by this profile in a recent publication written by Allan Burney:

> Pilot Profile. Douglas Bader
> Although he flew Hurricanes during the Battle of Britain, Douglas Bader was a great advocate of the Spitfire and had his own specially-marked example. Immortalised by the film '*Reach for the Sky*', Bader lost both legs as a young pilot officer, but returned to duty at the start of World War 2. He was given command of No 242 Squadron in June 1940 and introduced the tactic of sending out fighter squadrons in pairs – known as the 'Big Wing'. Bader had a personal Spitfire Va with distinctive markings D-B. He preferred to engage the enemy from short range using machine guns, and for a long time resisted having to fly a cannon-armed aircraft. In August 1941, he was forced to bale out of his Spitfire over German-occupied France. He was captured and, after a number of escape attempts, was sent to Colditz where he spent the rest of the war as a PoW. [He was awarded a DSO and Bar, DFC and Bar.][11]

But this is really not revisionist as Brickhill had dealt in elegant detail with all these issues and remains the standard source. In his film, Gilbert managed to pick up this information about Bader and juggle it to a greater or lesser extent, sometimes for convenience and to save costs, using the device of a documentary narrator to quickly skim over some of the events.

The flying scenes that become the next sequence in the *Reach*

---

11 Allan Burney (ed.), *Famous Fighters of World War 2*, Coxy Media, UK, 2015, 29.

for the Sky movie are particularly well executed by Gilbert, starting with Bader's first mission over Dunkirk where he 'bags' a 109 enemy plane. Studio shots of Bader/More and other pilots in their cockpits are skilfully intercut with camera gun footage from actual dog-fights and specially shot footage of aircraft in flight provided by the Shuttleworth Archival Collection. The effect to the cinema audience was compelling and crowds flocked to see the film when it was first released.

Gilbert very carefully follows Brickhill's powerfully visual description in his book:

> He [Bader] rammed stick and rudder over and the Spitfire wheeled after them. A 109 [Messerschmitt] shot up in front; his thumb jabbed the firing button and the guns in the wings squirted with a shocking noise. The 109 seemed to be filling his windscreen. A puff of white spurted just behind its cockpit as though someone had used a giant flit-gun. The puff was chopped off … for a moment nothing … then a spurt of orange flame mushroomed round the cockpit and flared back like a blow-torch. The 109 rolled drunkenly, showing her belly, and in the same moment he saw the black cross on its side. It was true. They did have black crosses. Suddenly it was real and the 109 was falling away and behind, flaming.
>
> …
>
> The heady joy of the kill flooded back as he slid out over the water towards England.[12]

Only a RAF fighter pilot could re-create the explicit detail and matter-of-fact emotion required in such a description and Paul

12 Brickhill, *Reach for the Sky*, 173.

Brickhill had been one. It is written in the best Hemingway-style and flourish, one simple active sentence following another. As such it was well imitated on film by the director.

The major scenes on the ground in the movie show how Bader was put in command of 242 Squadron at Duxford; a Hurricane squadron of war-weary depleted Canadian pilots forced to leave most of their supplies in France when they evacuated. The Canadian flyers are reluctant to accept an English commanding officer 'without legs'. In a dramatic flying scene (an ironic echo of his earlier crash scene without the crash), Bader/More demonstrates his flying ability to them and then shows his aggressive ability to cut red-tape with the higher authorities to obtain vital supplies and equipment. These two actions win the total respect and affection of the squadron. Thus, they are ready for action against the enemy instead of sitting around endlessly waiting. Through these short, sharp sequences, Lewis Gilbert reveals the significant and specific qualities of Bader's wartime leadership.

In one of these scenes, Bader/More is called before Air Chief Marshall Sir Hugh Dowding, head of Fighter Command, for sending an abusive almost violent message to a stubborn, by-the-rules bureaucrat. But even Dowding, at the top of the RAF chain of command, falls for Bader's mixture of charm and aggression and agrees to give him what he wants.

Bader is correctly depicted by Gilbert as leading his men from the front – also a classical stereotype of a wartime hero in the movies that was to be used on many occasions as 'the proving himself' sequence used in many standard movies about war, including the portrayal of Guy Gibson in *The Dam Busters*, the first film adaptation of Brickhill's three books.

For our entertainment as a mass audience, Gilbert presents the usual merry and wild mess scenes (also found in *The Dam Busters*). During such high jinks and joking camaraderie in the

Canadian mess, two new recruits arrive and Bader introduces one of them as Pilot Officer Nicholson.

In real life, Flight Lieutenant James Nicholson, depicted in the film as merely a rookie pilot, won the Victoria Cross for bravery in the Battle of Britain. On 16 August 1940 Nicholson was flying a Hurricane of 240 Squadron when he was hit by a Messerschmitt Bf 110. He was wounded and started to bale out, but when another enemy aircraft came into his sights, he remained in the cockpit and continued firing until he had shot it down.

Badly wounded by this time, he baled out and landed near Southampton where he was accidentally fired on by the local Home Guard. Nevertheless, he recovered from his severe wounds and went back into active service. As a humble man, he felt he did not deserve the accolades and fame he received from the award of the VC. He was shot down again in May 1945 and his body was never recovered. (As late as May 2015, to mark the 75th Anniversary of the Battle of Britain, an RAF Typhoon jet was named in his honour and painted in the original colours from 1940. In the summer of 2015, it flew alongside a Hurricane at an air show in the United Kingdom.)[13] In the film the young actor playing his role appears in the Canadian mess scene only briefly. The events of his great bravery are not depicted in *Reach for the Sky* as a film. Everything is centred on Douglas Bader's life.

Bader's wife Thelma appears in the mess scene when the two young rookies arrive. She tells her husband: "They are so young". "I'll look after them", the intrepid leader replies. "Yes", she adds, "but who will look after you?" Here, Gilbert uses almost the same dialogue as in Brickhill's book. As a popular chronicler of

---

13 Taylor Downing, 'War on Film. Reach for the Sky', *Military History Monthly*, Issue 59, August 2015, 64.

historical event, Brickhill often recreated dialogue, thus using a fictitious device.

The next important scene, later used in other films and television dramas, shows the Canadian squadron under Bader listening to Churchill's famous radio broadcast, 'their finest hour', during the Battle of Britain. But the Canadians are kept on standby until the impatient Bader receives a phone call to 'scramble' and intercept a massive German bomber force over Kent. Gilbert uses authentic Luftwaffe footage here intercut with Pinewood's special effects to create 'some powerful aerial combat sequence' to thrill the cinema audience.[14]

The narrative then follows Bader getting to know his commanding officer Air Vice-Marshall Trafford Leigh-Mallory (played by the well-recognised character actor of military types, Ronald Adam, in a cameo part – even if his name is not well known), commander of Group 12. Bader, using charm and forceful persuasiveness, explains that his Canadian squadron had shot down twelve enemy planes in the Battle of Britain. If they had had three times as many fighter planes involved, they could have shot down three times as many. It was a simplistic but innovative idea and Leigh-Mallory goes along with Bader's ideas. The narrator of the film then informs the audience that Bader was soon leading five squadrons called the Duxford Wing.

The Battle of Britain is a victory for the British as Adolf Hitler postponed his plans to invade England. Bader becomes a Wing Commander – yet another rapid promotion – and is sent to Tangmere to take over command of three Spitfire squadrons. Brief scene after brief scene – Gilbert moves the story swiftly along at a cracking pace.

About a year after the Battle of Britain in a mission over France, Bader's Spitfire collides apparently with a Bf 109 and

---

14 Downing, 'War on Film. Reach', 65.

the tail is sliced off. As his plane plunges to earth, he struggles to bail out, but his inflexible artificial foot gets caught. In a supreme effort, he unstraps his artificial leg and leaves it in the cockpit. This is convincingly depicted by the special effects the director uses at Pinewood studios. Bader parachutes safely to earth, but is immediately taken prisoner by German troopers. The scene as a whole ironically echoes Brickhill's own real-life experience, also in a Spitfire, when he was shot down over Tunisia in North Africa.

Bader is immediately placed in hospital, but the German authorities allow a replacement leg to be parachuted in by a passing British bomber. He soon persuades his doctor to bring his artificial legs to his bedside and plans an escape by night through a third-storey window of the hospital using an improvised rope made of almost all of the bed sheets in the ward tied together. (After the war, a German sent Bader a photograph taken the day after he had escaped showing the rope made of sheets with the caption: 'Bader escaped from the hospital in St Omer'.)[15]

It was a daring breakout, typical of the Bader public persona. He was half-carried by a courageous member of the French

Kenneth More as Bader in escape scene, Reach for the Sky

15 Brickhill, *Reach for the Sky*, 257.

Resistance to a safe house. Soon after, however, he is captured while hiding under hay in a barn at the back of the house. The elderly farmer and his brave wife are marched off by searching German troopers. Bader/More, as he is taken away, protests that they did not know he was hiding in their barn. It is a harrowing scene, felt intensely by the cinema audience, as the old folk are taken away to be shot for aiding the enemy. These scenes follow step-by-step those in Brickhill's book. The film's narrator recounts that Bader was moved from one prison camp to another in Germany as he continued trying to escape and defy his captors. Ever defiant, he ends up in Colditz Castle after a stay in Stalag Luft III in Sagan where Paul Brickhill was incarcerated.

Colditz Castle lies in Saxony to the south-east of Leipzig. The castle still dominates with its huge stone walls and austere roofs. It is perched high on a rock overlooking the Zwickau Mulde River which gives it a romantic aura. It was largely rebuilt in the sixteenth century as a fortress in the opulent Renaissance style. For five years during World War II, it was a notorious prisoner-of-war camp. It was a place to which the Germans dispatched the most recalcitrant officers of the British and Allied force such as Group Captain Douglas Bader, DSO and Bar, DFC and Bar.

Despite its reputation, ironically it had a number of successful escapes. While surrounding terrain would have proved too difficult for Bader, he joined in gleefully in the almost daily game of cat-and-mouse. Most escapees were brought back – escape was the easiest part; getting out of Germany was infinitely more difficult, especially for a man with 'tin-legs'. The ingenuity of the many escape plans kept up morale. [16]

---

16 See Introduction by James Holland, in Major PR Reid, *Colditz. The Full Story*, The Folio Society, London, 2015, xx.

Some action involving Bader at Colditz would have enhanced the final stanza of Gilbert's film. But no doubt there were budgeting decisions that limited his scope. As it stands, the ending of his film is a little disappointing and jingoistic in tone. Despite this, the scenes of the Battle of Britain and Bader's recovery from the first aeroplane crash of 1931 have turned it into a classical film. Gilbert's film does not, however, deal with Bader's time in Colditz beyond mentioning in the voice-over narration that this was where he was finally placed by German authorities. The image of the bleak fortress believed to be inescapable is not used at all in the film.

Bader

When Bader – in real life – arrived in Colditz in 1943, his wooden chess set, when searched by the careful German guards, revealed one thousand German Reichsmarks, three home-made compasses and – probably from Stalag Luft III – seven maps, all equipment for his next planned escape! Ever defiant at Colditz and involved in several failed escape schemes, Bader was finally liberated with all the other prisoners by the Americans in April 1945.

Although frequently frustrated and difficult to be handled by prison guards and authorities, Bader remained in Colditz Castle until its relief as a Second World War prison camp. At the time, there were 1,300 officers imprisoned there. Lee Carson, an intrepid woman newspaper correspondent, somehow found her way to Colditz, met with Douglas Bader who proudly escorted her to the castle's vaulted attic to show her the two-seater glider they had secretly built there. It was a newspaper scoop for Carson and she took a photograph. Bader explained that it would have been their next form of escape that he hoped to use as its co-pilot:

> The glider reposed on its polished skid, a symphony in blue and white check; its wings glossy and taut; its controls sensitive, balanced, easy to the touch; a tropical bird, it looked as if it needed only a gentle breeze to float it easily off the ground. It filled the attic. Its total span from wing-tip to wing-tip was thirty-three feet. It was a beautiful piece of craftsmanship and astonished all who saw it.[17]

Thus Douglas Bader had dreamed in his cell of reaching for the sky again, but it was too late – the war was over. It is a great pity that Gilbert did not find a place in his film for this ironic image. Before the prisoners including Bader vacated the castle, the attic was locked securely again.

In the second last scene in the film, Bader returns to Thelma in their idyllic country cottage for a brief romantic reunion. He told her, however, that he wanted to get off 'for one last fling' before the war was technically over, thus destroying the moment once again for the long-suffering Thelma. The war ends when the Japanese surrender before Bader can get into the act. The last triumphal scene shows him leading a celebratory fly-past over London in September 1945.

Bader

17 PR Reid, *The Latter Days at Colditz*, Cassell, London, 2003, 316.

This scene stands in stark contrast to the sombre final scene in *The Dam Busters* when the solitary figure of Guy Gibson (Richard Todd) quietly walks back in the dark of the night to his lonely room to write painful letters to the loved ones of the many men he had lost. Grief not triumph is the theme of this last scene.

* * *

The film *Reach for the Sky* is clearly of its time as a splendid tribute to past glory of winning the war. Lewis Gilbert makes Bader the perfect hero and Kenneth More plays the part with great gusto which was like the real-life character in some aspects while considerably softening some of his more negative aspects. Brickhill brings them out more in his book.

While Gilbert starts his film in 1928 with Kenneth More (the youthful Bader) joyfully riding his bike to Cranwell to begin his RAF cadetship and looking romantically and idealistically to the sky and ending with the triumphal and spectacular fly-past over London in 1945, Brickhill explores in greater depth Bader's ancestry and birth, his period as an infant in India, his childhood at Kew, at Temple Grove school and his winning a scholarship to St Edward's (that Guy Gibson also attended). He also gives a much deeper study of his previous sporting career before loosing his legs and his romance and marriage to Thelma. Nevertheless, Gilbert glances at these matters deftly and economically to maintain the pace and tension of the movie.

Brickhill picks up, briefly, on Bader's post-war career with Shell Petroleum Company and his business air-tours, up to about 1954 and until the book was published. He summed up Bader post-war in his usual manner:

> People are too easily deceived by Bader's swashbuckling. Underneath is a generosity easily touched by other

> people's adversity so that he finds it difficult to walk past a beggar without wanting to help him. He lost a lot of money lending to old associates after the war. Now he prefers to give rather than to lend. He is still as much a man of extremes as ever, blowing hot or cold in enthusiasms, an intensely loyal friend, an uncompromising foe.[18]

As Brickhill hints, there was a rougher arrogant side to Bader. But both the book and the film are of the first half of the 1950s where positive wartime propaganda persisted. 'Bader in his immaculate RAF uniform and flying gear was the perfect hero for his time'.[19]

Brickhill's immensely successful story of Douglas Bader's struggles to regain his status as a fighter pilot after his terrible accident remains inspirational for many disabled people. Reports of this proliferate in the media of mass communication. For example, the *Canberra Times* in 1972 reported 'Legless boy finds a hero': 'Melbourne, Wednesday Colin Stephenson 14, hopes to become as renowned as the British wartime ace Douglas Bader'. Two weeks before, Colin had lost both his legs after falling from a train near Dimboola in country Victoria. His father had given him Australian Paul Brickhill's book *Reach for the Sky*. The doctor compared Colin's injuries as similar to those of Bader, much earlier in 1931. Colin read Brickhill's book as he lay in bed at the ironically named Footscray and District Hospital. He had also fractured his skull, broken his left elbow and had severe cuts to his face.[20]

Reach for the Sky, while of its time in the British Empire

---

18 Brickhill, *Reach for the Sky*, 370.
19 Downing, 'War on Film. Reach', 65.
20 'Legless boy finds a hero', *Canberra Times*, 20 January 1972, 3.

period of the first half of the 1950s, comes spectacularly out of its time as an inspiration to the physically disabled and, as well, as an acutely accurate portrait of the dashing wartime culture and legendary status of the Royal Air Force and the enemy coast ahead.

CHAPTER 11

FACT OR FICTION: THE GREAT ESCAPE

We will remember the comradeship, the freedom of mind, the rare moments of community spirit; we will forget the wet days, the wet weeks, the days when it was an effort to do anything, the days when it was an effort to do nothing, and our bunks seemed the only escape.

– Guy Morgan, *Only Ghosts Can Live*, 1945[1]

Guy Morgan was an English POW repatriated from Germany in 1944. His sentiments here, from his book in the first published account after World War Two of life in a German concentration camp, closely reflected those of Paul Brickhill, the Australian POW at Stalag Luft III

1 Cited by Taylor Downing, 'War on Film: The Captive Heart', *Military History Monthly*, Issue 67, April 2016, 60.

in Sagan. Morgan was to write the script for the feature film *The Captive Heart* (1945, directed by Basil Dearden), the first of the POW films – a genre of film making that went on with a flourish to *The Wooden Horse* (1950) and *The Colditz Story* (1955) and several others before coming to a peak with *The Great Escape* (1963) based on Paul Brickhill's book.

Production for *The Captive Heart* began even before the end of the Second World War, but was not released until March 1946. The film painted a realistic, documentary-style black-and-white portrait of the harsh destructiveness of life in a POW camp at a time when tens of thousands of men (like Brickhill) who had seen out the war incarcerated in prison camps were finally returned home. At the time there was a tendency to dismiss their wartime experience. The propaganda purpose of *The Captive Heart* was to show the extent of the loss suffered and the sacrifice made by such men.

While the book *The Great Escape*, sensationally well received, was first published in March 1950 (and before in shortened form as *Escape to Danger* with Conrad Norton in 1947), it was not lavishly filmed until 1962 and released in 1963. Yet like Paul Brickhill's depiction of POW life in Germany in book form, it profoundly influenced a whole popular cycle of wartime concentration camp genre films, notably Jack Lee's *The Wooden Horse* (1950) – a British film in documentary style with overtones of black-and-white Film Noir – similarly with *The Colditz Story* (1953).

John Sturges' film (*The Great Escape*) hit the screens as an all-star colourful action saga structured like an open-ended thriller with strong echoes and structural similarities with the director's earlier hits *Bad Day at Black Rock* and *The Magnificent Seven.* The escape script is an anthology of genre clichés established in several British prisoner-of-war dramas of the fifties except that there is a formidable American presence.

On the other hand, the films *The Dam Busters* and *Reach for the Sky*, both on smaller budgets and in black-and-white, were produced in a more understated natural and very British style of documentary romantic realism, nevertheless with powerful images of British Empire Imperialism. They consciously strove to create a microcosm of England behind barbed wire.

While the use of some composite characters began in both *The Dam Busters* and *Reach for the Sky* as films, most were closely wedded to the notions of authenticity and documentary realism as a form of film drama. And yet, as the playwright and screen writer Robert Bolt once wrote: 'If you want facts you must go to a library and not to the theatre [or cinema]'.

The extravagant dangers that were to face James Bond had their start with Sturges' film with the casting of the enemy as incompetent 'goons'. In the end of *The Great Escape,* Steve McQueen's star presence dominates. Even though it was a star vehicle for a bevy of American and British screen performers, each with his own 'big' scenes, Sturges' integrating organisation of his film was brilliantly achieved and drew heavily on Brickhill's account of the mass escape for ideas, authentic detail and inspiration. The main events of the book were neatly dovetailed into the film with great imagination and balance. Some events, of course, needed to be made more dramatic and thus, to some extent, were fictionalised.

> Can there possibly be any historian of the Second World War, or even just a military buff (at least living in the former western Allied nations), who has not seen the epic 1963 film "The Great Escape", featuring American actor icon Steve McQueen? Some of the millions of viewers have also probably read the 1950 account on which the movie was (loosely) based, by British [*sic*] author Paul Brickhill, himself a prisoner-

of-war in Stalag Luft III camp at Sagan in Silesia.
– Lawrence D Stokes, Dalhousie University[2]

While Stokes has made the usual error that other reviewers and historians have made in referring to Paul Brickhill as a British rather than an Australian author, he captures the overwhelmingly enduring legend that John Sturges' film *The Great Escape* created that blurred the edges of reality and historical truth with entertaining and thrilling drama including dollops of fiction, as did David Lean's *Bridge on the River Kwai* (1957) and his *Lawrence of Arabia* (1962).

The Great Escape in its book and feature film forms has created ironic cyclical overtones in the extent of the literary career of the author as they form the precise book ends of 1950 and 1963. The film followed the year after Brickhill's last major literary work and the release of his first and only thriller novel *The Deadline*, whereas 1950 was his first golden year as a popular author with the initial success of his finely-measured and well-researched history of his own experiences of incarceration and of those of other POWs in Stalag Luft III North Compound at Sagan in German Silesia.

Unlike the movies *The Dam Busters* and *Reach for the Sky*, *The Great Escape* was only loosely based on Brickhill's book. But like them, it became an unforgettable classical war movie. Nevertheless, both *The Dam Busters* and *Reach for the Sky*, as films, contained composite, partly fictionalised protagonists and sequences in which historical time was concertinaed as a device to maintain the pace of the filmic narrative.

Steve McQueen, the iconic American actor with a striking

2 Lawrence D Stokes, review of '*A Gallant Company: The True Story of "The Great Escape"* by Jonathan F Vance, John Gresham Military Library series, New York, ibooks (distributed by Simon & Schuster) 2003, xxi.

presence, had top billing and yet he played an entirely fictitious character oppositional to the main theme and story. *The Great Escape* did not follow the traditional, more modest documentary approach in black-and-white of the other two earlier movies of Brickhill's books. It was not so obsessively British in tone and world-view as were the Imperialistic tones set by the two English directors, Michael Anderson and Lewis Gilbert.

Instead, John Sturges, an experienced American director and producer, used the prisoner-of-war camp as a colourful backdrop for an exciting adventure plot which turned his film into a perennial repeat late night television favourite after its theatre release in 1963.

The Great Escape was the longest, most expensive and biggest money-making POW picture of them all, apart from David Lean's *The Bridge on the River Kwai* (1957). As producer-director John Sturges handled *The Great Escape* with an original gusto. The screenplay offered some ingenious variations on the Great Escape usually applied to many other earlier movies of the barbed-wire-tunnel-digging genre.

Film scene with Richard Attenborough & Steve McQueen

In Panavision and De Lux Color the picture started light-heartedly, maintained an engaging pace with never a dull moment and ended in a tragic, but uplifting manner. No one could sleep through its lively sequences. In it Sturges contrasts British soldiers' and airmen's hierarchical collective and ensemble efforts to escape by grit and grace with the insouciant individualism of their fellow allied prisoners, especially the fictitious US officer played by Steve McQueen and the larrikin Australian pilot played by American actor James Coburn with his inauthentic attempt for a broadly Australian accent (to stretch the imagination on the part of the cinema audience).

McQueen was born in Indiana in 1930, a so-called juvenile delinquent who was abandoned by his father as an infant, sent to Reform School, escaped and was gaoled, became a sailor, lumberjack, poker player and a US Marine. Key scenes, such as those in the so-called cooler (solitary confinement punishment) reflected his own life experiences as a lonely, rebellious troubled adolescent with no family.

He studied acting in New York after his service in the Second World War at the Neighbour Playhouse. After making his film debut as an extra in 1956, he quickly graduated to leading roles, starting with the success in the television series *Wanted Dead or Alive* (1958). He then made a successful leap to lasting movie fame on the big screen.

For *The Great Escape,* Sturges was particularly anxious to obtain Steve McQueen since he had created a taciturn, ice-cool loner image in the screenplay by James Clavell. McQueen was ideal in age, style and stature for the American character. Moreover, by the early 1960s McQueen was eminently bankable, the 'coolest of all film stars, with rugged good looks and ice-blue eyes'[3] – there was a good possibility for him to turn the fairly standard escape story into a big hit as William Holden had done in Billy Wilder's ironic prison camp film *Stalag 17* (1953). For his performance, Holden won the Academy Award for best leading actor.

As it turned out, *The Great Escape* was to be McQueen's first major career high and was followed by *The Sand Pebbles*

---

3 Derek Winnert (gen. ed.), *The Ultimate Encyclopedia of the Movies,* Carlton Books, London, The Museum of the Moving Image, 1995, 129.

(1966), *Bullitt* (1968), *The Thomas-Crown Affair* (1968) and *Papillon* (1973). In all of these hit movies, he was to play similar roles to the icy, iconic one he performed to a tee in *The Great Escape*. His acting range was limited to the one central image of the cool guy – but it worked magnificently in the film of Paul Brickhill's book when it was released in 1963 to an eager waiting public.

Yet he was most reluctant to accept Sturges' offer to play in it, having played in a dud, lifeless war movie a little earlier. What clinched the deal was that Sturges, to entice the actor, agreed for him to perform most of his own stunts on the German motor bikes in the exciting climatic sequences of the film. As a macho star, McQueen often insisted on doing his own stunts. In *The Great Escape* he not only rode his own bike – in the escape sequences dressed in a borrowed German uniform – he also rode one of the pursuers' bikes. These episodes involved fast riding along roads and across attractive summer-grassed fields.

In many ways, *The Great Escape* is simply a thrilling adventure drama and only incidentally a war film from beginning to its spectacular upbeat ending. But characters are not paste-board figures. They are precisely differentiated by an ensemble collection of outstanding character actors very carefully chosen by Sturges.

In the 1960s, feature filmmakers, especially Americans, were obsessed with size, epic themes, wide-screen colour and sometimes almost three-hour running times and all-star casts as effectively displayed in *Lawrence of Arabia* (1965), *The Guns of Navarone* (1961), *El Cid*, (1961) and *How the West Was Won* (1962). All this, in part, was to counter the impact of television and increase diminishing cinema audiences.

In war movies like *The Man Who Never Was* (1955) and *Cockleshell Heroes* (also 1955), both colour films, the ambitious scope was realised. *The Man Who Never Was* was even in

Cinemascope. The casts were a mixture of leading British and American actors. Frequently, the British actors had to play roles with the right *Boy's Own* qualities and stiff upper lip of British officers as expected by cinema audiences; while the American actors were required to play reluctant heroes, more individualistic and egalitarian, sometimes with an eye to the main chance, like the characters William Holden played in both *Stalag 17* and *The Bridge on the River Kwai.* James Garner and Steve McQueen in *The Great Escape* followed this pattern with James Coburn playing a similar Australian larrikin and individualistic type.

Sturges well understood and appreciated the acting styles of McQueen, Garner and Coburn as well as Charles Bronson, having used all four as gunmen heroes in his successful and suspense-filled Western epic *The Magnificent Seven* a few years before in 1960. With *The Great Escape*, he used much the same approach of exciting action sequences from start to finish with sharp editing and intercutting in each of the rapid-fire scenes. Even the movement of the loaded trucks of prisoners speeding across the picturesque Bavarian countryside in Germany to arrive at the newly-built prison camp at Sagan resembles or echoes the galloping group of gunmen-horsemen approaching the Mexican village as their destination with the accompaniment of stirring music.

The Great Escape was highly successful as a film in spreading a judicious blend of political diplomacy and Allied fervour on an unusually broad canvas, including the casting of leading German actors in the smaller feature roles of the German characters. In his casting of players, Sturges was without a doubt masterly. He successfully avoids cameo-in-and-out style performances of sometimes fading stars as found in Darryl F Zanack's extravagantly turgid *The Longest Day* (1961) – aptly titled from an audience point-of-view – with

'43 International Stars'. It was a film that deals with the Allied invasion of 'Operation Overload' in Europe on 6 June 1944. The reconstruction of this event was two years in the making.[4] As a blockbuster, it failed since the cast were not integrated as a whole with an even balance and sharply defined and compelling characterisation as found in *The Great Escape*. In *The Longest Day*, cinema audiences played spot the star, or "Where's Wally" to prevent being totally bored, whereas all the actors cast in *The Great Escape* were at the top of their form like Richard Attenborough and Donald Pleasence, or nearing it, like Charles Bronson and David McCallum.

Steve McQueen headed the cast in the film's titles and other publicity with James Garner and Richard Attenborough – two Americans and one Brit. Next came the phrase 'in The Great Escape', followed by 'co-starring James Donald, Charles Bronson and Donald Pleasence, two Brits and one American, a neat balance. After that came James Coburn, an American Hans Messemer, a German, David McCallum, Gordon Jackson, both Scots, John Leyton, an Englishman, and Angus Lennie, another and smaller Scot who played a humorous, but finally tragic figure with what was described as 'prisoner-camp fever' – a serious form of depression, fatalism and suicidal tendencies that, as Paul Brickhill had pointed out, was not an unusual problem in POW camps. This made one American, one German and four Brits. The supporting cast was made up of distinguished German and British character actors.

4 Tom Perlmutter, *War Movies*, Hamlyn, London, 1974, 127; 128-39 contain images from the film.

Paul Brickhill is given pride of place by Sturges in a separate frame of the opening titles informing the cinema audience that the film is based on his book. James Clavell with WR Burnett wrote the distinguished screenplay as an action story, but with constant reference to the main ideas and themes expressed throughout Brickhill's chronicle.

Elmer Bernstein is recognised in the titles as the musician composer. His dominant music captures the light and shade of the story and, in critical parts of the film, the stirring music adds to the excitement, as used similarly in *The Magnificent Seven*. The film contains abundant music throughout, whereas the musical score of the more documentary style of Brickhill's books made into films – *The Dam Busters* and *Reach for the Sky* – is sparsely used so as to emphasise the more natural sounds of planes revving up, cars screeching, the boots of men marching and so on. In contrast, Bernstein's music harmonises constantly with human movement, characterisation and tension in each scene and indeed provides a musical chronography of the action. It is more than background music and almost becomes another character in a well conceived and dynamic plot. The music is memorable – easily recognisable by listeners many years later (as was, however, "The Dambusters March").

The screenplay is cleverly written by James Clavell (author of the best-selling novel *Shogun*) and highly experienced WR Burnett who wrote the screenplays for *Little Caesar* and *The Asphalt Jungle*. The screenplay, after being revised particularly on the demands and requirements of Steve McQueen, nevertheless draws heavily and appropriately from the key themes and ideas found in Brickhill's work, together with the convincing details represented visually in shorthand in the carefully constructed set and costume design. Clavell provides autobiographical touches as he was himself a prisoner-of-war in a Japanese prison camp.

In the overall impact of the screenplay, respect is shown for

Brickhill's chronicle of prison camp life, capturing its essence of confinement and claustrophobia together with its more humorous characteristics as found in RC Sherriff's remarkable and hugely influential 1929 play *Journey's End* about the existence of officers in the confines of a frontline dugout in World War I. *The Great Escape* as a screenplay falls into the long tradition begun by *Journey's End* in 1929.

The screenwriters of *The Great Escape* did not adapt the Brickhill's text chapter-by-chapter as the screenwriters of *The Dam Busters* and *Reach for the Sky* had done in their documentary style and reverential approach. Instead, *The Great Escape* screenwriters turned it inside out before it was fit for the screen. They avoided pretentious documentary-style voiceover narrative as was used in the two earlier films of Brickhill's books. They were intent on lifting out of Brickhill's book content that emphasised the day-to-day social life of the prison camp with its detailed factual descriptions of the work of the escape factories. They moulded a fine, exciting adventure story that would turn it into a tightly dramatic suspenseful film.

Nevertheless, all the fascinating details which Brickhill so clearly wove into his evocative descriptive writing can be found in a visual form in the design of the exteriors and interiors of the set. Much was captured of the content in the book. Yet, it is more in the background than the foreground in this exciting movie thriller. In such design, they were helped enormously by the magnificent drawings by artist Ley Kenyon, a POW himself in the North Compound. These are found in certain editions of Brickhill's *The Great Escape*[5] and also in the earlier book *Escape to Danger* by Brickhill and Norton.

Kenyon provided a detailed layout of the entire North

5 Brickhill, *The Great Escape*, 1951 – the year Sturges purchased the film rights.

Compound identifying all of its barracks (101 to 119), the theatre, the Appell Ground, the kitchen, the fire pool, the tract of the three attempted escape tunnels ("Tom", "Dick" and "Harry" – the latter used in the mass escape), the hospital, the prison (the cooler), the coal store, the guard room, the sentry towers, the warning wire, the barbed wire enclosure fences and the forest beyond. All of this was faithfully recreated for the film – they are all there somewhere. Particularly well used was the section drawing of the escape tunnel "Harry" as well as other sketches.[6]

The sparse, incisive dialogue and fine character delineation do the rest. Each scene is active rather than passive, in a similar way to Brickhill's prose style, so as to build tension and suspense like John Sturges' earlier work in his fine thriller *Bad Day at Black Rock* that has brooding silences with intimations of an impending explosive climax, starring Spencer Tracey as a weary middle-aged war veteran hero and Robert Ryan as a murderous racist villain in control of the railway-side hamlet together with a hand-picked cast of expert and highly experienced American character actors. In this case, the small Texas desert rundown railway hamlet Black Rock becomes every bit as confining and as sequestered a world as Stalag Luft III for the one-armed baffled ex-soldier played ably and naturally by Tracey. He travels there by train on behalf of the American Republic to deliver the military medals of a dead brave American soldier to his Japanese farmer father, only to find the old man has mysteriously disappeared from the place and no one is prepared to admit even to his very existence. Everyone in the isolated tiny desert town acts suspiciously or violently. The mystery and the threatening situation quickly develops from there. The middle-aged hero finds innovative but desperate ways of coping

6 Fly leaves in Brickhill, *The Great Escape*, London, Readers Union, Faber and Faber, 1952.

and resisting the small isolated violent world as do the officer inmates of the German prison camp. Both films address, in quite different ways, the lasting impact of international war. Bad Rock is confining as is Stalag Luft III.

What the scriptwriters, Clavell and Burnett, achieve in *The Great Escape* is to extract the basic ideas and events from Brickhill without ever really throwing aside the rest and yet still providing an entirely fresh framework by mixing the plot around, concertinaing time and place. They keep as many as possible of the original protagonists together with their historical authenticity and backgrounds, but invented some more fictitious or composite characters to keep a strong dramatic line going which takes the story creatively in a few new directions. Fact and fiction are carefully interwoven and sometimes fused together so that the uninitiated cinema goers who have not read Brickhill's book come easily to the legend created on the screen as historical reportage best in a dramatic form.

And yet Sturges had marked trouble with the screenplay as the film was being made and shaped, partly because of the troublesome, difficult actor Steve McQueen who did not think his character was strongly enough written and defined in an individualistic manner. He threatened to resign from the film blackmailing the whole project and operation. He did not want to be simply one of the ensemble of heroes that the other actors were playing, but demanded to stand out more definitively. He was reflecting on his part in *The Magnificent Seven* where he was not so dominant on the screen, just one of Sturges' ensemble. His demands were met as his character was fictitious anyway. Events were introduced to suit his ambitions without necessarily spoiling the storyline. James Garner, in his memoir, argues that four more writers were brought in over Clavell and Burnett and about a dozen drafts were produced until McQueen became happy and satisfied with it all.

The actors in the main and secondary parts still wound up improvising their own dialogue to improve their scenes and make them more authentic.[7] Nevertheless, the results were particularly good when the film was shown to cinema audiences.

Hilts, the baseball loving character played by McQueen, is often seen as real rather than fictional. Most people don't know what Paul Brickhill thought of the film, but it is clear from his experience with different forms of the media of mass communication that he well understood the difference and mainly stood out of the way of filmmakers. His close friends at the time of the film's release in Australia, however, noticed that he was most angry with the inclusion of the character Hilts played by McQueen as it muted the scale of the tragedy at the end of his well-told story – the execution of fifty escapees under direct order of Adolf Hitler. He would have been excited that his ideas and wartime experiences had had such a massive and sustained impact on the world at large. The greater part of his story was never discarded in the movie which does capture neatly Brickhill's tremendous vitality and generosity of spirit.

Unlike Sturges, Brickhill placed some emphasis on the ethnic variety of the North Compound: Australians, New Zealanders, Canadians, Dutch, Poles, French, Czechs and Norwegians, all united by their ranks in the Royal Air Force, including those who had escaped occupied Europe to join the war in England. Brickhill created a much stronger multi-ethnical world in his book than Sturges created in his film, perhaps apart from the character played by Bronson. In other words, the Anglo-Celtic predominated almost completely.

The fictitious elements of the film are crystal clear. There were no Americans in the actual escape (despite the parts played by Garner and McQueen). All the Americans at Stalag Luft III

7 Garner & Winokur, *The Garner Files*, 71, 78-82.

had been transported to other camps before the tunnels were finished and the escape actually occurred. There was never a motorcycle chase (even though it became the most memorable sequence in the film) and there was no attempted spectacular escape by a training aeroplane as the characters played by the blinded Donald Pleasence and James Garner did in the film. This dramatic event too was pure fiction.

The bike McQueen used was actually an ahistorical 1961 Triumph 650 painted green and dressed up with Nazi insignia including swastikas. McQueen, in character as Hilts, did much of the stunt driving himself, including the sequence of the German chasing him. The whole memorable scene to cinema audiences was to give McQueen a lasting super-star status around the world. This was in part because of his 'super cool' unique screen presence and in part the brilliance of the stunt sequence in its own right. Viewers are probably not aware that McQueen did not do the final leap over the massive wooden and barbed-wire barrier, supposedly on the Swiss border and close to freedom. His close friend and stunt driver Bud Ekin made this jump from a wooden ramp out of camera range. He flew sixty-five feet and twelve feet off the ground. Such was the illusion of film-making! While McQueen desired and even demanded unsuccessfully to do the stunt himself, the film insurance company would not allow it and neither would John Sturges as director.[8]

Exciting high-speed chases on film were a keynote of McQueen's super-cool performances. They were later adopted in an even more spectacular and less realistic manner in all the highly popular James Bond film series. Such exciting sequences have their origins in *The Great Escape*.

In filmmaking, the documentary-style black-and-white semi-realistic and authentic approach to wartime history lost

8 Garner & Winokur, *The Garner Files*, 79.

its supremacy which had existed in the 1950s and early 1960s and Brickhill's own work was mixed up in it all, but did not fade so quickly in terms of reprint publications of his books.

At the end of the roll-over of introductory titles of the film, Sturges provided a written claim that: 'This is a true story. Although the characters are composites of real men, and time and place have been compressed, every detail of the escape is the way it really happened'.[9] Obviously, a Hollywood hyperbole that was slightly misleading, although perhaps not intended to be so. James Garner later pointed out: 'Almost everything in the movie is accurate, though some incidents are condensed and a few characters are composite. It was such a good story that the director John Sturges didn't have to take liberties'.[10] But he certainly did with the motor bike and training plane incidents which added memorable colours to the storyline.

The Great Escape was far more ambitious in Panavision and colour than the two earlier gritty, documentary-style reality films of Brickhill's books. Its running time was 165 minutes whereas *The Dam Busters* was 120 minutes and *Reach for the Sky* was 134 minutes. These films were shot in black-and-white to allow the integration of original footage of World War II bomb trails. None of the three films, however, were excessive in running-time considering their content. All were economic and precise in rapid story-telling. All were favoured by casts of outstanding character actors who provided sharp characterisations that were, on the main, most convincing.

Paul Brickhill would have seen another historical inaccuracy in *The Great Escape* that almost exhaustively deals with two segments of the North Compound's inmates – integration of

9 *The Great Escape*, The Mirisch Company Inc. Panavision DVD. Running time approx. 165 minutes, colour, 2000.

10 Garner & Winokur, *The Garner Files*, 71.

the American and the British. Brickhill cast his net to haul in real characters from a much larger range of ethnic origin:

> A mixed lot, the diggers [of the escape tunnels]. They came from nearly every British country, from America [until they were removed to a different camp before the mass escape] and France, Poland, Norway, the Argentine and Czechoslovakia.
>
> From Wales there was Shag Rees, the little man with thick black hair and a nose that had been broken so often it was getting to be a habit. His friend, 'Red' Noble was a red-headed Canadian, built like a navvy with a slow gentle drawl and nearly always a half-grin on his face.[11]

And so his description continues. Such characters may have ended up on the cutting room floor with the thematic emphasis on the two Americans, three or four Scots and the rest English apart from the Australian making the film Anglo-Saxon-Celtic in its cultural values throughout. Only Charles Bronson in the character he played seemed European in ethnic background.

The most predominant reason for historical inaccuracies in the filming of *The Great Escape* was doubtless to allow the director to cast a speed-obsessed American star Steve McQueen as Virgil Hilts, The Cooler King, in the leading role and thereby increase its box-office appeal enormously to audiences in the United States, but his appeal became international in nature. His characterisation moved into a super-hero status of indestructability and optimism.

The British films of the same POW movie genre, set in

11 Brickhill, *The Great Escape*, 1951, 91. Reference pages taken from this edition appear in the text.

various places in Germany, consciously strove to create a sequestered microcosm of cultural England with its social class hierarchies behind barbed wire where these attitudes of class could maintain and even improve morale and discipline. Everybody was prepared to obey orders from the commanding officer down. Military discipline and morale were two sides of the one coin. They were glorified. The boredom, deprivations and dangers of incarceration were minimised or played down, apart from climacteric endings, in favour of good humour to strengthen the idea of British resilience and the known outcome of war; eccentricity and xenophobia became patriotic attributes and various quips in the dialogue served to promote a nostalgia that was fast fading into dream-like qualities, especially in *The Captive Heart.*

On the other hand, the American film *Stalag 17* created an unruly and democratic microcosm of the diverse culture of the United States behind the ever-present wire cage with a hostile alien and ruthless world on the outside as well as behind the omnipresent sentry towers with their searchlights and dangerous mounted machine guns. The internal human sequestered environment within *Stalag 17* reflected the independent idiosyncrasy of the egalitarian American characters and their regional differences which are in fine display in the comic sequences. William Holden's cocky cynical character dominates proceedings as the enterprising capitalist POW and manipulator with an eye to the main chance who makes life bearable for most in the camp by his many money-making betting enterprises and schemes. His potato peel still makes a potent bootleg whiskey. As well, as the broad humour of the script turns to tense drama his reluctant heroism is finally exposed. His 'anti-hero' character is not dissimilar to that of McQueen's Virgil Hilts in *The Great Escape.*

While Sturges may have borrowed his humorous whiskey-brewing scene on Independence Day from *Stalag 17*, to be fair, it is also clearly chronicled in a slightly different manner in Paul Brickhill's 1950 book:

> Roger [Bushell] wrote home, 'It can't last much longer. This is definitely our last Christmas in the bag.' Grimly true for him.
>
> On the last day of the year the 'X' chiefs threw a raisin wine party in 110 and by evening appel [the German checking assembly] the world was sweetness and light. Canton and Bob Tuck charitably got on each side of a prominent tunneller and carried him on appel, his leg making movements about six inches above the snow. They held him up, swaying, in the ranks, but when Pieber [the guard] came past, counting [the POWs], the tunneller swayed out of their grip, and staggered to one side.
>
> 'Please stop moving,' said Pieber severely. 'I cannot count you properly.'
>
> ''Tisn' me moving,' said the tunneller, focusing desperately. ''Tis you.'
>
> There weren't any more raisin wine brews after that (pp.140-1).

In Brickhill's account 'hooch' – British distilled rather than American – was banned after a drunken POW was caught in the open and shot low down in the stomach, but fortunately survived. Sturges and his scriptwriters expanded on both incidences, the latter when the character played by the Scottish actor Angus Lennie as Willie, Hilts' solitary cooler friend, was tragically shot trying to escape by climbing the wire. As Hilts, McQueen shows an intensely emotional response by knocking a guard to the ground and ending up in the cooler again bouncing his baseball against the prison wall and catching it in his glove.

In actors, Sturges looked for a sense of authenticity; they could, therefore, draw from their experience of the Second World War or in similar earlier films to shape their various characters into some depth and sharpness. Some actors had even been POWs. Donald Pleasence, who played Blythe The Forger, was himself held in a concentration camp in Germany after being shot down in an RAF bomber. His character was clearly inspired as a composite from Brickhill's 'Chapter XI. The Forgers'. Like the sequences in Sturges' film, the book chapters are short and to the point. Pleasence's character was mainly based on Tim Walenn:

> Walenn had that methodical and precise nature which, if you didn't know it before, is essential for good forging. He had a smooth, unruffled face – and hid most it it behind a spreading, Jerry Colonna-type moustache which revolted every artistic feeling in the compound. Artists liked to work with him because he was so unfailingly courteous (p.120).

Walenn never went blind because of the forging work, but the Pleasence character did before the escape took place in the film. In reality ironically, Walenn was one of the fifty murdered by the Gestapo. As Brickhill put it: 'It was a terrible list … The ever-courteous Tim Walenn was on it (p.229).

The German actor Hannes Messemer who played von Luger, the Stalag Luft III commandant, was captured and placed in a Russian camp. Messemer closely modelled his character on Brickhill's real Colonel von Lindeiner – they were visually alike. Til Kiwe played Frick and Hans Reiser played the Gestapo agent Kuhn. They had both been military prisoners of the Americans in real life.

James Clavell, the best-selling novelist who co-wrote the

screenplay, had been in a Japanese POW camp during World War II. His experiences there formed the basis of his book *King Rat* which, like Paul Brickhill's book, was later filmed successfully in the same genre under the same title. Wallace Floody, a former POW at Stalag Luft III, was hired as *The Great Escape*'s technical director and gave an unqualified approval of the film's brilliantly conceived set in the Bavarian forest. He found that Sturges with the film's technical crew had designed it in such a manner that they had achieved an 'authenticity that was too real for comfort'. In his twelve-week stay in Germany in the set's camp, he began to believe he was back in the real camp. The set-makers had closely followed Brickhill's descriptions and Ley Kenyon's illustrations.

In fact, Sturges achieves a masterly stroke when casting actors for his film, setting aside Steve McQueen's box-office prowess. English stalwart actor Richard Attenborough was absolutely right for "Big X" Bartlett and he plays it right down the line of Brickhill's original portrayal of Roger Bushell, the intrepid head of the "X" escape organisation. Attenborough's portrayal is the closest of all to Brickhill's characterisations and not really a composite character at all, despite the alteration of his surname in the film.

In the opening sentences of 'Prelude' at the beginning of *The Great Escape*, Paul Brickhill introduces Roger Bushell as the predominant protagonist of the whole work. He appears on most pages: 'Roger Bushell had just turned thirty … He was a big tempestuous man, with broad shoulders and the most chilling pale-blue eyes I ever saw'. Brickhill recounts how Bushell had been an international skiing champion and had an accident, being gashed wickedly in the corner of his right eye. 'After it had been sewn up the corner of his eye drooped permanently and the effect on his look was strangely sinister and brooding' (p.17). Despite being much smaller in physical build,

Richard Attenborough carefully captured these characteristics using make-up to form the necessary scar tissue on his face. Attenborough read Brickhill's book in his preparation for the part and studied it carefully. His characterisation of the real-life Bushell is splendidly achieved as a linchpin to the drama as Michael Redgrave does as Barnes Wallis in *The Dam Busters.*

Attenborough made his stage debut in 1941 and his first appearance on celluloid was in a similar patriotic war film, Noel Coward and David Lean's *In Which We Serve* (1942), as the panic-stricken working-class stoker of HMS *Torrin* and for a while he continued to specialise in 'other ranks' working-class military types – sometimes Cockneys and cowardly characters. After actual service in the Second World War (a factor Sturges was looking for in his choice of actors where possible), Attenborough graduated into upper-class and middle-class complex military and sometimes neurotic leadership roles in such films as *Guns at Batasi* (1964) for which he won the BAFTA best actor award. It was filmed soon after *The Great Escape*. His two characters in these films had a similar complex intensity,[12] although his part in *The Great Escape* was more heroic and resourceful.

Apart from Attenborough's distinguished and influential background in the film industry by the early 1960s as a producer as well as an actor, John Sturges chose him especially to play the key central role of Bartlett because he was an actor who could always be relied on to produce a polished, sustained and dominating nuanced performance of psychological complexity as he had done in such diverse films as *Brighton Rock* (1948) – playing a vicious gangster psychopath that was genuinely frightening. In *The Great Escape* he effectively heads the cast, at least of British actors, by making a grand entrance as a

12 Lloyd & Fuller (eds), *The Illustrated Who's Who,* 18.

handcuffed prisoner in a well-guarded Volkswagen and then, with great authority, almost immediately initiates the escape plan that is at the centre of the filmic story. In his portrayal, he does not neglect the obsessive, abrupt and overly-determined side of his character, making several insensitive demands on his overworked POW underlings and subordinates. This follows the same lines as Brickhill had explored thoroughly in his 1950 book. In this important sense, Sturges is faithful to Brickhill's intention.

Charles Bronson, now gradually moving towards permanent stardom after several supporting roles especially in Westerns, plays Danny Velinski, the so-called Tunnel-King, that is, the chief tunneller leading the physical work side of the escape enterprise. While very much a composite character, he carries a pivotal character role in the plot based on his real-life experiences as a hard-working Polish descent coal miner before he came into the film acting business. His physical presence and obvious muscularity convey to the audience the idea that he is capable of all the skills needed of an experienced manual labourer in a dangerous context.

The scenes of him working in the tunnel are most convincing as is the gradual development of the characterisation of his growing claustrophobic fears in confined spaces that make his escape scenes through the tunnel so suspenseful and chilling. As a composite character, he perhaps represents Paul Brickhill with his known handicap of claustrophobia; a non-Britisher and generalised European with an accent not easy to define; and one of the three successful escapees represented in the film. Thus he becomes one of the two Norwegians who escape by Swedish ship in real life, even though no Norwegians are recognised specifically in the screenplay. One small detail is that his military uniform looks different and could be perhaps Norwegian.

The third successful escapee who reaches the Spanish border

in the film was represented by the actor James Coburn as Sedgwick, The Manufacturer. He is presented as an Australian, but in reality he was Bram "Bob" Van Der Stok (or Vanderstok) a Dutch airman who escaped to occupied Holland by train (not as Coburn does in the film riding by bicycle through France to Spain). Van Der Stok was aided through Belgium and France by members of the Resistance south to the Spanish border and freedom by getting to Madrid and the British consul who sent him to Gibraltar where he was flown back to London. 'It was four months since he crawled out of the tunnel', wrote Brickhill (p.235). Time and place, however, were rearranged by Sturges as he admits in the titles: 'times and places have been compressed'.

The great irony of the 'Great Escape' was never really addressed in the film – that none of the British or supposed Americans were successful in their escape attempts. This was left to two Norwegians and one Dutchman who were never properly acknowledged or acclaimed. In the opening of his book chapter 'Some Came Home', Brickhill carefully records: 'In June [1944] a letter came in the prisoners' mail with two prearranged fictional names, Rocky Rockland (in Norwegian, Bergsland) and Jens Muller [both Norwegians] had made it back to England via Sweden'. He points out: 'It was a perfect escape'. On the morning after the breakout, they got to Kustrin near Frankfurt on Oder by train and changed trains there to reach the port of Stettin without detection. They met some Swedish sailors and stowed away on their boat which was about to return to neutral Sweden. The Germans had checked the ship, but did not locate the well-hidden stowaways. At dawn the next day, they landed in Sweden and a little later the RAF flew them back to England. More romantically, the character played by Charles Bronson and his companion commandeered a small rowing boat and travelled by river to Stettin and thus to neutral Sweden.

Brickhill reports that the Dutch pilot Van Der Stok, who was eighteenth out of the escape tunnel, had travelled alone wearing a modified dark-blue Australian Air Force greatcoat, Dutch naval trousers and a beret. He took the crowded train from Sagan to Breslau. He changed trains twice and got to Holland without detection where, with the help of resistance fighters, went south through Belgium and France to Spain (pp.232-5).

Cinema audiences were led to believe an Australian escaped – but in reality only an Australian greatcoat worn by Van Der Stok reached England – and two ill-defined Europeans, one of whom (Bronson's actor companion) seemed to the audience to be British. Thus it was not strictly true 'that every detail of the escape was the way it really happened', as the film loudly announced.

Brun "Bob" van der Stok (Vanderstok)

Another fictitious event was when Bronson and partner travelled rather romantically by rowboat down river and climbed directly from it up the steps of a Swedish ship at the end of their journey – pure invention by the scriptwriters.

In real life, a great Australian surfer from Manly, a seaside suburb of Sydney, took part in the so-labelled Great Escape. Unfortunately, he was not so lucky as the fictitious Australian character in the film played by Coburn. He did not escape over the Spanish border. Instead, he was one of the fifty executed under Adolf Hitler's direct orders.

Held in the Williams family collection is a photographic record taken by the International Red Cross of Australian POWs incarcerated in Stalag Luft III. Of the thirty-one men in the image with the backdrop of the pine forest, outside the camp, most are in uniform. Paul Brickhill is prominent, third from the left in the front row, immaculately in uniform as usual. John Williams of Manly is in the back row, also third from the left. Like Brickhill, he has a neatly clipped RAF moustache favoured by the British pilots.

The last portrait of Squadron Leader John Williams was taken, sadly, as a mug shot by the Kripo or Nazi police in Reichenberg Police Station in German-occupied Czechoslovakia shortly after his capture along with his school friend Flight Lieutenant Reginald "Rusty" Kierath. Both young men attended North Sydney Church of England Grammar School ("Shore").[13] Paul Brickhill reported their capture in precise terms in the 'Aftermath' chapter of *The Great Escape:*

> Willy [John] Williams, Johnny Bull, ["Rusty"] Kierath and [Jerzy] Mondschein were caught trying to cross the Czech border near Reichenberg and after interrogation and several days in the cells they were taken away from Reichenberg at four o'clock on the morning of March 29th [1944] and not seen again. They were cremated that same day at Breux. They certainly weren't killed trying to escape again. Baatz, the local Gestapo chief, had signed the order for their cremation the previous day. [John] Stower also vanished from Reichenberg Gaol (p.256).

Previously on the night of 24-25 March 1944, John Edwin Ashley Williams was one of the seventy-six Allied airmen who

13 See Louise Williams, *A True Story of the Great Escape. A Young Australian POW in the Most Audacious Breakout of WWII,* Allen & Unwin, Sydney, 2015.

escaped from the POW camp at Sagan near the German-Polish border. John was twenty-four years of age at the time – the same age as Paul Brickhill when he volunteered for the RAAF in Sydney.

John was born in New Zealand and, as a child, moved with his family to Australia. The Williams family settled in Manly. The sound of the surf could be heard from where they lived close to the Ocean. Young John was soon to be attracted to the beach and the water. In 1935 he joined the Manly Surf Life-Saving Club and soon became involved in swimming, surfboard riding and rowing. He was a member of the rowing crew that won the 1935-36 Australian Junior Surfboat Championship. In all respects, he became an outstanding surfer. After a high school education at Shore, he matriculated and entered the Faculty of Medicine at the University of Sydney in 1938. Before sitting for the First Year final examinations, he left for the United Kingdom having won a place, similarly to Paul Brickhill, in a pilot training scheme, but in Scotland, not Ottawa where Brickhill trained. In other words, Williams joined the RAF directly before the Second World War began. After achieving his wings, he began his flying career in the RAF observing the great dramatic events at the start of the war in Europe.

Williams rose quickly in ranks to Squadron Leader due to his strong leadership potential and intelligence. He transferred to the Royal Australian Air Force (RAAF) in reverse order to Brickhill who was transferred from the RAAF to the RAF in England and flew in English squadrons.

In North Africa like Brickhill, Williams, who was quite an outgoing character, chose to fly missions wearing shorts and sandals in the Desert Camp rather than the approved flying kit that Brickhill always flew in. John became regarded in the Desert as a heroic flying ace with a number of kills to his credit. He was awarded the Distinguished Flying Cross for his outstanding service.

When the RAAF 450 Squadron was formed and sent to North Africa, John flew Kittyhawks. Like Paul Brickhill, he was shot down. This occurred during a dangerous strafing mission. After he was captured he found himself in the North Compound of Stalag Luft III where Paul Brickhill was later to join him. Clearly, they got to know each other well.

John worked with great enthusiasm and dedication for the "X" Organisation, helping to build the 110-metre long tunnel. He was among the two hundred men selected by the "X" Committee to escape and was allocated by lot 31 and thus was the thirty-first to come through the tunnel. He was the Chief Supply Officer (to some extent like the James Coburn composite Australian character in the film version). Among his tasks was the location of the timber to shore up the tunnel. Many of John's comrades complained of sore backs as John pinched many of their bed boards or slats for use in the tunnel to avoid it collapsing because of the sandy soil. In the film this situation was graphically demonstrated by the POW played by English stalwart actor Nigel Stock (playing one of the Australians) suddenly collapsing through the weakened upper bunk to the floor in the Compound. Through this small humorous scene, Sturges supplied a light-hearted anecdote and moment for the eager cinema audience. (The stoutish Stock also played an Australian bomber pilot in the film version of Brickhill's *The Dam Busters* – he had featured roles in several other British war movies and later played Dr Watson in the famous television Sherlock Holmes series with Jeremy Brett.)

John Williams was thus one of the seventy-six men to make their way through the escape tunnel. John and his old schoolmate from Shore days, Reginald "Rusty" Keirath, were caught on the Czech border in the town of Most. With two others, Jerzy Mondschein and Leslie Bull, they became known as the Most Four in the tragic legendary annals of the Great Escape.

As recounted, Hitler was violently enraged by the mass escape and eventually ordered the execution of fifty of the escapees although he wanted to execute all of them at first.

He was talked out of this by Göring who feared English reprisals in POW camps for Germans in the United Kingdom.

Williams, Keirath, Mondschein, a Czech pilot in the RAF, and Bull were taken to a nearby forest and shot. Their bodies were cremated at Most. General news of the atrocities was known in Sydney although the names of those executed were withheld. The Williams family, living in Manly, feared the worst. They were eventually advised of John's fate.

Before the mass escape: Paul Brickhill (front row 3rd from left); John Williams (back row 3rd from left), later executed under Hitler's order (International Red Cross photograph Stalag Luft III, courtesy Williams family)

The ashes of the fifty executed were taken back to Stalag Luft III. The intention was for them to serve as a stern warning to other prisoners there who may have been planning to escape. After the war, the ashes were taken from the Sagan cemetery plot and placed in a memorial near the Polish city Posnan.[14]

No one was brought to justice for the execution of the Most Four, even though a thorough-going investigation was carried out after the war and twenty Gestapo officers were found guilty and sentenced to death. Another memorial to the Most Four today occupies a prominent place in the Most cemetery.

The name of John Williams appears on the Manly Life Saving Club's Honour Roll for World War 1939-1945. The honour roll held in the Club Rooms at South Steyne is probably the most unusual type of honour roll in Australia. Names are inscribed on the surfboard once owned by Pilot Officer Geoffrey Cohen of the RAAF – the first member of the Manly Club killed in action on service in the Second World War. The board bears the names of every member of the Manly Club who served.[15] And only recently acknowledged on the Manly War Memorial in The Corso is Squadron Leader John Edward Ashley Williams RAAF.

***

The John Sturges' film *The Great Escape* blends fact with fiction.

James Garner, the second, perhaps underrated, star of the movie, played an American in the RAF, Bob Hendley, The Scrounger – in real life, Major Johnny Dodge, The Artful Dodger, as Brickhill put it (p.19). His portrayal had subtle light touches and gentle good humour towards his eccentric bird-watcher room mate Blithe The Forger (Pleasence). Garner's part is the most co-operative and innovative person, obtaining all kinds of useful objects including a camera for The Forger

14 'John Williams', in Stan Vesper, *Those who served. Surf Lifesavers at War*, Playright Publishing, Carringbah, 2015, 60; also for a fuller version of the life of John Williams, see Williams, *A True Story of the Great Escape*.
15 Reg S Harris, *Heroes of the Surf. Fifty Years History of Manly Life Saving Club*, MLSC, Sydney, 1961, 74. This page also contains a photograph of the Honour Board 1939-1945.

and for the escape plan by bribing the guards with chocolates and coffee from Red Cross parcels or subtly blackmailing them.

While Garner's part is composite in nature incorporating efforts in real life undertaken by several individuals at Stalag Luft III, there were strong autobiographical elements that made his performance authentic and believable. Garner had served bravely in the Korean War as a rifleman in the most dangerous frontline positions on the 38th parallel. After recovering from wounds for which he received two Purple Hearts, he became, like his character Hendley, a hustler who could bribe, barter his way around anything. After leaving hospital, he wrote:

> I decided to turn our area [at the base in Korea] into a first-class recreation center. To do that I had to scrounge materials and supplies from other [better provided] units on the base. They weren't always inclined to cooperate, so I had to give them an incentive: if they didn't come up with what I wanted, they didn't get their mail. Soldiers become unhappy when they don't get their mail, so they usually gave me what I asked for including what we needed to build a bar and keep it stocked with whiskey.[16]

Thus in Garner's performance in *The Great Escape* a real-life experience becomes art and Garner fitted the shoes of the character Hendley with great ease and authenticity.

Unlike the part played by McQueen as the independent uncooperative Hilts, The Cooler King, Garner's part is strongly cooperative with the escape plan and his part in it, while Hilts (McQueen) was in the cooler when the escape plan is formulated and his loner character was at first alienated from

16 Garner & Winoker, *The Garner Files*, 30-1; 76.

it. He made escape attempts without the authority of the "X" Organisation until much later in the film where he joins in enthusiastically and provides a significant contribution to the escape itself, helping many on the outside of the tunnel to make their successful escape by a rope signal from the tree hideout. By this time, he becomes more than a reluctant hero and a vital problem-solver of the escape group in difficult circumstances. In these sequences he displays an authentic composite character vaguely in line with Paul Brickhill's text.

The quality of the film production was a key to its lasting success and appeal to the widest of audiences internationally. The film was shot on location entirely in Europe. A complete camp resembling the destroyed Stalag Luft III camp – the North Compound – was rebuilt near Munich in Germany almost in its entirety based on Ley Kenyon's splendid line drawings in Brickhill's book as well as the author's splendid descriptions of the camp structure.

Exteriors for the nicely varied escape sequences were shot in the Rhine district and near the North Sea. McQueen's famous motorcycle pursuit scenes were shot in Fussen on the picturesque sunny Austrian border. While it was heavily snowing and cold in the actual escape, the film constantly portrays the sunny green of summer. Interiors were filmed at the Bavarian Film Studio near Munich.

Hundreds of male extras were recruited from a university in Munich. They were the right age and appearance in Anglo-Saxon terms to portray the POW inmates of the camp. To save time in the casting schedule for the more intimate scenes, Sturges gave parts to wardrobe personnel, his script clerk and other employed technicians not required for certain days. All enthusiastically took the roles as film extras to cut costs. When the Bavarian studio backlot proved too small for certain key open-air sequences, permission was obtained from the West German government to shoot in a national forest near the studio.

Pines damaged or removed during the shooting were replaced by the planting of two thousand small pine trees that have now grown tall. Like the real Stalag near Sagan, the false Stalag near Munich in the forest was dismantled and disappeared from the face of the earth after the feature film was released.

Authentic World War II German military equipment and uniforms were obtained from many junkyards and second-hand stores across Germany. These included 1940s vintage cars, trucks and some of the motorcycles that were carefully restored to running order for the exterior motorised scenes particularly outside the prison camp, adding to the feel of authenticity.

For the railroad sequences, a railway engine was hired and two condemned rail cars were purchased and restored to run on the rails. James Garner in his memoir mentioned that such filmed sequences were carried out on rails beside an ordinary busy commercial track – the Munich to Hamburg line – with other commercial trains passing regularly and dangerously by. Again, authenticity was heightened as the film's keynote or, at least backdrop.

The tunnel set, described by Scottish actor David McCallum in his interview in *Return to The Great Escape* documentary as being impressively built with its rail trolleys in a long hangar-type building, was so effective that in the film's first première screening the audience were found to be still gripping their seats at the end of the showing. Like Paul Brickhill – as is often claimed – they were so badly affected by the claustrophobic tunnel. In a sense, these thrilling sequences and their effect on the cinema audience was a subtle tribute by Sturges to the original author of *The Great Escape* – Paul Brickhill – together with Charles Bronson's singular composite performance in the tunnel affected by claustrophobia.

These scenes or sequences in the film number thirty-two minutes of the screening time of 165 minutes. Some sequences lasted five minutes.

The momentum was well-maintained and never let up. Sturges' experience as an editor and cutter came to the fore. No scene or sequence was overly long, nearly all being less than twelve minutes, thus maintaining the tension of a thriller. Nothing dragged on. The opening sequence of the trucks containing the prisoner travelling quickly and recklessly across picturesque green-pastured scenery to Sagan is almost happy, accompanied by Elmer Bernstein's thrilling upbeat music, as is the arrival at the newly-built camp.

This is followed by a series of humorous individual "Keystone" escape attempts and the main characters are introduced and established in closer wider or close-up, more intimate studies in group scenes. James Donald, sternly stiff-upper-lipped and starkly blue-eyed as an aristocrat, is Ramsey, Senior British officer (Group Captain HM Massey, DSO, MC in real life) interviewed by Commandant von Luger (Messemer) in his office and thoroughly warned against escape attempts. The policy is clearly explained: We are putting 'all rotten eggs in the same basket' – as extracted from Brickhill's account. The commandant is a sympathetic portrayal by Messemer and runs close to Brickhill's text.

It looks harmless enough until ... Under the stove the entrance to "Harry" (by Albert Comber, AWM ART34781.012)

The arrival of Steve McQueen as the American hot-shot pilot shows him as rather separate from the others, underlining his individuality of character and purpose. He stands and walks aside from the others on the wire-warning boundary already silently plotting to escape himself. Attenborough, though, has the biggest entrance of them all as Bartlett (Bushell). He is accompanied by the Gestapo in an imposing open Volkswagen car and then presented handcuffed to the commandant with veiled threats while the proud Luftwaffe officer shows his distance from the evil Gestapo, the true villains of the piece who reappear in the more deadly of the escape sequences later in the film. For example, when David McCallum's character is shot dead beside the railway line. While McQueen's character is an invention, Attenborough's is closest to Brickhill's text as Bartlett (Bushell).

The comic "Keystone" attempts to escape by Bronson and the others enliven the opening sequences for the cinema audience in an entertaining manner and set the scene, in contrast, for the precise organisation of the escape committee under Bartlett's authoritarian direction, re-establishing strict and inflexible hierarchical order by the British authorities. Soon the well-organised three-way tunnelling gets going in three places under the stresses of spot inspections by the so-called "ferrets" and the organised reactions to them to cover up escape sounds – 'Singing in Tune', a chorus directed by character actor Nigel Stock as an Australian pilot.

Guards are tempted, especially by Garner (who obtains the camera for The Forger, Blight/Pleasence). In Garner's performance there are strong echoes of William Holden's 1950s performance in *Stalag 17*. The tunnel collapses in another frightening sequence and the claustrophobic theme is well established. The Independence Day scene breaks the tension with the comic heavy drinking of 'bootleg' whiskey with Gordon Jackson doing the Highland fling; this is suddenly followed by the small Scot's tragic attempt to go over the wire and his death by an efficient burst of machine-gun fire, establishing the death-threat theme inherent in any escape attempt. The audience thinks: Is it worth it? In the same scene, McQueen's character shows his bravery and his love for his little Scottish friend of an earlier Cooler sequence. This scene reveals, for the only time in the film, the limited acting skills of the film star in question. As a result of knocking down guards about to shoot, McQueen is hauled off to the Cooler again for his individualistic courageous action, while the other POWs stand by baffled, unable to move. They helplessly witness the tragedy, fearing for themselves.

After more tense sequences, the escape begins to take shape and Virgil Hilts (McQueen) discovers that the tunnel exit is twenty feet short of the forest cover, detailed originally by Brickhill. He bravely innovates using a rope signal lying across the open ground and works selflessly to get the majority of the men out before escaping himself. By this act, he is the hero of the hour, thus fulfilling the difficult actor's demands to stand out in the film beyond the required ensemble approach that James Coburn and James Garner adhere to co-operatively.

The escape sequences are beautifully blocked in by Sturges, providing a pleasing variety of tense moments: the tragic railway platform shooting of David McCallum on the run down the track near the stationary train; the fictitious flight escape of Garner and Pleasence; the crash landing; when Bronson and his companion calmly escape down the river to the North Sea port by rowboat; the motorbike pursuit involving McQueen that is the highlight; the French Resistance shooting of German officers in the open-air café while Coburn, as the super-cool Australian, hides behind the counter and looks on and then continues his successful triumphal escape; as well as several other exciting sequences that maintain the film's momentum to the end.

The capture of Attenborough and his offsider Gordon Jackson is followed by the three ominous trucks heading in different directions leading to the muted, but effective massacre scene. For a while the film darkens to real human tragedy. But the film ends on a brighter, more optimistic note after the names of the murdered fifty are solemnly read out by James Donald (as Senior

RAF officer Ramsay) to the assembly of captured men with the recaptured McQueen taking cool strides to the Cooler carrying his usual baseball and glove. The end titles then roll over.

Intriguingly, John Sturges purchased the film rights of Paul Brickhill's book as far back as 1951 soon after it was published as 'the first full account of the greatest prison-camp escape of them all' that Brickhill had dedicated to 'The Fifty'. While several years had 'softened the memory, they had never faded' for Brickhill, nor did he think they would ever (p.11).

Sturges became dedicated to this cause from the time he read the book, but the experienced director faced great difficulties for several years and various obstacles in Hollywood, capital of the worldwide film industry. It took him more than a decade to get the picture made. The major Hollywood studios were reluctant as there were no female characters and because they estimated it would be far too expensive to shoot.

In the meantime, the American *Stalag 17* and the British *The Wooden Horse* were released to acclaim and box-office success in the early 1950s along with several other similar prison camp stories like *Albert RN* and *The Captive Heart*. Hollywood producers viewed Brickhill's story as just another one in an already crowded field.

It seemed that Sturges had missed the boat. Sam Goldwyn was famously prompted to complain: 'What the hell kind of escape is this. Nobody gets away!' But by 1962 after the huge success of *The Magnificent Seven* which followed on from *The Gunfight at OK Corral* and, earlier, *Bad Day at Black Rock*, John Sturges was hugely bankable and the Mirisch Brothers and United Artists put up $4 million in capital to make the picture.[17] But Paul Brickhill had waited too long to see the film as his literary career had wound up almost completely and fame gradually slid

17 Garner & Winokur, *The Garner Files*, 71-2.

away from him, even though he was strongly acknowledged in Sturges' film and the literature surrounding it.

Since the filming of *The Great Escape* was delayed until the early 1960s, the argument that it was a watered-down version of Brickhill's largely factual account is accurate enough. It is, as occasionally claimed, an anthology of the genre clichés established in the many British and even the American prisoner-of-war camp dramas of the 1950s.[18]

But what a persuasive and wonderfully executed anthology that suddenly broke free at the climax in the famous McQueen motor bike pursuit sequences with their stunning stunt work. And yet Brickhill's book, as well as *The Wooden Horse* and *The Colditz Story* in the early 1950s, laid the foundations and provided all the factual evidence on which a good anthology of behind-the-barbed-wire could be based as a highly rated, entertaining and lasting film classic which continues to survive its fame when other similar films have disappeared almost entirely – even the great performance of Peter Finch, Brickhill's closest friend, as an

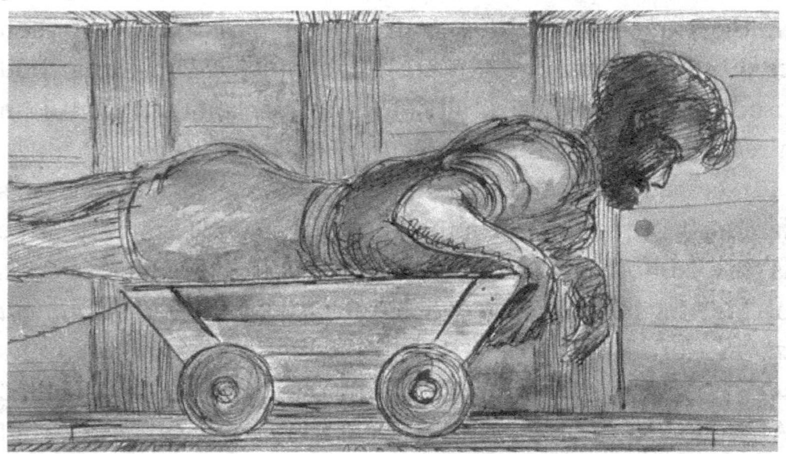

Rolling down to the working face: the tunnel Stalag Luft III (by Albert Comber AWM ART34781.015)

18 Phillip Bergson, 'The Great Escape', Anne Lloyd & David Robinson, *Movies of the Sixties*, Orbis Publishing, London, 1983, 62-7.

Australian POW being crucified in a Japanese prison camp in *A Town Like Alice.*

Coda

The film versions of Brickhill's *The Dam Busters*, *Reach for the Sky* and *The Great Escape* were highly successful in their time in the British and International box office and, as time went by, became esteemed classic films of the Second World War, as well as being an outreach of the lasting achievements of the non-fiction work of Paul Brickhill and open tributes to him as a bestselling, highly-regarded writer of the immediate post-Second World War period of English and indeed international literature. It is, however, little known, or has been forgotten, that his last book and first and only work of thriller fiction was also given a television version of some prominence at the time. This means, of course, that there were four rather than three films of his books, all of which have survived and can still be watched today. Three were major achievements with the fourth a minor one.

The film rights of *The Deadline* or *War of Nerves* (as it was titled in America) was sold directly to Hollywood and obviously in the wake of the brilliant box office returns of *The Great Escape*. At the time of its sale in America, the intention was to turn *War of Nerves* into a major feature film of the contemporary thriller genre popular in the 1960s and 1970s with films like *North by North-West* (1960), *The Heroes of Telemark* (1968) and *Funeral in Berlin* (1969) as well as the James Bond international intrigue thrillers based on Ian Fleming's series of novels in the 1950s and 1960s. Instead, the Hollywood moguls decided in their sometimes bizarre wisdom to turn Brickhill's thriller into a telemovie or teleplay as part of the prestigious anthology series The Chrysler Theatre, then hosted on a regular basis by the comic Bob Hope.

War of Nerves was, nevertheless, provided with a distinguished cast with Irish actor Stephen Boyd as the hero Robert Mackay and French matinee idol Louis Jourdan as the arch-villain Phillipe Tabor, as well as a cast of well-known and experienced actors. The director was Sydney Pollock. The story was filmed at Universal Studio in 35mm. Mark Roberts adapted Paul Brickhill's novel to fit the short time-slot. It was aired on Friday, 3 January 1964 at 8.30pm and ran for 55minutes and watched by a large American audience in prime time.[19] It is doubtful that it was ever shown in Australia on television in 1964. As a telemovie it was quickly forgotten about.

Brickhill sets his story in contemporary Paris in 1962. Robert Mackay as energetically played by Stephen Boyd (as an American) was in the book a young Australian visitor to France, out for a good time on a three-week holiday. He enters a Left Bank café, saunters up to the bar, orders a drink, casts a knowing look around the room and spots a beautiful young woman making an urgent telephone call. All this is faithfully rendered in the teleplay as is the next moment when two shots ring out. A man slumps over a table, dead – and a tall assassin escapes after grappling with Mackay in the doorway. Another victim of the current Algerian crisis is murdered – a daily occurrence that Parisians were facing at the time. Robert Mackay, an eye-witness and an innocent abroad, is drawn into the political conflict. The victim is an Algerian businessman and his assassin is a terrorist Brickhill calls Ben Chakry.

The police find that Mackay is the only person in the café able to recognise the killer. While the plot thickens and the excitement builds in Brickhill's book, there is little chance it

---

19 War of Nerves, <www.tv.com/bob-hope-presents-the-chrysler-theatre/war-of-nerves-131901/>.

can develop particularly well in a fifty-five-minute teleplay. Nevertheless, as continuously underlined in the dialogue, only Mackay can identify the assassin and the entire Paris police force is mobilised. Mackay thus becomes a target for the Algerian terrorist group (the *OAS, Organisation de l'Armée Secrète*). In the book the search intensifies with sudden twists and turns, but not in the film where the villain played smoothly by Louis Jourdan is fatally shot by the female protagonist in a side street climax near the café. The assassin is killed in a police trap led by a Maigret-like police inspector. Brickhill's hero, like James Bond, is victorious in the end and so wins the young woman.

Sydney Pollock, the director, did his best to create the feel of Paris at night and the cast give a vigorous performance to keep it interesting. The American director, who was born in 1931, cut his teeth with such teleplays with small budgets and then went on to bigger and better things with films like *This Property is Condemned* (1968), *They Shoot Horses, Don't They?* (1972), *Absence of Malice* (1982) and *Out of Africa* (1990).

For Brickhill's *War of Nerves*, he built the atmosphere well in the opening stanzas and also extracted some good performances from the cast, but in the end it leads nowhere.

It was a sad minor ending for Brickhill on film. Without being able to write again, at least in published books, for the rest of his life's struggle, Paul Brickhill had to fight his own 'war of nerves'. But both the books and the film versions derived from them stand as a lasting memorial to his creative ability to write what people wanted to read especially in the immediate post-war period when he had significant international success as an Australian writer of note.

He had interested untold readers in the real-life epics of men whose password was raw courage and who gambled everything for freedom or death and the directors of the films based on his books achieved the same end.

BIBLIOGRAPHY

By Paul Brickhill:

- Books -

(and Conrad Norton), *Escape to Danger*, London, Faber & Faber, 1946

The Dam Busters, London, Evans Brothers Ltd, 1951

Escape – or Die. Authentic Stories of the R.A.F. Escaping Society, London, Evans Brothers, 1952

The Great Escape, London, Evans Brothers, 1950

The Great Escape, London, Faber and Faber 1951

The Great Escape, London, Faber and Faber, Readers Union, 1952

Reach for the Sky. The Story of Douglas Bader D.S.O., D.F.C., London, Collins, 1954

The Deadline, Sydney, Collins, 1962

War of Nerves, New York, Morrow, 1963

- Chapters -

'Tunnel to Freedom', in Charles S Verral (ed.), *True Stories of Great Escapes,* vol.1, Surry Hills, Reader's Digest, 1983, 167-82

'Seconds to Live', in Verral (ed.), *True Stories of Great Escapes,* vol.2, 267-83

'Escape or Die', in Verral (ed.), *True Stories of Great Escapes,* vol.2, 310-50

- Articles -

'Getting to Grips With Amazing Bader', *Examiner* (Launceston), 27 March 1954

'The Bomber Fought for The Lives of Its Crew, and Won', *News* (Adelaide), 3 December 1945

'At Last the Night Came For A Dash To Freedom', *News* (Adelaide), 5 December 1945

'He Joined his Friend On a Parachute', *News* (Adelaide), 6 December 1945

'Berlin Family's Drab Xmas Outlook', *Mail* (Adelaide), 22 December 1945

'Doctors Fight To Save Europe From 'Flu', *Newcastle Sun*, 22 December 1945
'POW Goes Back --- How the Germans Have Changed', *News* (Adelaide), 24 December 1945
'Glassy-Eyed People of Berlin Have Now Ceased to Care ', *Newcastle Sun*, 28 December 1945
'Battle in Berlin – To Save Europe From Disaster Worse Than War', *News* (Adelaide), 29 December 1945
'Do "Jungle Drums" Guide Jews?', *Mail* (Adelaide), 12 January 1946
'Russian Zone of Germany is Making Speedy Recovery', *Newcastle Sun*, 22 January 1946
'Jewish Exodus Organised', *Telegraph* (Brisbane), 10 January 1946
'Russians Watch Germans In Big Political Struggle', *Telegraph* (Brisbane), 24 January 1946
'Germans Do Well For Food', Dortmund, Feb. 3, *Telegraph* (Brisbane), 4 February 1946
'Nazi Leaders Plotting To Rat on Mates', *Mail* (Adelaide), 16 February 1946

- Primary Sources -

Attestation Papers & Service Records, National Archives of Australia (NAA), Canberra:
~ Bain, Donald, 4134, 1st AIF
~ Service Record, WWII, Brickhill, F/Lt PCJ, 403313, RAAF
~ Statements by Repatriated or released RAAF Prisoners of War taken at No 11 PDRS Brighton, England, 1945, 408513, Australian War Memorial (AWM), Canberra
First World War and Second World War. 16 Recruitment Posters from the collection of the Australian War Memorial, AWM, 2014
Crowley, FK. *Modern Australia in Documents*. Volume 2 1939-1970, Melbourne, Wren Publishing, 1973
Jones Papers, DRL 3414, AWM
The Falcon. The Journal of North Sydney Boys High, 1926-1934

- **Books** -

Aplin, Graeme, SG Foster, Michael McKernan & Ian Howie-Willis (eds). *Australians. A Historical Dictionary*, Broadway, Fairfax, Syme & Weldon Associates, 1987

Bauer, Lt-Col Eddy. *Marshall Cavendish illustrated encyclopedia of World War II : an objective, chronological, and comprehensive history of the Second World War*, vol.1, pt 13, London, Orbis Publishing, 1978

Beck, Deborah. *Hope in Hell. A History of Darlinghurst Gaol and the National Art School*, Crows Nest, Allen & Unwin, 2005

Bond, Barbara A. *The Times Great Escapes*, Glasgow, HarperCollins, 2015

Burgess, Colin. *Australian's Dambusters. The Men and Mission of 617 Squadron*, Loftus, Australian Military History Publications, 2013.

Burney, Allan (ed.). *Famous Fighters of World War 2*, Midlands, Coxy Media, 2015

Cooper, Alan W. *The Men who breached the dams. 617 Squadron, 'The Dam Busters'*, Barnsley, Pen & Sword Aviation, 2013

----. *Beyond the Dams to the Tirpitz. The Later Operations of 617 Squadron*, Barnsley, Pen & Sword Aviation

Curthoys, Ann, AW Martin & Tim Rowse. *Australians from 1939*, Broadway, Fairfax, Symes & Weldon Associates, 1987

Cyprian, Tadeusz & Jerzy Sawicki. *Nuremberg in Retrospect. People and Issues of the Trial*, Warsaw, Western Press Agency, 1967

Dams, Carsten & Michael Stolle. *The Gestapo. Power and Terror in the Third Reich*, trans. by Charlotte Ryland, Oxford, Oxford University Press, 2014

Dundy, Elaine. *Finch, Bloody Finch. A Life of Peter Finch*, New York, Holt, Rinehart and Winston, 1980

Durand, Arthur A. *Stalag Luft III. The Secret Story*, New York, Simon & Schuster, 1988

Eberhardt, Kim. *A Falcon Century. North Sydney Boys High School 1912-2012*, Crows Nest, North Sydney Boys High School, 2012

Faulkner, Trader. *Peter Finch: A Biography,* Sydney, Angus & Robertson, 1979
Fleming, Thomas. *The Great Escape,* EBSCO Publishing, 2002
Foucault, Michel. *Discipline and Punish: The Birth of the Prison,* trans. by Alan Sheridan, New York, Pantheon, 1977
Gammage, Bill. *Narrandera a Shire,* Narrandera, Bill Gammage & Narrandera Shire, 1986
Garner, James & Jon Winokur. *The Garner Files,* New York, Simon & Schuster, 2011
Gibson, Guy. *Enemy Coast Ahead – Uncensored. The Real Guy Gibson,* Manchester, Crécy Publishing, 2013
Hall, Ken. *Australian Film. The Inside Story,* Dee Why, Summit Books, 1980
Harris, Reg S. *Heroes of the Surf. Fifty Years' History of Manly Life Saving Club,* Sydney, MLSC, 1961
Hatch, FJ. *The Aerodrome of Democracy: Canada and the British Commonwealth Air Training Plan 1939-1945,* Ottawa, Department of National Defence, 1983
Head, Dominic (ed.). *The Cambridge Guide to Literature in English,* Cambridge, Cambridge University Press, 2006
Herington, John. *Air War Against Germany and Italy 1939-1943,* Canberra, Australian War Memorial, 1962
Hetherington, John. *Forty-Two Faces,* Melbourne, FW Cheshire, 1962
Higgs, Colin & Bruce Vigar. *Voices in Flight: The Dambuster Squadron,* Barnsley, Pen & Sword Aviation, 2013
Hyams, Jay. *War Movies,* New York, Gallery Books, 1984
Jary, Christopher. *Portrait of a Bomber Pilot,* Barnsley, Pen & Sword Aviation, 2012
Johnson, Tony. *Escape to Freedom,* Barnsley, Leo Cooper, 2009
Kennedy, Brian & Barbara Kennedy. *Sydney and Suburbs. A History and Description,* Frenchs Forest, Reed, 1982
Kent, Jacqueline. *Out of the Bakelite Box. The Heyday of Australian Radio,* Sydney, Angus & Robinson, 1983

Kesey, Ken. *One Flew Over the Cuckoo's Nest,* The Folio Society, London, 2015

Lawther, Rebecca (ed.). *Dambusters. The Raid Sixty-Five Years On,* Barnsley, 2008

Lloyd, Ann, & Graham Fuller (eds). *The Illustrated Who's Who of the Cinema,* Hornsby, Child-Henry, 1983

Lloyd, Ann & David Robinson (eds). *Movies of the Sixties,* London, Orbis Publishing, 1983

Longerich, Peter. *Heinrich Himmler,* trans. by Jeremy Noakes & Lesley Sharpe, Oxford, Oxford University Press, 2012

McFarlane, Brian Geoff Mayer & Ina Bertrand (eds). *The Oxford Companion to Australian Film,* South Melbourne, Oxford University Press, 1999

Mitchell, Claire. *Through the Heads To Balmoral,* Sydney, Sydney, Claire Mitchell, 2015

Mooney, Christopher. *A Powerhouse of a Man. Tom Farrell,* Melbourne, Brolga Publishing, 2015

Moran, Albert & Tom O'Regan. *The Australian Screen,* Ringwood, Penguin, 1989

Moran, Albert & Chris Keating. *Dictionary of Australian Radio and Television,* Lanham, Maryland, The Scare Crow Press, 2007

Pearson, Simon. *The Great Escaper: The Life and Death of Roger Bushell,* London, Hodder & Stoughton, 2013

Peck, Ira. *The Battle of Britain,* New York, Scholastic Book Services, 1969

Pentland, Geoffrey & Peter Malone. *Aircraft of the RAAF 1921-78,* Melbourne, Kookaburra Press Technical Publications, 1971

Perlmutter, Tom. *War Movies,* London, Hamlyn, 1974

Perry, George. *The Great British Picture Show,* London, Pavilion Books, 1985

Pike, Andrew & Ross Cooper. *Australian Film 1900-1977,* Melbourne, Oxford University Press, 1980

Pollon, Frances (compiler & ed.). *The Book of Sydney Suburbs,*

Pymble, Cornstalk Publishing, 1996
Quinlan, David. *Quinlan's Film Directors,* London, BT Blatsford Ltd, 1999
Rees, Peter. *Lancaster Men. The Aussie Heroes of Bomber Command,* Crows Nest, Allen & Unwin, 2015
Reid, PR. *Colditz. The Full Story,* London, Macmillan, 1984
----. *The Latter Days of Colditz,* London, Cassell, 2003
Ross, John (ed.-in-chief). *Chronicle of the Twentieth Century,* Ringwood, Viking, 1999
Sherriff, RC. *No Leading Lady. An Autobiography,* London, Victor Gollancz, 1968
Simpson, Geoff. *Guy Gibson Dambuster,* Barnsley, Pen & Sword Aviation, 2013
St Leon, Mark. *Circus in Australia Printed Ephemera 1833-2008,* Penshurst, Mark St Leon & Associates, 2008
Storey, HM. *History of North Sydney High School 1912-1962,* Crows Nest, North Sydney Boys High School, 1962
Sun Newspaper Ltd 1910-1929, Sydney, *Sun* Newspapers Ltd, 1929
Sweetman, John. *The Dambusters Raid,* London, Cassell, 2012
Thorning, Arthur G. *The Dambuster who Cracked the Dam. The Story of Melvin 'Dinghy' Young,* Barnsley, Pen & Sword Aviation, 2013
Thornton, Gordon. *Bomber Command 1939-1940. The War Before the War,* Barnsley, Pen & Sword Aviation, 2013
Vader, John. *Spitfire,* Purnell's History of the Second World War Weapons Book, no 6, London, Macdonald & Co, 1970
Vesper, Stan. *Those who served. Surf Lifesavers at War,* Carringbah, Playright Publishing, 2015
Ward, Chris & Andreas Wachtel. *Dambuster Crash Sites. 617 Dambuster Squadron Crash Sites in Holland and Germany,* Barnsley, Pen & Sword, 2013
Williams, Eric. *The Wooden Horse,* London, The Reprint Society, 1950
Williams, Louise. *A True Story of the Great Escape. A Young*

Australian POW in the Most Audacious Breakout of WWII, Sydney, Allen & Unwin, 2015
Winnert, Derek (gen. ed.). *The Ultimate Encyclopedia of the Movies*, London, Carlton Books, 1995
Young, Brigadier Peter (ed.-in-chief). *World War II. Battle of Britain*, no 13, 1978

- Articles / Chapters / Theses -

Allmon, William B. 'The Man Behind the Great Escape', *World War II*, vol.17, Issue 3, 2002, 1-6
Axford, Edward. 'Eyes on the Glamour Boys', *The Home*, an Australian Quarterly, June 1941, 16-17, 60
----. 'Catalina Patrol', *The Home*, March 1942, 12-19
Britain, IM. 'Finch, Frederick George Peter Ingle (1916-77)', *Australian Dictionary of Biography (ADB)*, vol.14, John Ritchie (gen. ed.), Carlton, Melbourne University Press, 163-4
Cassuto, Leonard. 'The Silhouette and the Secret Self. Theorising Biography in Our Times', *American Quarterly*, vol.58, no 4, December 2006, 1249-61.
Couser, G Thomas. 'Genre Matters: form, force, and filiation', *Life Writing*, vol.2, no 2, 2005, 123-40
Downing, Taylor. 'War on Film. The Dam Busters', *Military History Monthly*, Issue 32, 2013, 40-43
----. 'War on Film. Reach for the Sky', *Military History Monthly*, Issue 59, 2015, 62-65
----. 'War on Film: The Captive Heart', *Military History Monthly*, Issue 67, 2016, 60-62
Dyer, Steve. 'Training the RAAF in Britain', *Journal of the Australian War Memorial*, no 8, April 1986, 11-19
'Embry, Sir Basil Edward', *The Concise Dictionary of National Biography*, vol.1, Oxford, Oxford University Press, 1992, 931
McCarthy, John. 'The "surrender" of aircrew to Britain 1939-45',

Journal of the Australian War Memorial, no 5, October 1984, 3-8
----. 'The Defence of Australia and the Empire Air Training Scheme 1939-42', *Australian Journal of Politics and History*, vol. XX, no 3, December 1974, 326-34
'Mountain out of a Brickhill', *People*, vol.4, no 6, 20 May 1953, 20-23
St Leon, Mark. 'Circus & Nation', Part II, PhD thesis, University of Sydney, 2006
Rossison, James. 'The political decisions and policy leading to the Royal Australian Air Force having no fighters for the coming war against Japan', PhD thesis, Faculty of Creative Industries, Queensland University of Technology, 2015
Walker, RB. 'Denison, Sir Hugh Robert (1865-1940)', *ADB*, vol.8, Bede Nairn & Geoffrey Serle, (gen. eds), Carlton, Melbourne University Press, 1981, 283-5
Washington, Judy. 'Tidal Swimming Pools of Lane Cove, 2 Greenwich Baths Pt 2', *Lane Cove Historical Society Newsletter*, no 167, July 2001, 1-6
Wilcox, Craig. 'Fall from the Sky', *Wartime*, Issue 58, 2012, 20-31

- Audiovisual / Websites -

"Obituary. The full life of Ley Kenyon', by Kendall McDonald, February 1991, <http://classicdivebooks.customer.netspace.net.au/Authors/Ley-Kenyon-Obituary,jpg>
'Paul Brickhill', by Steve Holland, http://bearalley.blogspot.com/2010/09/paul-brickhill.html
Reach for the Sky, DVD, 136 minutes, black/white, Pinnacle Productions, (original 1956)
The Dam Busters, DVD, black/white, 120 minutes, 2010 (original 1954)
'The Dambusters 1954 otr australian radio', 26 episodes, <https://archive.org>
The Great Escape, DVD, approx. 165 minutes, colour, The Mirisch Company Inc., 2000 (original 1963)

The Long March to Freedom, DVD 3-part documentary film, produced and directed by Stephen Saunders, 2012

War of Nerves, <www.tv.com/bob-hope-presents-the-chrysler-theatre/war-of-nerves-131901>

Wilcox, Craig. 'Brickhill, Paul Chester (1916-1991)', *Australian Dictionary of Biography,* Australian National University, http://adb.anu.edu.au/biography/brickhill-paul-chester-14647/text25780, published online 2014

INDEX

ACKNOWLEDGEMENTS

Thanks are due for the provision of valued information by all those who kindly responded to public appeals in articles in the *Mosman Daily*, *Manly Daily* and elsewhere: Margot Minchin (ex-wife of Paul Brickhill), Helen Waddington, Marianne De Souza, Ilona Watson, Louise Williams, Peter Tyree, Syd Bateman, Kate Ellis, Diana Noel, Anthony Clancy, Tony Humphrey, Margaret Chessell, June Imre, Alan Jones, Sue Meares, Nicholas Goodall, Sandra Frearson, Dennis O'Brien.

The help of the following individuals and organisations is much appreciated:

- Margaret and Beatrice Brickhill for their keen and steadfast interest in the project and for their ready provision of Brickhill family photographs and other useful family memorabilia;

- Denise Gaudion, of the Port Stephens Family History Society, for encouragement, support and the provision of useful information;

- Janet Ramsland Bain for providing documentation of the life of her father Donald Sackville Bain of the *Sun* newspaper;

- Dr Alan Hewson for continued support, encouragement, discussions and provision of relevant background literature;

- Richard Fleming for the provision of his father's RAAF diary and photographs;

- The biographers of Peter Finch: Trader Faulkner and Elaine Dundy;

- Glennis Haradasa of Manly Village Public School for her interest and the provision of relevant source material;

- Wendy Holz, librarian, Information and Access, State Library of NSW, for promptly making available primary documents from the collection, as well as other librarians on duty from time to time;

- The librarians and archivists of the Australian War Memorial, Canberra; the Auchmuty library of the University of Newcastle; National Library of Australia;

- Lane Cove and Mosman Libraries (especially the enthusiasm, helpfulness and energy of Lavinia Foote Morid and Naomi Bassford, Local Studies Collection of Lane Cove library;

- Mark Zocchi and his staff at Brolga Publishing always ready to oblige and support.

I wish to recognise the constant encouragement and support of all members of my family. My wife Marie well deserves a special tribute for her computing and editing the text through its several drafts – above all, her constant encouragement and many valuable suggestions.

* * *

ABOUT THE AUTHOR

John Ramsland OAM, born in Manly in 1942, is Emeritus Professor of History (The University of Newcastle, Australia) and the author of over twenty books and at least 120 articles, reviews and invited chapters in edited books. He has written widely on social, cultural and educational history, Aboriginal Studies, child social welfare, marine history, historical biography, the impact of modern industrial warfare and on the historical significance of sport.

Brave and Bold (2008, Brolga Publishing) won the prestigious NSW Writer's Centre Open Book award. He has won various other awards in History and honoured in 2012 with a Lifetime Achievement Award of the Wollotuka Institute of Aboriginal Studies (Newcastle) for his mentorship and supervision of postgraduate Indigenous students. *To Climb the Hill* was Highly Commended in the Heritage Awards of 2016.

His articles, reviews and academic papers have appeared in well-regarded publications in many countries establishing an international reputation.

In 2006 he was awarded the Medal of the Order of Australia 'for services to the community, particularly through historical research in the areas of child poverty and abuse, the Indigenous experience and institutional life in colonial Australia and to education'.

BOOKS BY THE SAME AUTHOR

with Brolga Publishing, Melbourne:

Remembering Aboriginal Heroes. Struggle, Identity and the Media (with Christopher Mooney), 2006; 2012

The Swiss Swagman. Theodor Müller's Nineteen Years in Australia (co-edited), 2007

Brave & Bold. Manly Village Public School, 1858-2008, 2008

The Rainbow Beach Man. The Life and Times of Les Ridgeway, Worimi Elder, 2009

Cook's Hill Life Saving & Surf Club. The First Hundred Years, 2011

From Antarctica to the Gold Rushes. in the wake of the Erebus, 2011

Venturing into No Man's Land. The Charmed Life of Joseph Maxwell VC World War I Hero, 2012

The Other Side of No Man's Land, Arthur Wheen World War I Hero, Scholar and Pacifist, 2015

Other book titles:

Entrances and Exits, 1 & 2, William Brooks, Sydney, 1972 & 1973

Adolf Hitler and German Nazism, William Brooks, Sydney, 1973, 1984

Benito Mussolini and Italian Fascism, William Brooks, Sydney, 1984

Children of the Back Lanes. Destitute and neglected children in colonial New South Wales, University of New South Wales Press, Kensington, 1986

The Struggle against Isolation. a History of the Manning Valley, Library of Australian History, North Sydney, 1987

Children of the Circus (with Mark St Leon), Butterfly Press, Springwood, 1993

With Just But Relentless Discipline. A Social History of Corrective

Services in New South Wales, Kangaroo Press, Kenhurst, 1996

Maitland Gaol, 1844-1998, Verand Press, Sydney, 2001; 2014

Custodians of the Soil. A History of Aboriginal-European Relationships in the Manning Valley of New South Wales, Greater Taree City Council, 2001

The Galloping Seahorse. University of Newcastle Rugby Union Club, 1954-2004, The University of Newcastle Rugby Club, Gosford, 2004

Gardiens de la terre dans la vallée de la Manning. Aborigènes et Européens en Australie, (translated into French by Valérie Djénidi), L'Harmattan, Paris, 2010

The Great Australian Silence Reigns. Aboriginal children and schooling in New South Wales, Australian National Museum of Education, Canberra, 2010

Neville Howse VC. Manning Pioneering Doctor and War Hero, Manning Valley Historical Society, Wingham, 2014

John Melville-Jones (ed.), *Ludovic de Beauvoir's Visit to Australia* (Contributor), Hesperian Press, Carlisle, WA, 2016

To Climb the Hill. A People's History of Newcastle East Public School 1816-2016 (Major Contributor, editor), Newcastle East Public School, Newcastle, 2016 (Highly Commended, Heritage Awards 2016)

Gretchen Poiner and Sybil Jack (eds), *Gardens of History and Imagination. Growing New South Wales* (Major Contributor), Sydney University Press, The University of Sydney, 2016

Flying Into Danger

by John Ramsland

ISBN 9781925367683 Qty:

RRP AU $(TBA) .....

Postage within Australia AU$5.00 .....

TOTAL* $________ * All prices include GST

Name: ....Phone:..

Address: ....

Email: ....

Payment: ❑ Money Order ❑ Cheque ❑ Amex ❑ MasterCard ❑Visa

Cardholder's Name: ....

Credit Card Number: _ _ _ _ _ _ _ _ _ _ _ _ _ _ _ _

Signature: ....Expiry Date: ....

Allow 10 days for delivery.

Payment to:

Marzocco Consultancy (ABN 14 067 257 390)
PO Box 12544
A'Beckett Street, Melbourne, 8006
Victoria, Australia
admin@brolgapublishing.com.au

Be Published

Publish through a successful publisher.

Brolga Publishing is represented through:

• **National** book trade distribution, including sales, marketing & distribution through **Macmillan Australia.**

• **International** book trade distribution to
  - The United Kingdom
  - North America
  - Sales representation in South East Asia

• **Worldwide e-Book distribution**

For details and inquiries, contact:
Brolga Publishing Pty Ltd
PO Box 12544
A'Beckett St VIC 8006

Phone: 0414 608 494
markzocchi@brolgapublishing.com.au
ABN: 46 063 962 443
(Email for a catalogue request)